The Moral Philosophy of
Josiah Royce

The Moral Philosophy of
Josiah Royce

ॐ

PETER FUSS

HARVARD UNIVERSITY PRESS
Cambridge, Massachusetts

1 9 6 5

© Copyright 1965 by the President and Fellows of Harvard College
All rights reserved

Distributed in Great Britain by Oxford University Press, London

Publication of this book has been aided by a grant from the
Ford Foundation

Library of Congress Card Catalog Number 65-11590

Printed in the United States of America

TO CAROL

We choose some fashion of life in the morning, and we reject it before night. Our devotional moments demand that all life shall be devotional; our merry moments that all life shall be merry; our heroic moments that all life shall be lived in defiance of some chosen enemy. But we are false to all these ideals, even while we pretend to have them.

(*The Religious Aspect of Philosophy*)

. . . to be bounded in a nutshell and to have bad dreams as well is of the essence of . . . finitude. . . .

(*The Spirit of Modern Philosophy*)

Preface

Royce's position in contemporary philosophical discussion is, to put it mildly, somewhat uncertain. He is often mentioned but rarely read. Among the older generation of current American philosophers, many acknowledge that Royce influenced them in their student days, but few would claim that this influence persisted. The historians of American philosophy invariably include Royce among the four or five "classic" American philosophers, generously accord him as much printed space as Peirce or James or Dewey, and then almost reluctantly observe that his chief philosophical doctrines, namely those having to do with his absolute idealism, are no longer viable. Yet occasional books, scholarly articles, and doctoral dissertations continue to appear, attempting, for the most part, to revive or create interest in this or that "neglected aspect" of his thought. In recent years several of Royce's major works have been reprinted in paperback, and more are promised. The editors of these reprints would have us believe that a "Royce revival" is about to take place.

The present study is motivated by the conviction that if such a revival is indeed in the offing, its greatest promise lies in an orientation toward Royce's moral philosophy. For understandable reasons, a systematic study of Royce's moral philosophy has not hitherto been attempted. Most of his major works expound a doctrine of metaphysical absolutism which seems to preclude an intelligible ethical theory at the very outset. Other works present normative doctrines of value and conduct whose theoretical foundation is far from clear. Royce's commentators have therefore treated what appear to be mere fragments of ethical doctrine in a correspondingly fragmentary way. Nevertheless, I believe that a careful examination of Royce's published works, in conjunction with a large body of unpublished writings, shows that Royce did develop an integrated, intelligible, and not implausible ethical theory after all—an ethical theory which in no way presupposes, moreover, an acceptance of his metaphysical absolutism.

In order to bring the structure of Royce's ethical theory into clear focus, I have found it useful to combine chronological presentation with systematic exposition. An understanding of the order in which Royce developed the various phases of his ethical theory is, I am convinced, indispensable to a full understanding of the nature of his ethical theory as a whole. But my primary concern is systematic. I have therefore sacrificed chronological development for topical coherence in several instances.

With one exception, I have made only passing mention of historical influences on Royce, chiefly because of his almost unbelievable intellectual voraciousness. It is probably no exaggeration to say that virtually every major, and countless minor, figures in the history of philosophy affected his thinking to some extent. What emerged in his writings was never quite original, yet never devoid of something unmistakably Roycean. Under such circumstances, to ask whether he was influenced more by Spinoza or by Kant, by Hegel or by Lotze, by Fichte or by Schopenhauer, seems to me a rather fruitless question. The one exception is C. S. Peirce, whose profound and catalytic influence on Royce's later doctrines of interpretation and the community merits special attention.

I have found that the effort to expound and to clarify the salient features of Royce's ethical theory has left me with but little room for extensive criticism. I have therefore confined myself for the most part to criticism "from within" Royce's conceptual and doctrinal framework, forswearing altogether the too ambitious task of essaying a definitive evaluation. In addition, I have not thought it appropriate to hold Royce accountable, in his own presentation of his doctrines, to the rigorous standards of analytic and terminological clarity and distinctness that have since come into vogue in Anglo-American philosophic discussion. While I personally believe that the adoption of these standards has benefited the enterprise of philosophy considerably, I am also inclined to think that their application, willy-nilly, to writers who lived prior to their inception, and who might not have accepted them had they known of them, could result in a refusal even to read these older writers, not to mention a disinclination to confront their thought sympathetically. That, it seems to me, would be unfortunate.

Yet no attempt to re-enter a past thinker's "universe of discourse" is ever wholly successful. Wherever possible I have let Royce speak for himself. But at certain significant points in his argument I have found theoretical gaps that needed filling, and language sufficiently obscure or misleading to warrant restatement in other terms. The risk of infidelity thereby incurred is comparatively small, I suspect, over against that involved in my attempt to treat Royce's ethics independently of his metaphysical absolutism. From Royce's point of view, this procedure may amount to downright treason. Yet he himself resolved to develop his ethical theory independently of metaphysical presuppositions—a resolve in which he occasionally weakened, to be sure. In further defense of this undertaking, I would add my conviction that Royce's ethical theory is both more attractive and more intelligible when freed of any significant association with his more familiar metaphysical preconceptions. If that is to fragment a body of thought whose originator's very motto was the organic interconnection of realms of inquiry, so be it. There still remains the possibility that the parts are worth saving even when the whole is not. It is a later generation's privilege to decide for itself what is living and what is dead in a philosopher's thought. To suppose otherwise is to dwell in an intellectual mausoleum, in which philosophers are buried whole.

Finally, a word in defense of my extensive use of Royce's unpublished writings. With rare exceptions, these writings are more than mere gropings in new directions as yet incompletely thought out. For the most part they are what appear to be final versions of lectures and addresses given by Royce at various universities and assemblies. Moreover, they do shed considerable light on the structure of Royce's ethical theory, particularly on its analytic rather than its substantive aspects. These writings are throughout continuous with Royce's published work at corresponding periods, and I have not found a single point of significant conflict between unpublished and published material.

I should like to think that this essay is not merely a study in Royce but a study in ethical theory as well. It is my belief that both Royce's conception of the major problem of moral philosophy and his attempt to resolve this problem are pertinent to contemporary discussion. But I shall have to let this investigation suggest that pertinence of itself, if it will, since I wish to avoid special pleading.

This study is a revised version of my doctoral dissertation at Harvard University in 1962. I am grateful to the members of the Harvard philosophy department for their critical supervision of the dissertation and for their subsequent encouragement to bring the manuscript to press. I am further indebted to my colleagues Professor Philip Wheelwright and Professor Oliver Johnson for their kind offer to read the manuscript and for their valuable criticisms and suggestions. My appreciation is due to Miss Eleanore Stone for her gracious and competent assistance in preparing the manuscript. Finally, I wish to thank Professor Gilbert Ryle, editor of *Mind,* for permission to quote from the H. A. Prichard article in Chapter Seven, the Macmillan Company for permission to quote from *The Problem of Christianity*, and Harvard University for its courtesy in providing me with leisurely access to the unpublished Royce material in its Archives.

Peter Fuss

University of California, Riverside
June 1964

Contents

PART III

THE STRUCTURE OF ROYCE'S MATURE ETHICAL THEORY

CONTENTS

PART I

ROYCE'S EARLY ETHICAL THEORY

Chapter One

THE PROBLEM OF ETHICAL THEORY

1. Ethical Realism and Ethical Idealism

ROYCE's first sustained discussion of ethical questions appeared in 1885, in a book somewhat misleadingly titled *The Religious Aspect of Philosophy*. At the outset, Royce defines the moral philosopher's fundamental task as that of providing a theoretical account of the moral distinctions men make in their everyday lives. The outstanding problem for the moral philosopher is to determine whether, and if so how, these distinctions between good and evil, right and wrong, may be theoretically justified.

In undertaking such an inquiry, the moral philosopher should avoid a metaphysical or religious *parti pris*. He should take for his "data" the opinions of reflective moral consciousness as he finds them, for it is these that he is attempting to understand and to explain.[1]

Surveying the history of ethical theory, Royce finds that on the whole moral philosophers have been singularly unsuccessful in discovering an acceptable rational justification for moral distinctions. Their efforts have tended to land them in one or the other of two warring doctrinal camps, which he designates as "ethical realism" and "ethical idealism." The ethical realist, as Royce describes him, insists that moral distinctions can be justified only by appeal to matters of fact external to the moral consciousness. The ethical idealist, on the contrary, is equally insistent that distinctions be-

[1] *The Religious Aspect of Philosophy* (New York, 1885), pp. 18–20.

tween good and evil, right and wrong, can be justified only by reference to the "inner consciousness" of the moral agent himself.[2]

As Royce gradually clarifies the nature of the controversy between the ethical realist and the ethical idealist, it becomes apparent that this controversy stems from the need, not always clearly recognized, to satisfy two possibly conflicting yet equally fundamental demands of our reflective moral consciousness. The first may be termed the demand for moral objectivity. It is the requirement that valid moral standards and judgments shall have a binding force upon the moral agent independently of his personal desires or whims. The second may be termed the demand for moral autonomy. It is the recognition that the binding force of valid moral standards and judgments must depend in the last instance upon the voluntary assent of the rationally self-legislative moral agent himself.[3]

Now it is Royce's contention that the controversy between the ethical realist and the ethical idealist is a conflict of one-sided positions. The ethical realist, in his determination to establish the objectivity of moral distinctions, has neglected the equally legitimate demand for moral autonomy. He has sought to ground valid moral distinctions in states of affairs external to the moral consciousness. Thereby he has denied to the individual the very meaning of his moral agency, namely, the human quest for ideal values and ideal moral relations whether the actual physical and social environment embodies these or not. It might even be said that the ethical realist has misconceived the nature of morality itself, for he has tended to reduce normative questions to factual questions, questions about what ought to be and ought to be done to questions about what is the case and is done. In

[2] *Ibid.*, pp. 22–31.
[3] "Moral objectivity" and "moral autonomy" are not Royce's terms. But in the senses specified they express quite accurately what Royce wishes to say.

Royce's own words, the ethical realist has mistakenly "founded the lofty *Ought* on the paltry *Is*." [4]

But the ethical idealist's position is equally one-sided. In his eagerness to safeguard the moral autonomy of the individual human person he has failed to provide a ground for moral objectivity. There are notoriously almost as many ethical ideals and obligation claims as there are persons. Unable to find any warrant for these ideals and obligation claims other than the fact that this or that individual asserts them, the ethical idealist has abandoned the realm of morals to private caprice and whim. Thus, whereas the idealist rightly charges the realist with irrelevance, the realist with equal cause convicts the idealist of arbitrariness. Neither has presented an adequate theoretical justification for moral distinctions.

The suspicion grows that the ethical realist and the ethical idealist are involved in an apparent antinomy peculiar to moral philosophy. Starting from equally plausible premises —the realist that the objectivity of moral distinctions must be established, the idealist that the autonomy of moral agents must be secured—they reach conflicting conclusions about the nature and ground of moral distinctions. Royce believes that the history of rival ethical theories repeatedly bears out this suspicion. His polemics against other ethical theories are designed primarily to show that this is so. We might briefly examine these polemics.

2. *Royce's Criticisms of Other Ethical Theories*

Royce devotes three chapters of *The Religious Aspect of Philosophy* to a critical survey of the history of ethical theories. Most of his critical analyses are neither thorough nor close, and occasionally there is some doubt as to whether he has really understood the views he is criticizing. The pur-

[4] *The Religious Aspect of Philosophy*, pp. 33, 59.

pose of his criticisms, however, is a restricted one. He is convinced that the controversy between ethical realism and ethical idealism is "endlessly repeated in the history of moral doctrines," [5] and it is the nature of this controversy that he wishes to elucidate. Our own purpose in examining these polemics is even more restricted: it is to elicit further indications of what Royce takes the problem of ethical theory to be. Thus we may better understand the structure of his own ethical theory as an attempt to resolve this problem.

a. Greek Ethics [6]

In Plato's *Republic* Royce finds the first self-conscious attempt to defend the validity of moral distinctions on moral grounds. Glaucon and Adeimantus are dissatisfied with both the Sophists' view that justice is a matter of arbitrary convention enforced by the will of the stronger, and the popular view that justice is desirable because the gods command and enforce it. Both views reduce morality to prudence. When the two men ask Socrates to defend the worthiness of justice for its own sake, they are eloquently expressing what Royce conceives as the ethical idealist's demand. But in Royce's estimation, Socrates, in spite of a noble effort, fails to answer them. Socrates compares the soul in sensual discord with the soul in rational harmony, and concludes that the unjust man will always be wretched. But that is at best a fact, if it be a fact, about man's nature. It fails to provide a reason why justice is intrinsically desirable, quite apart from its alleged consequences. Socrates has no valid ground for calling unjust the man who insists that "his life of conflict and danger is fuller and sweeter in its lurid contrasts and in its ecstasies of sensuous bliss, than are all your pale, stupid joys of blank

---

[5] *Ibid.*, p. 33.
[6] What follows summarizes Royce's discussion in *The Religious Aspect of Philosophy*, pp. 34–38, unless otherwise indicated.

contemplation." [7] In Royce's eyes, the first would-be ethical idealist has ended in the camp of the ethical realist.

After dismissing in somewhat cavalier fashion the contributions of Aristotle and the Epicureans to the problem at issue as negligible,[8] Royce briefly considers the Stoic view that there exists an ideal Universal Reason to which all men ought to conform, and which they ought in active brotherly concert to realize on earth. Royce credits the Stoics with a high ethical ideal, but he questions the theoretical adequacy of their position. What, Royce asks, is the binding force of the Stoic's obligation claim? On the one hand, the alleged existence of, or desire for, Universal Reason does not of itself establish that it is the highest good or that I ought to work for it. If, on the other hand, Universal Reason triumphs inevitably, I am under coercion, not moral obligation, to serve it. Royce's contention is that the Stoic, no less than Socrates, has fallen prey to the realist-idealist dilemma.

b. Christian Ethics [9]

Royce next examines the ethics of Jesus. Well aware that Jesus was not an ethical theorist but the teacher of a salvationist doctrine compounded of human brotherhood and divine love, Royce, nevertheless, finds the structure of this ethics philosophically illuminating. Like Greek popular morality, this is an ethics founded on theology. But unlike its predecessor, it makes moral distinctions dependent, not "on the mere fact of divine reward or vengeance," but on "a peculiar and necessary relation between God and his creatures." This relation is one of love, and it is to constitute at once the "highest sanction for all good acts" and the "ultimate motive" for right action. Love of and duty toward one's

[7] *Ibid.*, p. 47.

[8] Aristotle because his position is too close to the Socratic-Platonic, the Epicureans because theirs is frankly an ethic of "selfish advantage."

[9] Quotations are from *The Religious Aspect of Philosophy*, pp. 39–48.

neighbor as a child of God are simply corollaries of this doctrine.

Admirable as he feels the doctrine of universal brotherhood and love to be, Royce finds its theoretical justification wanting. Its theological premise, the idea of God as a loving Father, is difficult if not impossible to establish on philosophical grounds, and for the philosopher it cannot be accepted on mere faith. Even if it be granted that Christian Love, like Stoic Reason, is a "physical or metaphysical truth," the question of its *moral* binding power on men is not answered. Conversely, from the point of view of ethics the Christian doctrine seems to put the theological cart before the moral horse. "The doctrine that God loves us is a foundation for duty only by virtue of the recognition of one yet more fundamental moral principle, the doctrine that unearned love ought to be gratefully returned." For this moral principle, in turn, theology cannot supply a theoretical warrant. Then what can? Surely not some generalization about human nature like the fact that men often feel gratitude. The alternative seems to be that the ideal of love is this or that individual's highest moral ideal. But that leaves moral judgments dependent on someone's private will. At this point a Christian ethical theory would find itself squarely in the middle of the realist-idealist antinomy. Once again the choice is between the realist's ethically irrelevant facts and the idealist's individually arbitrary ideals.

c. *"Moral Sense" Theories* [10]

Royce proceeds to a general critique of attempts to justify moral principles by appeal to an innate "moral sense," usually referred to as conscience. Once again his criticisms are neither close [11] nor, by his own admission, original. Never-

---

[10] Quoted passages are from *The Religious Aspect of Philosophy*, pp. 50–57.
[11] With the exception of some remarks about Butler, Royce does not discuss any one "moral sense" theory in detail.

theless, Royce's criticisms of this form of ethical theory provide an illuminating background for his own theory of the role of conscience in the moral life. His main concern is to show that conscience conceived as an *instinct* or a mere *feeling* [12] provides no foundation for moral distinctions. To this end he adduces four considerations:

(1) The consciences of various individuals in various cultures are found to conflict. This being the case, it is difficult to see how an appeal to any one or several of them could serve as rational warrant for ethical distinctions. "If there are several consciences, and all conflicting, then the choice among these can only be made on the ground of something else than a conscience."

(2) An individual's conscience may and often does give rise to conflicting principles of action. Two of the introspectively most evident claims of conscience are justice and benevolence. Conscience rebels against the attempts of some moralists to reduce either of these felt moral obligations to the other. Yet it dictates now one of them, now the other, in a manner that can only be described as "confused and uncertain." Royce does not mean to impugn the legitimacy or ultimacy of conscience as the individual moral agent's guide in urgent matters of practical conduct. He insists, however, that as such it cannot answer philosophical questions and cannot "make a system of morals." "It is the starting-point, not the guide, of moral controversies."

(3) It is extremely difficult to distinguish moral conscience as a feeling from other feelings not regarded as moral, such as a sense of propriety, a respect for custom, or shame over having committed an offense against etiquette.[13]

[12] The very legitimate question whether Shaftesbury, Hutcheson, Butler, et al., understood by "conscience" or "moral sense" an instinctive or affective faculty and, if so, in what sense, will not be raised here because our concern is not with the justice of Royce's criticisms but with ascertaining his own positive orientation.

[13] Royce writes: "You ride using another man's season ticket, or you tell a white lie, or speak an unkind word, and conscience . . . never winces. But

To this objection the common reply that although it may be mistaken for other, non-moral feelings, conscience, where and when it *does* exist, is still infallible, offers no defense. "For if the question can arise whether a given impulse in me, which I take to be the voice of conscience, really is the voice of infallible conscience or not, then this question cannot be decided by an appeal to conscience itself."

(4) "Moral sense" theories, in common with the other theories previously examined, fail to meet the need for an ethical justification of moral distinctions. Even assuming for the moment the existence of an internally consistent, universally uniform, and readily distinguishable moral sense, it would still fail, as a mere "psychological fact," to *justify* moral distinctions. My conscience, Royce maintains, cannot by itself make clear to me that it is morally right to obey its dictates regardless of what these are.

We insist then that one of the first questions of the moralist must be, *why conscience in any given case is right*. Or, to put the case otherwise, ethical doctrine must tell us why, if the devil's conscience approves of the devil's acts, as it may well do, the devil's conscience is nevertheless in the wrong.[14]

Royce's conclusion is that "moral sense" doctrines once again oscillate between equally unsatisfactory forms of ethical realism and ethical idealism.

---

you bow to the wrong man in the street . . . or you tip over a glass of water, and then you apologize for your shortcoming all day long" (*The Religious Aspect of Philosophy*, p. 54). This seems to me a good example of how a psychological argument may be brought to bear against an ethical theory which itself depends for its plausibility, if not for its validity, on psychological arguments. Cf. p. 56, where Royce rejects "even Antigone's sublime test" of eternality as adequate to distinguish conscience from non-moral feelings, for a similar psychological reason. The sense of agelessness is as often as not a geographical or historical prejudice. "Nothing feels older than a well-established custom, no matter how recent it may be."

[14] Italics Royce's.

d. Evolutionist Ethics

Royce next examines what was perhaps the most popular ethical doctrine of his own day, Spencerian evolutionism.[15] Royce outlines the Spencerian doctrine as follows. Both man's physical and social environments are subject to laws of constant evolution of higher out of lower forms of life. Through experience we are able to discover, admittedly with some difficulty, the goal toward which this evolutionary process tends. This goal is to serve as our moral ideal and, once formulated, is to provide us with an adequate basis for a moral code. Such a theory clearly belongs in the realist camp, for it seeks to justify moral distinctions ultimately by appeal to supposed facts about the structure of the external world. Royce offers two distinct but related criticisms of this theory:

(1) Evolutionism "confuses the notion of evolution with the notion of progress, the conception of growth in complexity and definiteness with the conception of growth in moral worth." [16] The characteristics usually put forward to define a stage in the evolutionary process as "higher"—greater complexity, definiteness, permanence, finality, and most successful adjustment of means to ends—are not of themselves *moral* characteristics. The very use, therefore, of terms like "progress" and "higher" begs rather than settles the question of what is worthy of moral approval. If it is then urged that we have a duty to hasten the realization of some future state because in it all men will be happiest, the question becomes one of moral binding force here and now. "Why should I work for future ages, if it is not already quite plain, apart

---

[15] He regards this theory as being more or less within the classic British hedonist-utilitarian tradition of Hobbes (*The Religious Aspect of Philosophy*, p. 66), Bentham (p. 68), and Mill (pp. 78f.). Some of Royce's criticisms are therefore applicable to the tradition as a whole.

[16] *Ibid.*, p. 27; cf. pp. 75f.

from any knowledge of evolution, that I ought to do what I can just now for my brother here?"[17] In short, the confusion of what will be with what ought to be is no less serious than that of what is with what ought to be.

(2) Evolutionism fails to provide a satisfactory account of the common-sense distinction between moral and prudential motives of action. Royce attributes to Spencer the view that it is in our own enlightened self-interest to be altruistic, for unless we cooperate with our fellow men in furthering the evolutionary design inherent in the social order we shall not attain our private ends.[18] To this form of egoistic utilitarianism, Royce objects that appraisals of moral worth have to do primarily with the motives of human actions, not with the circumstances incidental to, and the consequences following upon, these actions. A clever man governed by selfish motives may realize that, his environment being what it is, he had better aid others in the achievement of their interests lest they thwart the attainment of his own. This realization may change the character of his actions, but not the moral quality of his motives. The latter are still selfish, and hence not held to be worthy of moral esteem. On the other hand, a man motivated by regard for the well-being of others is generally regarded as deserving of moral praise even when his actions, for any reason whatever, fail to bring about the intended result.

Royce concludes his attack with the flat assertion that an ethical theory based on the scientific facts of evolution is no ethical theory at all. The facts in all likelihood are true. But they inform us as to available means of action, not as to the moral worth of the ends to which action is directed. "Those who investigate evolution are doing much to further the realization of ethical ideals, but they cannot make or find for

---

[17] *Ibid.*, p. 76.   [18] *Ibid.*, p. 68.

us our ethical ideals."[19] In a display of the sharp wit he occasionally manifests, Royce remarks:

The whole [evolutionist] undertaking resembles that of a man who should try to show us that the truth of the law of gravitation clearly indicates that we all ought to sit down.[20]

e. Ethical Theory Founded on Pity or Sympathy

Having examined, and rejected, a species of utilitarian ethics that would "define unselfishness as a useful means to a selfish end," Royce now considers a theory that would "make unselfishness a self-evident goal of conduct, by founding unselfishness on the direct revelation of the emotion of Pity." He finds Schopenhauer to be the best spokesman of this doctrine, and expounds his position as follows.[21] The emotion of pity or sympathy is the only unselfish emotion in man. It is not reducible to any other, more selfish emotion. It is a psychological error to suppose that in pity we feel another's suffering as ours; it is just the peculiarity of pity that it is fully empathic. We suffer *with* and therefore *in* another, feeling his pain as his and not as ours. However, the psychological account of pity as a uniquely nonegoistic impulse does not fully explain its significance in the moral life. For in the concrete experience of pity a deep metaphysical insight is gradually and imperfectly revealed, namely, the real and essential oneness of all men. It is because pity not only coincides with unselfish feeling but actually exposes, when reflected upon, the very "illusion of selfishness" that it has the

---

[19] Ibid., p. 85. Royce notices that Spencer occasionally admits the Kantian categorical imperative as the foundation of his moral system (p. 83). "With Kant's principle assumed," Royce argues, "we already have attained, apart from any physical doctrine of evolution, the essentials of an ethical doctrine to start with; and we need no doctrine of evolution to found this ethical doctrine, but need it only to tell us the means."

[20] Ibid., p. 80.

[21] Ibid., pp. 85–94.

dignity and authority of an ultimate principle of moral conduct.

Now Royce himself considered the overcoming of the "illusion of selfishness" to be a necessary prerequisite of genuinely moral conduct.[22] Nevertheless, he is sharply critical of Schopenhauer's particular theory. From the very outset, Royce refuses to concern himself with the metaphysical penumbra of Schopenhauer's ethics.[23] Royce does, however, devote a good ten pages to a psychological counteranalysis of the emotion of pity.[24] Schopenhauer would have it that a genuine feeling of pity for another's suffering always leads one to seek unselfishly its alleviation. Royce replies that taken by itself pity is a more or less indeterminate impulse. As a rule, acts moral or otherwise do not follow upon such an impulse directly. Much depends on the act of reflection that usually follows the feeling but precedes the acting upon it. "For most people," Royce observes, "the first reflection that follows upon strong pity is no unselfish one at all. It is very simply the precept: 'Get rid of the pain that your neighbor causes you to feel.' " It may be true that the first spontaneous impulse of pity makes me feel your pain as yours and not as mine. But your pain unquestionably causes me pain, and it remains a moot question which of these pains I will be more concerned to remove, and in what manner. Sympathy, as often as not, leads one at last to recoil in terror from the pathos of another's condition. Pity is liable to end in hatred of suffering and contempt for the sufferer—or, worse still, in what Royce brilliantly describes as "the selfish love of the office of comforter."

Through the emotion of pity, then, the "illusion of selfishness" is as likely to be strengthened as overcome. An emotion

---

[22] *The Religious Aspect of Philosophy*, pp. 146ff.
[23] The latter's metaphysics is high-handedly dismissed in one sentence with the remark that it "was a rotten enough tub for a wise man to go down to sea in," *ibid.*, p. 94.
[24] *Ibid.*, pp. 95–105.

so deceitful and capricious can hardly be trusted as an adequate principle of moral action. And once again Royce enters his caveat against the ethical realist:

> Even if sympathy were always unselfish, never capricious, perfectly clear in its dictates, there would remain the other objection. Sympathy is a mere fact of a man's emotional nature. Anyone who has not this emotion you declare to be an incompetent judge. And so your last foundation for [moral principles] is something whose worth is to be demonstrated solely by the fact that it exists.

f. Hedonism [25]

Hedonism, even in its so-called "universalistic" form, is Royce's *bête noir*. This theory, as Royce understands it, holds that the value of anything is determined by the amount of aggregate happiness which it produces. The hedonistic ideal of the good life, therefore, is universal happiness, conceived as "an aggregate of states that would exist in the various separate individuals." The only moral limitation placed upon the individual is that in pursuing his own pleasure he ought not to interfere with others who are pursuing theirs.

Royce believes that the hedonistic ideal cannot withstand critical scrutiny. He offers three arguments to this effect. The first is the familiar psychological argument that the deliberate pursuit of happiness as a conscious end is self-defeating, for "present reflection upon happiness interferes in most cases with happiness." Royce concedes that this argument by itself is inconclusive. It merely affords a "first suggestion that the hedonistic ideal of life has some inner contradiction in its very nature."

The second argument, on the face of it, is likewise an appeal to an alleged psychological fact. It is that the imaginative experiment of supposing the hedonistic ideal of uni-

---

[25] *Ibid.*, pp. 185–211. The James quote is taken from "The Dilemma of Determinism," *Unitarian Review* (September 1884).

versal contentment attained inspires in most men nothing but a feeling of *tedium vitae*. Human nature is such that it would suffocate if the hedonist Utopia ever did become a reality. Royce here quotes William James with enthusiastic approval:

> To our crepuscular natures, born for conflict, the Rembrandt-esque moral chiaroscuro, the shifting struggle of the sunbeam in the gloom, such pictures of light upon light are vacuous and expressionless, and neither to be enjoyed nor understood.

Royce adds that a life in which striving for goodness, devotion, heroism, and love were absent would be a life in which neither morality nor human happiness as we now envision it would have any meaning. The implication is that what men understand by the good life, however varied their conceptions of it may be, cannot be encompassed by terms such as pleasure or contentment in any of their ordinary senses.[26]

The third argument once again appeals to a supposed fact about human nature. It is directed against any ethical theory proposing an individualistic moral principle. According to Royce, human society is so constituted that private satisfaction or contentment is a goal for whose attainment we can have no reasonable hope, and for which our very desire is, under normal social conditions, eventually superseded. Social processes of interpersonal criticism expose individual self-satisfaction and self-complacency as an illusion. The individual no sooner feels that he has achieved inner contentment than his fellow men point out his inevitable limitations and shortcomings. His self-esteem is wounded to the core, his satisfaction gives way to dissatisfaction. If he were more self-reliant than he is, he might greet the contempt of other men with indifference. But in fact he is not. If he could

---

[26] Royce may be suggesting that if the hedonist claims that by goodness we *mean* pleasures or contentment and by rightness what is conducive to pleasure or contentment, he has misdefined ethical terms. If that is Royce's point, it is directed against hedonism as a "metaethical" theory.

revert to the blissful ignorance of his former self-satisfied state, perhaps he would. But in fact he cannot. The recognition and approval of others are essential to his well-being. From this point on, he surrenders the right to determine his own worth as an individual to a moral point of view beyond his private self. His awareness of his ties with his fellow men becomes so strong that hedonism, "whose life-blood is the insistence upon individual states as such," no longer can provide him, if it ever could, with a viable principle of moral conduct. The whole notion of the self-fulfillment of isolated individuals, singly or in aggregate, loses its meaning for him.

This argument is designed to tell against hedonism as a species of "ethical individualism" by appeal to alleged facts about human nature. Now as we have seen, it is Royce's own contention that no fact about human nature or about the state of the world, as such and by itself, establishes the validity of any moral ideal or principle. This is the plight of the ethical realist. But the converse of this proposition, namely, that no such fact constitutes an adequate basis for the refutation of a moral ideal, offers little comfort to the ethical idealist. Stubborn facts need not refute a proposed moral ideal; it is quite enough if they deprive the latter of the feasibility of pursuing it, and hence of its rational persuasiveness. An ethical theory that not only ignores the factual conditions under which men live but actually proposes a moral ideal by which men *cannot* consistently live is, to say the least, implausible.

More strongly put, the attempt to live by an individualistic ideal involves one, if Royce's analysis of human nature is correct, in a "living contradiction." Royce expresses this most clearly in criticizing the ideal of personal heroism (he calls it "titanism") as a form of ethical individualism:

In short, just what the heresy of Prometheus asserts to be the perfect, namely, the complete and all-sided development of life, just that can belong only to the general, not to the individual life. It says that I, the narrow, limited self, who am dependent for every quality of my life on constant living intercourse with other people, must become perfect, independent, practically infinite. But to ask this is to ask that I destroy myself, and my Titanism with me.

3. Ethical Skepticism

For Royce the inevitable outcome of this inventory of conflicting ethical ideals and their respective failures to find theoretical justification is ethical skepticism. Yet the appalling instability of ideals, Royce observes, is not a problem for ethical theorists alone.

The problem is one of daily life. We choose some fashion of life in the morning, and we reject it before night. Our devotional moments demand that all life shall be devotional; our merry moments that all life shall be merry; our heroic moments that all life shall be lived in defiance of some chosen enemy. But we are false to all these our ideals, even while we pretend to have them. And the most disheartening aspect of the whole matter lies in the fact that we cannot prove even our faithlessness to be unworthy, unless we can bring ourselves steadfastly to accept some ideal by which our faithlessness itself can be judged. And this would imply that we are no longer faithless.[27]

Royce believes that he has at last "reached the root" of ethical skepticism. It consists in asserting "that all choice of ideals is an accidental caprice, that ideals have no basis but this caprice, and that a moral code depends for its successful propagation wholly on the personal persuasive force of the man that happens to have it and to teach it."

For a clear and definitive statement of this ethical skepticism, Royce refers us to the appendix of Arthur Balfour's *A Defence of Philosophic Doubt*, entitled "On the Idea of a Philosophy of Ethics." [28] Royce devotes only three pages to

[27] *The Religious Aspect of Philosophy*, p. 127.
[28] (London, 1879), pp. 335–355.

quoting from and paraphrasing Balfour's view, and he makes no effort directly to controvert it here. Nevertheless, it was ethical skepticism, and in particular Balfour's version of it, that Royce took to be one of his primary tasks as moral philosopher to attempt to overcome. It would be well, therefore, to present Balfour's position more fully than Royce himself does, so that we may learn more about the nature of that self-imposed task. Moreover, there is a distinctive feature of a theory of ethical skepticism that deserves particular attention. All the other ethical theories discussed above advanced the claim that they had provided or could provide an adequate theoretical basis for the universal acceptance of a moral ideal or principle. Royce's various criticisms of these theories quite properly assumed that the burden of justifying such a claim rested with them. The attempt to overcome ethical skepticism, on the contrary, places the burden of proof squarely upon the critic, as Royce is well aware. Hence it will come as no surprise that Royce's moral philosophy begins to take on a constructive rather than a polemical character just at the point where it is confronted by Balfour.

According to Balfour, scientific judgments and ethical judgments deal with fundamentally different subject matters. The former state facts or events, real or hypothetical, whereas the latter do not. It is axiomatic that the foundational propositions of an ethical system must themselves be ethical, and neither scientific nor metaphysical. "In other words, if a proposition announcing obligation requires proof at all, one term of that proof must always be a proposition announcing obligation, which itself requires no proof." It follows that the origin of a fundamental ethical belief cannot furnish a reason for accepting it. No amount of psychological or anthropological evidence concerning the history of moral ideas, the nature of moral sentiments, and the like can serve to confirm or refute a fundamental ethical proposition. Now an ethical proposition, as Balfour defines it, is one prescribing an action with reference to an end. In a system of such propositions, the fundamental proposition states an end which the person who accepts that system regards as final, chosen for itself alone. When two such systems conflict, preferences between them can be defended only in terms of a proposition contained in neither system.

On the basis of this analysis of "ethical systems," Balfour finds no criteria for distinguishing among moral, nonmoral, and immoral systems. The result is of course the core of his skeptical position. In defense of it, Balfour examines two of the most common criteria put forward as definitive of moral as opposed to nonmoral and immoral systems—universality and the approval of conscience—in order to see what possible bearing they might have on obligation. His answer is that they have none whatever. There are only four senses in which a moral law may be said to be universal: (1) All men regard themselves as bound by it. Universality in this sense may be dismissed as being a scientific assertion (and a discredited one at that) which, as such, cannot provide the foundation of an ethical system. (2) All men *ought* to regard themselves as bound by it. Universality in this sense involves one in an infinite regress of universal moral laws, each obliging all men to be bound by the preceding one. (3) *We* think that all men ought to obey it. But "we" is merely a misleading way of saying "I." *I* am bound by the law held by me whether it is universal in this sense or not. Other men are *not* bound by a law held by me whether it is universal in this sense or not. (4) All people of "well-constituted minds" regard themselves as bound by it. But "well-constituted" must be defined either in moral or in nonmoral terms. If the former, that is, if it is taken to mean something like "holding the one true moral system," the assertion that moral laws are universal becomes a "frivolous and merely verbal matter." If the latter, that is, if "well-constituted" refers to some nonmoral characteristic like being sane, well-educated, Christian, or scientific, then universality in this sense, being a questionable scientific assertion, cannot afford a basis of obligation.

The appeal to conscience, Balfour asserts, fares no better. The supposed existence of a special faculty announcing moral laws does not validate them, even if it is accompanied by sanctions of remorse, self-approbation, and the like. Conscience in this sense is merely one more external authority. Why *should* conscience be obeyed? Because it is intrinsically right to obey? But then the authority derives its validity from a moral law beyond itself. Because it is conducive to our happiness to obey? But then the authority derives its validity from, in Balfour's terminology, an "ethical but nonmoral law" beyond itself.

To repeat, the question which Balfour is raising is on what grounds, if any, an "ethical" system can be established as "moral" over against those that are commonly regarded as immoral and nonmoral. An ethical system, as we saw, consists of ultimate propositions prescribing ends in themselves for which, as such, no further reason can be given, and a body of dependent propositions prescribing actions conducive to these ends. "If, for instance, revenge against a particular individual is for me an end-in-itself, a proposition which prescribes shooting him from behind a hedge may be one of the subordinate or dependent propositions belonging to that particular system." On what grounds could the view be *defended* that this is an immoral system and that a moral one is to be preferred? Balfour finds none. The moralist has the choice either of merely reasserting what is for him the ultimate end of action, or of adducing further characteristics of his system, such as "the sanction of conscience, the emotion of approval, the expectation of reward, the feeling of good desert, [and the] glow of conscious merit." But these and any other conceivable characteristics of what we regard as a *moral* system, whether they be taken as the causes, the ends, or simply the marks of good action, afford no *grounds* or *reasons* for moral obligation.

Balfour draws several concluding corollaries from his argument, two of which are of special interest here. The first has to do with the proper role of the moral philosopher. His task is not to account for the origin of moral ideas; that is the job of the psychologist. Nor is it to prove the fundamental propositions of any system of morals; that he cannot do. Nor is it to justify the preference of one ultimate end over another when these conflict; that he cannot do either. Nor, finally, "has he any but a subordinate part to play in expounding or deducing the derivative rules of morality"; that requires minor premises, usually of a scientific nature, the validation of which lies within the sphere of sociological investigation. Rather, Balfour contends, "the important duties of the moralist . . . arise from the confused state in which the greater part of mankind are with regard to their ethical first principles." His job is not "to prove them or deduce them, but to render them explicit if they are implicit, clear if they are obscure." His method, accordingly, should be "casuistical, and not dogmatic."

The other corollary worthy of note is that, according to Balfour, "there are only two senses in which we can rationally talk of a moral system being superior to the one we profess." The first is superiority of form, meaning that it is more coherent, more consistent, or more closely conforming to a model of the ideal structure of any ethical system. The second is superiority of content. But in this sense, Balfour contends, "superior" can only refer to a system of which we are as yet ignorant, but would adopt if we knew of it. "The superiority indicated is a hypothetical superiority."

It is noteworthy that there is a striking resemblance between Balfour's ethical theory and more recent noncognitive ethical theories on at least five important points: (1) the radical distinction between ethical propositions on the one side and scientific and metaphysical propositions on the other; (2) the impossibility of providing any theoretical justification for fundamental ethical propositions, that is, those announcing ultimate ends; (3) the impossibility of resolving conflicts between rival ethical systems on rational moral grounds; (4) the restriction of the sense in which one moral system can be said to be "superior" to another to considerations of formal consistency on the one side, and, on the other, to the purely hypothetical possibility that further knowledge *may* lead to a change of personal attitude; (5) the restriction of the legitimate role of the moral philosopher to helping people become more clearly aware of their own moral commitments and avoid systematic confusions.

Now since Balfour's position clearly anticipates the currently popular noncognitivist orientation in ethics, Royce's efforts to avoid and overcome this position may well be of more than historical interest. Royce states in no uncertain terms his reluctance to accept as final the skeptical outcome of Balfour's theory:

> Thus viewed, the moral world seems essentially chaotic. Each end, if chosen, has its own way of marshaling acts as good and bad. But one end cannot establish itself theoretically over against another. The warfare among them is practical, but is not rationally judged or ended . . . for one another they have, not arguments, but anathemas . . . no proof, only assertion and condemnation.[29]

It is precisely the "plausible and yet dreadful pessimism" to which the position in question leads, which Royce, both in the remainder of his discussion and in his later moral philosophy, wishes to overcome. His first attempt to do so will be the subject of the next chapter.

[29] *The Religious Aspect of Philosophy*, p. 130.

Chapter Two

ROYCE'S EARLY SOLUTION

As MIGHT be expected, Royce's own attempt to provide a theoretical justification for moral distinctions is designed to avoid both horns of the dilemma in which the ethical realist and the ethical idealist find themselves. His strategy, in brief, is to agree with the idealist that moral distinctions can be justified only by reference to the ideal aims of moral agents—but not on the level proposed by the idealist. Royce argues that the very fact that our ends do conflict, both intrapersonally and interpersonally, is reason enough for the reflective moral agent *not* to derive from any one of these ends a definitive standard of moral distinctions. Instead, the moral agent properly so-called adopts as his ultimate standard of moral judgment the formal principle of the harmonization of conflicting ends of action. Once he has adopted the principle of harmony, the moral agent recognizes that the pursuit of private and limited, when opposed to interpersonally overarching, ends of conduct is morally indefensible.

In this way Royce believes that he, unlike the realist and the idealist, is able to account for both the autonomy of moral agents and the objective character of moral distinctions in a manner that satisfactorily answers the ethical skeptic. In addition, he believes that he is able to shed light on the classic egoist-altruist controversy, to account for the common-sense distinction between prudential and moral conduct, and to establish a sound basis for certain specific obligation claims. Let us examine Royce's early solution in some detail.

1. The Principle of Harmony

The point of departure of Royce's constructive ethical theory is probably unique in the history of moral philosophy. It is an argument designed to show that in a genuine *experience*[1] of moral skepticism a commitment to an ultimate ideal of moral conduct is invariably made. Under what conditions, Royce asks, do we actually experience moral skepticism? At least two conditions are necessary. The first is the existence of interpersonally conflicting ends of action. The second is the apparent impossibility of establishing any one of them as worthier of fulfillment than any other. But these two conditions, Royce contends, are not sufficient for a really thoroughgoing experience of moral skepticism. The conflict between two (or more) conflicting ends must be felt to occur *within ourselves* in such a way that, for the moment at least, they become *our* ends. In the absence of this third condition we would not experience moral skepticism at all.

Had we the will to choose the one end alone, we should unhesitatingly choose it, and should not see enough of the opposing will to be skeptics . . . Had we neither will at all in mind, did we realize neither one of the opposing ends, we should be feeling no hesitation between them. Our doubt arises from the fact that momentarily and provisionally we are in the attitude of assuming both. Our indifference is not the indifference of ignorance, but of knowledge, not of failure to understand either end, but of readiness to realize both ends.[2]

[1] I have underlined this word to call attention at the outset to a possible source of confusion as to what Royce is about here. As I understand him, he is not attempting to refute a philosophical theory of ethical skepticism by psychoanalyzing its proponent. Rather, he is analyzing the conditions under which a moral agent experiences for himself the moral skepticism of which a theory like Balfour's is the philosophical expression.

[2] *The Religious Aspect of Philosophy* (New York, 1885), pp. 133–134. By "realizing an aim" in this context I take Royce to mean "make real for oneself" rather than "achieve" or "attain its object."

In support of this argument, Royce briefly adduces a psychological and what he calls a "philosophical" consideration. From contemporary psychological investigations, Royce draws the "now generally accepted principle" that there is a psychological connection between conceiving of or remembering an act and performing that act. This connection is exemplified particularly in the phenomenon of imitation. "An act is performed, we witness it, we see or know how it is done, we conceive the effort that would lead to the performance of it, and forthwith this conception becomes the performance." Similarly, there is evidence to indicate that in many cases "the idea immediately aroused by a word [is] a sort of dramatic reproduction of the act expressed by the word." Royce sees no reason why this should not apply "even to general resolutions."

If two opposing fashions of action are present to our minds, and if mentally we are trying to realize them both, then mentally we are seeking to reproduce them both. Our skeptical hesitation between them expresses our effort to attain mentally both these ends at once.[3]

But Royce is not content to rest his argument on a "bare accident of the psychological structure of our minds." He holds it to rest on a "philosophical necessity" as well.

Who would know what it is to have an end unless he actually had ends himself? Who can realize a given end save by somehow repeating it in himself? And so it is rationally and universally necessary that one should realize the end of a moral system by reproducing in himself the will that accepts this end.

From this analysis of the experience of moral skepticism, Royce draws the "somewhat unexpected" conclusion that an ultimate moral ideal is implicit in the experience all along. That ideal is the harmonization of conflicting ends. If absolute moral skepticism were possible without destroying itself, it

[3] *Ibid.*, pp. 135–137.

would not really be total absence of moral aim, but would rather be the neutrality that would result from a provisional acceptance of all the conflicting aims in the world of action. Absolute ethical skepticism . . . would still presuppose an end, namely, the effort to harmonize in one moment all the conflicting aims in the world of life . . . Absolute skepticism would thus be founded on absolute benevolence. *Its own aim would be harmony and unity of conduct.*[4]

Royce's argument might be restated as follows. There is a "higher good," superior by its very nature to whatever relative goodness might attach to each of the individual warring aims considered by itself. This higher good is desired and recognized as such whenever a person "lives through," as one might say, the experience of attempting to make two or more conflicting ends of actions his own. The ideal situation of which he then invariably conceives is one in which both (or all possible) aims would be pursued in perfect harmony, without sacrificing or compromising any one of them. Once it is seen that a still higher end, beyond the harmonious achievement of all possible special ends, is inconceivable, the latter (let us, for the sake of brevity, call it harmony) is accepted as the ultimate moral ideal. This ultimate moral ideal or principle serves henceforth as the definitive criterion by reference to which actions and their motives are to be morally appraised.

Royce then seeks to defend the ideal of harmony as plausible in the face of the perennial antinomy he has discovered besetting theoretical ethics. The ethical idealist, who would preserve the normative character of moral distinctions at all costs, is generally confronted by two kinds of objection. The first is directed at the nature of the moral ideals proposed. Since the idealist formulates them in complete disregard of facts about men and the world in which they live, they are likely to be unattainable and hence so impractical that it is

[4] *Ibid.*, p. 138.

not worth while to pursue them. Royce maintains that the ideal of harmony is not subject to this objection. Since, by hypothesis, I know *what* is to be harmonized, namely, conflicting aims, and since my actions affect those aims, I can "direct my actions *toward* the attainment of universal Harmony"[5] regardless of whether universal harmony can ever be fully attained. The second sort of objection is directed at the manner in which the ethical idealist supports the ideals he proposes. The only rational warrant for any ideal I happen to have is that I choose it. The same is true of your ideal. Should these conflict, the preference of one over the other can be made only on arbitrary and subjective grounds. Royce contends that this objection likewise does not affect his ideal. Harmony is not one of the warring goals, chosen for whatever reason. It is the goal of achieving all of them to whatever extent that is possible. The rational warrant—and indeed the only one possible—for the goal of harmony is that anyone who fully experiences the existing conflict of special goals thereby inevitably makes it his ultimate goal. To be sure, the experience mentioned is a necessary condition of anyone's being able or willing to accept the ideal of harmony: Royce insists on this point. But if not everyone has this experience at least once in his lifetime, the conclusion is not that harmony is a capricious ideal, but that not everyone has a moral experience.

The ethical realist, who would preserve the objectivity of moral distinctions at all costs, is in turn faced with two kinds of objection, one as to the nature and the other as to the warrant of his proposed ideals. Since the realist looks only to what is in fact the case for his alleged moral ideal, his ideal tends to be devoid of any significantly normative character. He announces some alleged truth about the world, and accompanies it with an injunction to conform to that truth. Claiming to present us with a moral ideal implemented by

[5] *The Religious Aspect of Philosophy*, p. 141.

moral principles, the ethical realist offers us instead a report about matters of fact implemented by maxims of prudence. In defending the ideal of harmony against this objection, Royce points out that harmony by its very nature has to do with ideal ends and not with facts. To be sure, *that* someone desires harmony is a matter of fact. It is also a matter of fact that a certain experience, namely that of conflicting ends, is presupposed for anyone to desire their harmonization. But the moral worth of harmony is not determined by these facts. It is determined instead by its peculiar relation to ends as such. Since all value-appraisals must have reference to ends, and since harmony is the ideal of pursuing and achieving in integrated fashion *all* ends, harmony qualifies as "the ideal of ideals." "It is the absolute ideal that arises," according to Royce, "out of the consideration of the separate ideals." It is for this reason that Royce feels justified in asserting that he is not "capriciously deciding upon the worth of physical facts as such," but instead "passing a necessary judgment upon ideals as ideals." [6]

The second kind of objection against ethical realism is closely related to the first. It is that the only rational warrant the realist is ever able to offer for his allegedly moral ideal is an appeal to some existing state of affairs. But that is no rational warrant at all. For no amount of knowledge about what is the case can ever of itself provide an adequate reason for saying that something ought to be the case. Royce's defense of harmony against this objection is implicit in what has been said already. The problem of supplying a rational warrant for pursuing any one end arises only when there is a multiplicity of conflicting ends, among which a choice must somehow be made. But if, as Royce maintains, the experience of conflicting ends invariably suggests one ultimate end transcending all of these, that ultimate end in turn neither can have nor does it require a further rational warrant. The ideal of harmony being, according to Royce, implicit in every genuine experience of trying to decide between conflicting special ideals, all that is needed is to make the former explicit.[7]

To recapitulate briefly: Royce considers one of the fundamental problems of ethical theory to be whether, and if so how, moral distinctions can be rationally justified in such a way as to warrant their objectivity and, at the same time, preserve their distinctively normative character. Previous attempts in the history of moral philosophy to solve this problem have tended either to sacrifice the normative character of moral distinctions to the tyranny of fact, or to abandon moral objectivity to the caprice of personal whim. The result, both on the level of theory and on the level of practice, has been moral skepticism—the conviction that moral distinctions cannot be rationally justified. Royce contends that this result is premature. A closer analysis of the thoroughgoing experience of moral skepticism discloses at its basis a moral ideal, the harmonization of conflicting ends of action, which does after all satisfy at once the demands of moral autonomy and of moral objectivity. The experience of conflicting ends of action is accessible to all men, and when it occurs it inevitably suggests to each man the ideal of harmony as the ultimate end of conduct. Although the perfect harmonization of all ends of action is no doubt unattainable under human social conditions as we know them, it can be approximated in interpersonal relations and is therefore not an impractical ideal. Thus Royce's strategy is to concede that personal ends of action do conflict, to uncover in the experience of moral conflict the will, however momentary, to reconcile these conflicts, and to specify as object of this will the ideal of harmony as the ultimate end of moral conduct.

[7] Cf. *ibid.*, p. 145: "If one doubts this ideal, then he doubts the very foundation of ethical doubt itself."

It then remains to formulate moral principles defining obligations in order to implement the end of harmony. The adequacy of Royce's solution will be discussed later in the chapter. It is useful first to examine several other considerations that Royce adduces to explain and defend his view.

2. Moral Insight

It is Royce's thesis that the conflicting ends of action of two or more men can be experienced by any one of these men as his own ends. When this experience takes place, the individual, Royce believes, tends inevitably to have as his highest end, if only for a moment, the harmonious fulfillment of these conflicting separate ends. On the assumption that he has analyzed the alleged experience correctly, Royce feels justified in referring to such a moment as "the moment of moral insight." [8] To explain further what he means by this "moral insight," and under what circumstances it may be found, Royce turns next to a more concrete examination of everyday interpersonal relations, and specifically of the common-sense distinction between egoistic and altruistic behavior. "Why," Royce asks, "is it easier for me to be selfish than unselfish?"

Because it is easier for me to realize my own future, and my own desire about it, than to realize the desires of my neighbor. My will is the *datum;* his the dimly conceived, remote fact. Hence it seems to me obvious that his will must be to me less significant than my own.[9]

[8] *The Religious Aspect of Philosophy*, p. 146.
[9] *Ibid.*, pp. 146–147. At this point I would like, once and for all, to beg the reader's indulgence with Royce's frequently rhetorical, archaic, and seemingly "entity-ridden" language. A generous measure of good-naturedness is needed to leap over this linguistic hurdle for the thought that may lurk beyond it. My own conviction is that Royce's thought is well worth it. I will do my part by admitting that, from the perspective of the contemporary philosopher, Royce's prose style is occasionally unforgivable.

Since this is the way we generally respond to our fellow men, Royce deems useless the efforts of moralists to tell us to cooperate because sometimes it is to our own advantage to do so, or because out of selfish cooperation may one day evolve pure unselfishness, or because we sometimes feel pity or sympathy for one another. None of these reasons is sufficient to induce a selfish individual to be unselfish. The root of the problem is the question whether or not men are condemned to selfishness, hence to mutual estrangement and ever-recurrent moral conflict.

A negative answer to this question is essential to Royce's argument. The possibility of what Royce has called "moral insight" into the interpersonal conflict of ends and the attendant purpose of harmonizing this conflict is conditional upon the possibility of an individual's experiencing these conflicting ends as his own. If it could be shown on psychological or epistemological grounds that this experience is beyond human capability, Royce's argument would be vitiated. It would be unreasonable to hold that men are morally obligated to pursue harmony if in point of fact they were incapable of pursuing it.

Royce observes that most of our more casual everyday contacts with one another occur on a thoroughly egoistical plane. On this plane we are conscious of others only as loosely organized masses of dispositions to behave in certain ways.[10] We see them as "industrious or lazy, honest or deceitful, polite or uncivil, useful or useless people," but never as the self-conscious persons we take ourselves to be. To see them this way is to see them "from without. Not their inner, volitional nature is realized, but their manner of outward activity; not what they are for themselves, but what they are for others." Royce points out that this form of "natural" and "imperfect realization" occurs even among people bound by close ties of affection. He cites the example of Lear, and

---

[10] *The Religious Aspect of Philosophy*, pp. 149–151.

adds that even lovers are often more concerned to elicit from one another an action, a tone of voice, a familiar gesture than to realize "the inner and more personal emotional life that is the cause of this way of behavior." [11]

But Royce insists that this level of interpersonal contact is not the only one we know. It represents the basis of the "illusion of selfishness," an illusion that Royce believes can be and on occasion is overcome. It is overcome through "critical reflection" upon the consistency of my view of my neighbor. I cannot consistently regard him as "a dead fact of nature, an automaton" since many of his actions force me to an awareness of him as a conscious and voluntary agent much like myself. But I cannot consistently arrest the process of recognizing him even there. Upon reflection, I am driven to realize that his conscious and volitional experiences are as real to him as mine are to me. But to be aware to that extent of my neighbor's reality, Royce concludes, is tantamount to being *concerned* with him, and concerned not only for my sake but for his own. Critical reflection at last forces me to say, "As he is real, he is as much an object for my effort as I myself am, in case I can affect him. Ours is one life." [12]

This, then, is what Royce understands by "the moral insight" that arises out of the process of interpersonal recognition. Reflection forces me to see that at the level of casual interpersonal contact my awareness of my fellow is confused, inconsistent, and incomplete. Since I cannot give up recognizing him altogether, this same reflection thereupon leads me "of necessity [to] resolve . . . to realize him wholly." And to treat him as if he were real in the fullest possible sense leads one quite naturally to treat him in a nonselfish way. Royce contends that other moral philoso-

---

[11] *Ibid.*, p. 152. Royce footnotes what seems to be a line from a popular song current in his day: "I'd give all my income from dreamland for a touch of her hand on my cheek."

[12] *Ibid.*, p. 154.

phers have neglected this element of reflective rationality in the development of moral consciousness.[13]

> In this process we see the beginning of the real knowledge of duty to others . . . It is the process by which we all are accustomed to try to teach humane behavior in concrete cases. We try to get people to realize what they are doing when they injure others. But to distinguish this process from the mere tender emotion of sympathy, with all its illusions, is what moralists have not carefully enough done.[14]

As I understand him, Royce is attempting to change the customary focus on the traditional problem of egoism and altruism. In the past, moral philosophers have tended to take either of two positions on this problem. One is that men are irremediably selfish because they do not in fact have any other-regarding impulses or interests. Proponents of this position, Royce has argued,[15] have usually confined themselves as moralists to inventing more or less spurious reasons why men ought nevertheless concern themselves with the welfare of others: for instance, that it is to their own advantage to do so. The other position is that men in fact do have other-regarding impulses. Defenders of this view have sometimes maintained that the reason these impulses ought to be followed and cultivated is that they are uniquely "moral" impulses. In reply, Royce has contended [16] that it makes no sense to call impulses as such "moral." Our impulses as such do not as a rule move us to act directly. They are mediated by reflection upon our interests. These overriding reflective interests may be egoistic or altruistic independently of whether the impulses they help to control are themselves

[13] *Ibid.* Royce might have made an exception here of Kant, at least. Royce's "treating men as real" is not very different from Kant's treating persons as ends in themselves.

[14] Foremost among these moralists, in Royce's mind, is, of course, Schopenhauer. It is quite likely that he was thinking of Hume, although he had not previously mentioned him by name.

[15] See the discussion of evolutionist ethics in Chapter One.

[16] See the discussion of Schopenhauer's ethics in Chapter One.

self-directed or other-directed (if it makes sense to speak of impulses in this manner at all).

Royce is arguing, I believe, that both positions have misconstrued the fundamental problem. It is of little use to tell a man that he ought to be unselfish—that is, moral—if, as the one side maintains, he is constitutionally incapable of being unselfish. On the other hand, even if he does have "other-directed" impulses, as the other side believes, these impulses do not by themselves make him a moral agent. For he is under no compulsion to act on them; if he were, he would be even less a responsible moral agent. Neither side, Royce believes, has looked in the right place. It is not a question of impulse but of insight. Let a man once get to *know* his fellow men as well as he knows himself, and, if he is rational and consistent, he will condemn his own selfishness as immoral. To be selfish is to be blind, but men are not necessarily blind. The task of the practical moralist is not to cajole men into being something they are not. Nor is it to tell them that they have been instinctively moral all along. It is to help them see.

Finally, Royce claims that his analysis of moral insight enables him to account for the common-sense distinction [17] between morally praiseworthy and merely prudential motives of conduct. The "illusion of selfishness" stems in part from my very natural feeling that my own "present state with its experiences, thoughts and desires" is more "real" to me, because more immediate, than anything else in the world.[18] But when I act for ends I postulate future states of myself "as certain to come, and as in some real relation" to my present state. So to postulate, that is, to extend the scope of my concerns beyond the present moment is, among other things, to be prudent. Critical reflection, however, finds no

---

[17] A distinction, it will be recalled, that Royce found it extremely difficult for the ethical realist to render intelligible.

[18] *The Religious Aspect of Philosophy*, p. 156.

rational warrant for regarding my own future states that I do not now experience as any more or less "real" than the present and future states of my fellow men which are not now my own.

Once I have understood that much, I realize that it would be inconsistent for me to pursue exclusively my own private ends because these are more "real" or more "important." I then see that my "self," regardless of the deceptive feelings of self-importance that might attach to it, has no rationally defensible prerogatives. It is then that I begin to appreciate "the oneness of life," the "one omnipresent, conscious struggle for the getting of the desired," which underlies moral insight. It is then that prudential conduct gives way to moral conduct.

As the prudent man, seeing the reality of his future self, inevitably works for it; so the enlightened man, seeing the reality of all conscious life . . . at once and inevitably desires, if only for that one moment of insight, to enter into the service of the whole of it.[19]

Royce immediately enters a caveat, however, against the optimistic assumption that once an individual has attained this moral insight, he will act on it from then on. The resolution to treat my fellow as I treat myself begins and ends with my full awareness of his reality—an awareness that is at best sporadic.

Passion may cloud the insight in the very next moment . . . Moments of insight, with their accompanying resolutions; long stretches of delusion and selfishness: That is our life.[20]

3. The "Spray of Aims"

Royce has attempted to show that what he has defined as the "moral insight" is an insight into "the oneness of all conscious life." The latter he has loosely characterized as the

[19] *Ibid.*, pp. 160–161.   [20] *Ibid.*, pp. 155–156.

universal "struggle for the getting of the desired." It remains
to be determined what men in fact desire and what, if anything, that has to do with what they ought to desire. Royce
does not wish to be misinterpreted. He is not arguing that
universal harmony already exists in latent form, waiting
merely to be recognized, because all men really have one
and the same aim. To Royce this is simply false. Each man
seeks what seems desirable to him: that is all that can be
said. "What aim is common to the whole life of any one of
us? Much less then is any aim common to all men." [21]

In the light of the "spray of aims" [22] which guide men's
actions, Royce regards as a "hackneyed error" [23] the fre-
quent attempts of moral philosophers to base their principles
on a revelation of some one thing for which men have
blindly striven all along. There is no one such aim or desire,
and the philosopher who pretends that there is merely incurs
the charge of dogmatizing. Royce considers a possible corollary of this dogma, namely, that all moral failing arises from
mere ignorance of what men really want, to be equally
mistaken.

One may want anything, and may know it very well. There
is no known limit to the caprice and the instability of the human
will. If you find anybody desiring anything, the only tolerably
sure and fairly universal comment is, that he will stop desiring it
by and by.[24]

Thus, to the question of what men in fact desire, Royce's
answer is: virtually anything. To the question of what men

---

[21] *The Religious Aspect of Philosophy*, p. 167.   [22] *Ibid.*, pp. 142f.
[23] *Ibid.*, p. 163. Royce cites as examples Bentham, Mill, Spencer, and
Clifford. He finds Mill, in his attempts to distinguish higher from lower
pleasures and to defend the former as morally preferable, driven "to the
worst subterfuge possible for so skilled a thinker, when he at last says that
the pleasure which seems the higher of two pleasures to the 'most of those
who have experienced both' is actually the higher. For thus, to keep up the
show of merely interpreting to men their actual will, Mill has to appeal to the
opinion of the majority, has to use a purely practical habit of deliberative
assemblies for the purpose of deciding a question of theory . . ." (p. 165).
[24] *Ibid.*, p. 168.

ought to desire, therefore, no satisfactory answer that is based merely on what they do desire can be given.

Yet the occasional overarching unity of interpersonal moral endeavor is as much a fact of our experience as is the inevitable multiplicity of personal ends of action. Royce's problem is to account for the possibility of the former while preserving his realistic recognition of the existence of the latter. Once again, he believes that this can be done only by way of his doctrine of "moral insight" and its attendant principle of harmony. On his view, to experience the interpersonal conflict of aims fully is tantamount to identifying oneself with those aims. But to identify oneself with conflicting aims is to demand their harmonization. Since the aims of men are various and conflicting, and since no one of them has a higher *prima facie* moral claim to be realized than any other, the only *moral* attitude that can consistently be taken toward them is one that seeks not their mutual exclusion but their harmonious satisfaction. Harmony, then, is not a universal desire. Rather, it is a moral ideal recognized as such in a moment of moral insight and attained, if at all, only by "hard work." [25]

Underlying Royce's insistence upon the "spray of aims" is his recognition of, and respect for, an irreducible human plurality. Royce never wavered in his conviction that men differ notably in regard to who they are, what they do in fact "live for," and how they ought ideally to conduct their lives. As we shall see, this conviction became decisive in his later community theory.

4. Moral Obligation

Royce's doctrines of moral insight and harmony constitute the pillars of his early effort to construct a positive ethical theory. Taken together, Royce believes, they give rise to two

[25] *Ibid.*, p. 162.

classes of duties, "one formal and provisional, the other permanent," [26] which comprise a basic framework for moral obligation. A brief examination of what Royce has to say about duty here will conclude the expository portion of this chapter.

The first class of duties has to do with what Royce calls "the moral education of our race." The experience of moral skepticism shows us only too clearly that we do not know what is the highest good for man, individually or collectively —if there is such a thing at all. But we do know that value is determined within the context of human purposes. If we are ever to discover a *summum bonum*, or several indispensable goods, to which we might be expected to give common rational consent, therefore, we must first come to know the plurality of human aims in all their vividness and in all their conflict. But that is possible only through what Royce has called moral insight. Royce has attempted to show that we are capable of obtaining this moral insight, even though the flightiness of our passional natures makes it difficult for us to preserve it. Thus he specifies as an elementary duty, binding on all of us, that we strive for moral insight, preserve it in ourselves, and extend it as much as possible among our fellow men. This obligation is formal and provisional in character because it underlies any and all particular duties that might later be specifiable. It is designed merely to bring men to what might be called the moral attitude, "to produce in men the moral mood, and so to prepare the way for the further knowledge of the highest good." [27] Even more simply put: the most elementary moral obligation incumbent on each of us is that we respect one another as rational and voluntary agents. [28]

As we have seen, moral insight, according to Royce, has the further consequence of convincing its possessor of the

---

[26] *The Religious Aspect of Philosophy*, p. 173. [27] *Ibid.*, p. 175.
[28] Cf. *ibid.*, p. 146.

need to work for interpersonal harmony. Royce takes it as virtually axiomatic that whatever *summum bonum* we might some day discover, it would have to be attained in common.

Therefore the sense of community, the power to work together, with clear insight into our reasons for so working, is the *first* need of humanity. Not what good thing men may hereafter come to see, but how they shall attain the only sense whereby they can ever get to see the good, is the great present human concern.[29]

But if making men "formally moral"[30] through the extension of moral insight is our primary duty, it is still only a provisional one. And if working for interpersonal harmony is indispensable for the subsequent realization of any alleged highest good, that is still only a tentative and rather abstract moral obligation. "To be sure, the ultimate aim of life cannot be merely the extension of the power to realize the wills that are active about us, but must at last be found by defining the course of action that best harmonizes these wills."[31] The second class of duties which Royce is attempting to establish, therefore, has to do with the permanent and more positive task of achieving harmony concretely.

Royce, however, is hard-pressed to give this task precise formulation. He argues that moral insight, once attained, would in effect constitute what he calls an ideally "universal will."

It would demand all the wealth of life that the separate selves now have; and all the unity that any one individual now seeks for himself. It would aim at the fullest and most organized life conceivable.[32]

The permanent obligation binding on all men, once their moral insight has been cultivated, is to "organize all life." By this Royce means:

[29] *Ibid.*, p. 175.   [30] *Ibid.*, p. 184.   [31] *Ibid.*, p. 174.
[32] *Ibid.*, pp. 194–195.

Find work for the life of the coming moral humanity which shall be so comprehensive and definite that each moment of every man's life in that perfect state, however rich and manifold men's lives may then be, can be and will be spent in the accomplishment of that one highest impersonal work.[33]

Yet Royce feels obliged to concede that we are as yet unable to know "the whole nature of that work," or to foresee the "complete organization." There are, however, certain cultural activities and institutions that even now indicate the direction in which the ultimate ideal might be sought. "Beauty, Knowledge, and the State are three ideal objects that do actually claim from those who serve them harmony, freedom from selfishness, and a wholly impersonal devotion." Royce here presents for the first time his favorite example of an approximation to the ideal he has in mind by reference to a community of scientific investigators—all of them exceptionally selfless, objective, fair-minded, and closely knit together.[34]

Royce believes that he has at last discovered an adequate basic criterion for moral distinctions. Moral insight leads us to conceive, however dimly and imprecisely, of an ideal "unity of life"; and, "this being the ideal, all is good that helps us in the direction thereof, and all is evil that drives us in the opposing direction." [35]

[33] *Ibid.*, p. 211.   [34] *Ibid.*, p. 213.
[35] *Ibid.*, pp. 214–215. The remainder of *The Religious Aspect of Philosophy* is not concerned with ethical theory as such. It is Royce's contention that all of us, as moral agents, demand some sort of "outer support" for our moral life. "We want to know that, when we try to do right, we are not alone; that there is something outside of us that harmonizes with our own moral efforts by being itself in some way moral. This something may be a person or a tendency" (p. 219). There follows, in the second half of the book, an investigation, metaphysical in the traditional sense and with religious overtones, of nothing less than "the nature of reality" in an effort to provide the desired "outer support." Here Royce develops his well-known argument for the existence of an Absolute from the fact of human error—an argument whose structure somewhat parallels his attempt dialectically to

5. Clarification and Appraisal

For Royce one of the primary tasks of the moral philosopher is to determine whether, and if so how, a reasoned justification of the moral distinctions made by reflective moral consciousness can be given. With his early constructive ethical theory now before us, it remains to ask how well Royce has succeeded in accomplishing his task.

Royce, as we have seen, was very much aware of "the difficulty of giving any reason for the choice of a moral ideal. Single acts are judged by the ideal; but who shall judge the judge himself?" [36] Equally dissatisfied with the ethical realist's and the ethical idealist's attempts to justify moral distinctions, Royce, nevertheless, was disinclined to accept the ethical skeptic's conclusion that our ultimate moral commitments are arbitrary. On his own terms, Royce cannot justify moral distinctions by appeal to matters of fact external to the moral consciousness. Against the ethical realist, Royce has argued that judgments of fact as such neither entail nor warrant moral obligations. Nor can Royce justify moral distinctions by appeal to any *particular* end of action willed by this or that individual. Against the ethical idealist, Royce has maintained that when these particular ends come into conflict, as they inevitably do, no one of them furnishes its own reason why it should be regarded as morally preferable to any other. Yet to admit, with the skeptic, that for each individual some personal end is final, that it

---

elicit fundamental moral principles from the experience of moral skepticism.

We shall have occasion in the Appendix to speak of the relation of Royce's metaphysical idealism to his ethical theory. For the present it is preferable to pass directly to a clarification and appraisal of Royce's beginnings in ethical theory, and then to develop the full structure of his ethical theory in its mature form. Once that is done, at least one of the terms of the relation just mentioned will perhaps have become clear.

[36] *The Religious Aspect of Philosophy,* p. 47.

marshals moral distinctions for him and for him alone, and that therefore moral judgments have at most a first-personal warrant—is for Royce tantamount to admitting that "the warfare of moral ideals" is a permanent condition of our experience.

Thus Royce's defense of the ideal of harmony as the foundational principle of moral conduct represents an attempt at once to escape the dilemma of ethical realism and ethical idealism and to answer ethical skepticism. His strategy is to make a concession to each of the three positions he is opposing, without accepting any of them fully.

(1) Royce concedes to the idealist that it is useless even to attempt a justification of moral distinctions apart from a consideration of the ideal ends of action willed by moral agents. For it is Royce's conviction that neither the notion of value nor the notion of obligation can be meaningfully defined out of relation with the reflective interests of rational beings. But when these several reflective interests come into conflict with one another, as they obviously do, the idealist is unable to give a convincing reason why the attainment of any one of them should be regarded as morally preferable to the attainment of any other. To Royce this is understandable, for at this level no such reason *can* be given. However, since the realization of each of these ends would have *some* value, and since the perpetuation of conflict among the persons willing them is destructive of their realization, the reasonable conclusion is not that any one of these wills should prevail, but that all of them should be harmonized as far as that is possible.

Crucial to an understanding of Royce's argument at this point is the distinction between a substantive ideal and a formal or procedural ideal. The essential difference between them is that they are logically on two different levels. A substantive ideal arises out of the desire to attain the fulfillment of a concrete, specific "first-order" interest such as acquiring greater social prestige, securing professional advancement, appropriating some beloved object, and so forth. A formal ideal arises out of the reflective awareness that none of us can successfully achieve any of these specific goals unless all of us commit ourselves to certain procedural principles necessary in order to prevent mutually destructive conflicts of interest. Thus the commitment to being reasonable in adjudicating value disputes, to respecting all persons *qua* persons regardless of their differing interests, and to securing a maximal harmonization of interpersonally conflicting particular ends is *different in kind* from the commitment to pursuing this or that personal goal.

Royce is suggesting, then, that the idealist, in his attempt to justify moral distinctions, has appealed to the wrong kind of ideal. Let the particular ideal of this or that person be what it may: health, wealth, honor, power, pleasure, triumph of country, or union with God. Let this ideal be ultimate in his personal system of values. It can at best constitute a moral claim upon him and him alone. Now the uniqueness of the ideal of harmony as "the ideal of ideals" lies in its distinctively formal or procedural character. It enjoins the taking of what might be called a second-order interest in interests (or personal ideals) themselves: namely, that all of the latter be satisfied as far as that is possible without mutual frustration. Whereas the several first-order interests and ideals carry conflicting claims that the attainment of each of their particular objects would be of greatest value, the second-order interest in harmony has for its aim the adjudication of these several claims to the mutual benefit of all concerned. The ideal of harmony is uniquely qualified to serve as ultimate standard of moral conduct, therefore, just because it does "rise above" conflicting special interests without simply abandoning them to their fate. To seek harmony is to seek the maximum of good in a world in which that maximum can be attained only in and through the harmonization of conflicting interests. When an autonomous moral agent voluntarily adopts the principle of harmony as his ultimate standard of moral judgments, he is satisfying to the highest possible degree the demand of reflective moral consciousness that these judgments be objective, impartial, and in some sense universally applicable.

(2) In view of the vehemence with which Royce attacks the ethical realist position, one might suppose that he rejects the position *in toto*. But this would be an oversimplification. Actually Royce agrees with the realist that determinations of matters of fact are relevant to the problem of moral justification, but disagrees with the realist's conception of how they are relevant. The realist argues that we can directly determine what men ought to do by determining matters of fact about human nature or its physical and social environment. This Royce refuses to accept. Morality is essentially a normative not a descriptive discipline. Neither moral judgments nor the standards or principles on which they are based are assertions of matters of fact. Neither can be justified by merely reporting what is the case in regard to man or his environment.

Yet in his defense of the principle of harmony as the ultimate standard of moral judgment and conduct, Royce himself, by his own admission, appeals to alleged matters of fact. He argues that men are in fact capable of unselfish action; that they occasionally do experience a full awareness of their fellow men as thinking and willing beings like themselves; that when they do experience this awareness they there and then invariably recognize as the highest ideal and standard of moral conduct the harmonization of all conflicting interests and ideals whose existence they know of or conceive; and that their having this experience is a necessary condition of their feeling the binding force of the moral obligation to pursue harmony.

Is Royce, then, adopting the very position he has so em-

phatically rejected? Is he attempting to prove that harmony
is desirable from the mere fact that men desire it under certain circumstances? Is he arguing that men have a duty to
develop other-regarding interests simply on the ground that
they are capable of having such interests? I do not think so.
Royce is not appealing directly to factual states of affairs in
order to justify normative conclusions. Instead, he is showing how human beings, reflecting on certain factual states of
affairs, are naturally led by themselves to reach certain
moral conclusions. This much is a matter of "moral psychology" rather than of normative ethical theory. Moreover, I do
not think that Royce, in spite of some misleading language,
has any intention of offering a strict demonstration of the
principle of harmony or a formal proof, in any commonly
accepted sense, of the validity of certain obligation claims.
Instead, I understand him to be offering, to borrow J. S.
Mill's happy phrase, "considerations . . . capable of determining the intellect either to give or withhold its assent to
the doctrine"[37] he is advocating. With the considerations
Royce thus adduces we are by now sufficiently familiar. Interpersonal interests and ideals conflict. No one of them has
prima facie a stronger claim to being intrinsically worthy of
fulfillment than any other. A reflective person, fully cognizant of this situation and concerned with the satisfaction of
any interest or the realization of any ideal, can refuse to
adopt as his ultimate principle of moral conduct the harmonization of all interests and ideals only at the cost of unreasonableness and inconsistency.[38]

As we shall see presently, Royce devoted a considerable
effort to an empirical analysis of human nature in order to

[37] *Utilitarianism* (London, 1895), p. 7.
[38] To be sure, terms such as "rational," "consistent," and "impartial" are
themselves normative, as Royce was well aware. But the implication to be
drawn from this is not necessarily that all attempts to justify moral principles are in the final analysis circular, but rather that whatever justification
these principles can have must come from within the broader context of the
moral life itself.

make his moral principles both more concrete and more plausible. But he never supposed that such analyses could be construed as validating or demonstrating ultimate moral principles.

(3) Royce was deeply concerned to find an adequate answer to theoretical ethical skepticism, specifically in the form developed by Arthur Balfour. Yet it is not immediately clear just what the focal point of the controversy between Royce and Balfour really is. Balfour begins by asserting that scientific propositions and ethical propositions are fundamentally different in kind, the former being descriptive, the latter normative. Royce obviously agrees.[39] Next, Balfour takes it to be axiomatic that the foundational propositions of any ethical system must themselves be ethical and not scientific or metaphysical, and draws the corollary that fundamental ethical propositions cannot be confirmed or refuted by any amount of psychological or other factual evidence concerning the history of moral ideas, the nature of moral sentiments, and the like. With this Royce evidently agrees as well. Balfour then argues that in any person's system of ends, one end is likely to be final or ultimate, and for no other reason than that this person chose to make it so. When the system of ends of several persons conflict, their rival claims to preference could be adjudicated only by a judgment or proposition contained in neither of them. But no proof can be given or required either for the judgment that declares an end to be final, or for the judgment that declares which of two ends is preferable. Even with that much Royce seems to agree. If I choose an end that is ultimate for me, neither of us can prove to the other one that one of the ends must be preferred.

Balfour thereupon subjects to criticism two criteria com-

[39] In his later writings, however, Royce did draw certain significant analogies between scientific and ethical propositions (cf. Chapter Six, section 3).

monly advanced as justifying the obligatory character of this or that moral principle: universality and the dictates of conscience. We recall that Balfour distinguishes four senses in which a moral law might be said to be universally binding, and rejects all four as either arbitrary or inconclusive. They are: (*a*) all men in fact regard themselves as bound by the law; (*b*) all men ought to regard themselves as bound by it; (*c*) "we" think all men ought to be bound by it; and (*d*) all men of "well-constituted minds" regard themselves as bound by it.

Now I think it is quite clear that Royce himself, in view of his criticism of other ethical theories, does not attempt to justify moral principles by appeal to moral conscience. It is equally clear that Royce does not attempt to justify moral principles as being universally binding in senses (*a*), (*c*), and (*d*). To hold any moral principle to be universally binding in sense (*a*) would be both factually incorrect (as witnessed by what Royce so eloquently describes as "the warfare of moral ideals") and in any case irrelevant to normative questions. To suppose that a moral principle is universally binding because *we* (or more accurately *I*) think all men ought to be bound by it (sense *c*) is arbitrary and groundless. Royce has insisted that one man's moral opinions or commitments have no binding force on any other man. And to appeal to "well-constituted minds" (sense *d*) in order to justify the universal binding force of a moral principle is equally vain. Royce would agree with Balfour that "well-constituted," if defined in moral terms, begs the question at issue; if defined in nonmoral terms, it cannot, being then a questionable factual assertion, supply a basis for a valid obligation claim.

Yet it does seem as if Royce wants to say that all men ought, at least ideally, to regard themselves as bound by one ultimate moral principle (sense *b*), namely, the principle of harmony. Balfour's objection to universality in this sense was that it involves an infinite regress of similarly universal moral laws, each obliging all men to be bound by the one preceding. Now Royce makes no attempt to answer this objection directly. Apparently he recognized its cogency to such an extent that he did not even claim that the universally obligatory character of the principle of harmony could be demonstrated. If so, the core of Royce's disagreement with Balfour, and thus with theoretical ethical skepticism in general, is not so much over the question whether or not ultimate moral principles can be theoretically justified. Balfour maintains that they cannot be justified; Royce concedes that they cannot be justified *in any strict sense,* that is, they cannot be demonstrated or proved. Rather, the disagreement seems to focus on the question of when a moral principle may properly be regarded as ultimate.

On this question, Balfour's position may be expressed in the form of two theses. The first is that a system of ethical beliefs rests ultimately on the stipulation of some one end as final, and that such a stipulation is arbitrary since no rational warrant for it is possible. The second is that when more than one end is regarded as final, no rational warrant in support of the preference of one over the other is possible. Royce's position, in turn, might be expressed in the form of two countertheses, designed to challenge those of Balfour in reverse order. The first is that the very recognition that ends of action do conflict, both intrapersonally and interpersonally, and that *prima facie* no rational warrant for morally preferring one over another is possible, provides a reflective person with reason enough *not* to stipulate any one of these ends as final or ultimate. The second is that for these very reasons the only principle of moral conduct that could be rationally and consistently adopted as ultimate is that of harmonizing conflicting ends of action to whatever extent that is possible. Since it may fairly be presumed that the harmonization of all ends of action to whatever extent possible would result in a state of affairs in which the maximum value would be achieved, the rational warrant for preferring one end of action over another is its greater conduciveness to harmony.[40]

Thus understood, Royce's argument has, it seems to me, considerable subtlety and force. If Royce is correct, the dilemma in which the ethical realist and the ethical idealist find themselves, while pervasive in the history of moral philosophy, is one of their own making. The major portion of the blame rests, perhaps, with the idealist. While correctly supposing that moral value and moral obligation are necessarily related to the ends of human desire or interest, he has nevertheless misconstrued the nature of this relation. He has mistakenly supposed that the moral consciousness can be identified with some one substantive end of desire or interest as found in this or that desiring consciousness. Confronted thereupon with an inescapable plurality of conflicting ends, each claiming to constitute the one and only truly moral end, the idealist has been unable to provide from within the moral consciousness itself any defensible criteria for resolving these warring claims.

No doubt it is in large measure the moral subjectivism and relativism resulting from the idealist's position that has led the ethical realist to suppose that if moral distinctions have objective warrant at all, that warrant must be found in some state of affairs external to the moral consciousness and to which the latter must conform. But in so supposing, the realist, instead of correcting the mistake in the idealist's position, makes an even more serious mistake of his own. For he thereby deprives the moral consciousness of precisely that which makes it moral, namely, that it itself, and not any of

[40] Royce resumed his controversy with Balfour some twenty years later. See Chapter Six below.

the various objects which it confronts, is the ultimate authority for the judgments it renders. Whereas the idealist has misconstrued the relation between the moral and the desiring consciousness, the realist, worse still, has misconceived the very essence of the moral consciousness itself.

But if the theory that Royce is proposing does resolve the dilemma of ethical realism and idealism, it weakens the force of ethical skepticism as well. For ethical skepticism—at least in the form defended by Balfour—accepts the terms of the realist-idealist dilemma. The skeptic correctly contends, against the realist, that judgments of fact by themselves are incapable of providing a warrant for moral distinctions. He aligns himself with the idealist in holding that particular moral distinctions made by this or that individual derive their sole justification from an end which he accepts as ultimate, as desired for its own sake. But recognizing thereupon that men are capable of arbitrarily desiring virtually anything for its own sake, the skeptic concludes that moral distinctions are arbitrary, purely subjective, and completely relative as well. It is this conclusion that Royce finds unwarranted. While admitting that men are *capable* of determining their interests arbitrarily, Royce denies that they do so *necessarily*. Their interests are modifiable upon reflection—modifiable above all through the very consideration that ends of interest do conflict. An individual (to use Balfour's own example) cannot upon reflection *sustain* as his ultimate end the attainment of universal revenge if he is at all reasonable and consistent, and if he has any insight whatever into the co-reality of his fellow human beings and into the problematic nature of value predications. In the final analysis, then, ethical skepticism stems from an uncritical acceptance of ethical idealism's misconception of the relation between the moral and the desiring consciousness.

If the preceding interpretation is correct, Royce's theory of the way in which and the extent to which moral distinctions may be justified resolves the apparent antinomy of ethical realism and ethical idealism and considerably weakens, as a result, the plausibility of ethical skepticism. But Royce's early ethical theory has other commendable features as well. In his discussion of moral insight Royce offers, it seems to me, one of the finest statements in the history of moral philosophy of what it means in practice to take a genuine moral attitude toward one's fellow men. Again, Royce's contention that discussions of egoism vs. altruism and prudential vs. moral conduct properly belong, not at the level of immediate impulses and desires, but at the level of conduct mediated by critical reflection and insight, seems to me to shed considerable light on these familiar distinctions of moral common sense. And finally, I find commendable Royce's recognition of human individuality in his insistence upon an irreducible plurality of personal ends of action.

Nevertheless, Royce's early ethical theory has several outstanding weaknesses. In the first place, Royce's penetrating account of moral insight is preceded by highly questionable arguments concerning how we are able to obtain such insight. Royce is correct, I believe, in holding that most of us can have and on occasion do have the experience of genuine concern for the well-being of others. Moreover, it may be conceded that this experience is an essential prerequisite of adopting a genuinely moral attitude toward our fellow men as persons in their own right. However, his two sketchily developed lines of argument as to how we come by this experience are unconvincing. The first, as we saw in section 1 of this chapter, was an appeal to a psychological theory of imitation prevalent in Royce's time. This theory held that to conceive or to remember an act or an idea involves a tendency to perform or reproduce the act or idea in question. Royce extended this theory to include the process of conceiving vividly the purposes or aims of others. But even assuming that this theory in its extended form could be satisfactorily confirmed, it would for Royce's purposes prove too much. What Royce wishes to establish as essential for there to be a community of moral agents is that each respect the goals of the other as *prima facie* valuable and worthy of fulfillment. What the psychological theory would, if valid, establish is that for anyone genuinely to conceive of another's goal involves his reproducing that goal within himself. But surely there is a difference between respecting the goals of others and sharing them. Surely Royce does not want to argue that I will be selfish and blind in regard to my fellow men if I do not adopt as my own, even for a moment, the purpose of being a saint, a dedicated schoolteacher, or a loyal servant of the state. It is not at all unusual for us to desire the realization of other people's goals without adopting these goals as our own. All that is required is that we respect those goals as the expressions of praiseworthy moral commitments.

Royce's second line of argument, namely, the one from "philosophical necessity," [41] is not really very different from the psychological argument, and seems to depend on the latter. When Royce asks, "Who can realize a given end save by somehow repeating it in himself?," the term "realize" is ambiguous. If by "realize" another's goal Royce means to adopt it, he is simply formulating a tautology and begging the question at issue. If he merely means (as I believe he does mean) appreciate and respect another's commitment as I respect my own, it is once again doubtful that that requires my adopting it.[42] When Royce toward the end of his life

[41] See section 1 above.

[42] The criticisms just offered are not meant to impugn Royce's implicit suggestion that the "moment of moral insight" carries at once a cognitive, an affective, and a conative thrust: cognitive in that one recognizes one's fellow men and their goals to be as real as oneself and one's goals; affective in that in and through such recognition one learns to appreciate their reality as voluntary agents striving for goals; conative in that one tends, in the face of this recognition and appreciation, to strive toward the others' realization of their goals. But, to repeat, one can strive toward the realization of another's goal without adopting it as one's own. Furthering another's end

developed his theory of interpretation, he discovered a more intelligible and convincing way of accounting for interpersonal concern over individual commitments. But that must await discussion in Parts II and III.

Consider, in the second place, Royce's account of the principle of harmony. His attempt to justify the harmonization of ends of action as a procedural or formal principle of moral consciousness seems to me well-conceived. However, I believe that moral consciousness recognizes more than one principle of this order as being constitutive of the moral attitude as such. In his later writings Royce himself, as we shall see in Chapter Six, gives a much fuller analysis of the moral attitude formally regarded. There he defends three other procedural principles—reasonableness, impartiality, and respect for persons—as being coequal with the principle of harmony.

A more serious objection to Royce's early doctrine is his failure to provide a more definite theory of moral value. It is the absence of such a theory, I believe, that is largely responsible for the tentativeness and the lack of clarity in Royce's view of what men ought to harmonize and how they are to go about it. He characterizes harmony in some passages as though it were the *summum bonum* itself, and in others as though it were merely a procedural moral rule governing the quest for an as yet unknown highest good. He sometimes speaks of the harmonization of conflicting desires, interests, aims, ends, and ideals, both on the intrapersonal and on the interpersonal level, as though these terms were simply interchangeable. He attempts to infer from the allegedly formal principle of harmony a class of substantive obligations (a dubious procedure to begin with) which turn out to be such vague injunctions as "organize all life" and "find work" which shall be comprehensive and definite

---

does not entail sharing that end any more than sensitively appreciating his reality entails becoming identical with him.

enough to engage the full nature of every individual to his greatest capacities. But Royce is forced to concede that neither the ideal organization nor the ideal work is known to us as yet. As a result, his class of "permanent" moral obligations is no less provisional than the duty of fostering moral insight as such. We are instructed, in effect, to take seriously the quest for the good life—an injunction that comes dangerously close to involving us in the infinite regress of aiming to find a satisfactory aim in life. To risk a crude metaphor: it is as though Royce were asking us to jockey for moral position without knowing where the inside of the track is.[43]

In his later reformulation of his ethical theory, Royce's methodology, as I hope to show, was considerably sounder. Before returning to ethical questions as such, he offered a detailed account of the formation of human personality in its social context. This account enabled him to distinguish more clearly between immediate impulses and desires, reflective interests, and systems of ideal ends or, as he called them, "life plans." [44] When he thereupon reconsidered the nature of the moral attitude from a formal point of view, he carefully left aside for the time being questions of substantive value and obligation.[45] Finally, he developed criteria of substantive value and right conduct, first from the point of view of the individual and then from the point of view of society as a whole.[46]

Nevertheless, Royce's conception of the fundamental problem of ethical theory remained essentially unchanged. He continued to seek a theoretical justification for moral distinctions—a justification that would satisfy at one and the same time the demands of reflective moral consciousness for moral autonomy and moral objectivity.

[43] The familiar slogan often used to characterize the spirit of American pragmatism, "We don't know where we're going but we're on our way," seems peculiarly apt for Royce here.
[44] See Part II.   [45] See Chapter Six.
[46] See Chapters Seven and Eight.

PART II

PSYCHOLOGICAL AND EPISTEMOLOGICAL PRESUPPOSITIONS OF ROYCE'S LATER ETHICAL THEORY

❧

Chapter Three

IMITATION

AFTER the publication of *The Religious Aspect of Philosophy* in 1885, there is no significant development in Royce's ethical theory as such for some twenty years. Royce devoted these years primarily to formulating and refining his idealistic metaphysics, the fullest presentation of which came in 1900 with the publication of *The World and the Individual.* However, Royce was never satisfied with metaphysical speculation alone. Time and again he looked to current developments in the various sciences for support of his general idealistic position. At least three motives prompted this growing emphasis on the concrete in Royce's philosophical career. One was the turbulent and pragmatically oriented California environment in which Royce was raised and which inculcated in him an ineradicable sense of realism in regard to the complex relations between man and man. Another was the general antipathy to aprioristic speculation characteristic of the European post-Kantian tradition in which Royce received his initial philosophical schooling. And the third was the volley of criticism which his contemporaries—many of them, like James and the young Dewey, pragmatically oriented—leveled against the abstractness, the rationalism, and the relative impersonalism of his early formulations of the idealist position.

But during these twenty years Royce did not neglect ethics altogether. There are indications that he realized that his doctrine of moral insight and harmony lacked the psychological and epistemological substructure needed to make it plausible. In any event, during the early 1890's Royce came strongly under the influence of the pioneer work being done in social psychology by such men as Durkheim and Tarde, J. M. Baldwin and Wundt. From that time until his death in 1916, Royce developed, and occasionally expanded into epistemological doctrines, various aspects of this social psychology in an effort to explain the formation and growth of the individual's social and moral consciousness. Out of this effort came theories of learning, of motivation, of personality, of interpersonal communication, and finally, toward the end of his life, the doctrines of interpretation and of community. It was largely on the basis of this new material that Royce reconstructed his later, more mature ethical theory.

Some of this material is scattered in a rather fragmentary fashion throughout Royce's published writings after 1890. A large portion of it is presented in greater detail and somewhat more cogently in a series of unpublished papers and lectures. In both forms it has received scanty attention from commentators and critics who, with several partial exceptions,[1] have neither examined it as a body of theory nor studied its influence on the rest of Royce's philosophy. The next three chapters, therefore, will form a more or less schematic presentation of Royce's social psychology and epistemology, focusing respectively on the role of imitation in the formation of individual consciousness, the role of reflection in the development of the sense of personal identity, and the role of interpretation in the achievement of our cognitive goals.

The most important conception emerging from this phase of Royce's philosophical investigations is that of the human

---

[1] Professors J. Loewenberg in the introduction to Royce's *Fugitive Essays* (Cambridge, Mass., 1920), which he edited, and J. Harry Cotton in *Royce on the Human Self* (Cambridge, Mass., 1954), are the only two Royce scholars who, to the best of my knowledge, have made a study of Royce's unpublished writings. Both men occasionally quote from these documents to clarify a passage in Royce's published works.

personality or self. While virtually all of the doctrines examined in these three chapters bear to a greater or lesser extent on Royce's conception of the self, his attempt to define the self independently of metaphysical presuppositions will constitute the focal point of Chapter Four.

1. Imitation and Learning

In the spring of 1893, Royce gave twelve lectures at Harvard entitled "Topics in Psychology of Interest to Teachers." [2] In them he manifested for the first time a concern with the imitative processes in human behavior that was to occupy his attention for several years. The immediate problem to which Royce addresses himself is how we learn universal concepts or general ideas. These he divides into four groups: class-concepts of objects (tiger, flower), qualities (redness), relations (equality, friendship), and scientific concepts (causation, time, law of nature). What is it, Royce asks, to have a general idea? When I have a general idea, say of a tiger, I may imagine a particular tiger I saw in a zoo, or a picture-book tiger, or a composite image of several tigers, or no picture at all, but only a verbal memory such as the description of a tiger in Blake's poem. But, Royce insists, "my understanding of the word *tiger* is something more than these mere images of tiger-pictures or of words . . ." [3] This "something more" is determined by "what I should do if I met a tiger at large, say strolling about in Harvard Square."

Royce generalizes from this instance to what might be called a modified behaviorist account of learning.

I begin to know what a tiger is when I know how to behave in a tiger's presence . . . Rational general ideas always involve

[2] These lectures are contained in folios 63–66 of Royce's unpublished papers in the Harvard University Archives. All subsequent references to Royce's unpublished writings pertain to this collection, hereafter abbreviated as H.U.A.
[3] H.U.A., folio 63, lecture 2, p. 23.

a knowledge on our part of the acts we rationally propose to carry out, of the typical responses we reasonably propose to make, in the presence of the things, of the qualities, or of the relations, whereof we have the general ideas . . .[4]

And again:

general names, in so far as they are understood by us, are epitomized suggestions of our conscious habits of conduct towards things.[5]

Royce offers a familiar example. When Marcus Aurelius was at war with the Danubians, he unloosed lions on the latter, hoping to terrorize them with "supernatural monsters" they had never seen before. But the Danubians, resorting to past experience, called the lions "dogs" and proceeded to club them to death.

But how do we first come by general ideas? Through a process of learning by imitation, Royce replies, and adds that this is to be the keynote of the whole series of lectures. "I get general ideas of my world, of its classes of things, and their relations, only when I either, first, imitate the behavior of my fellows in the presence of these things, or second, imitate the structures and the relations of the things by deliberate acts of my own." [6] The first kind of imitation is more or less self-explanatory. It ranges all the way from the first crude attempts of a child to learn a language by reproducing the sounds made by its parents, to an adult's learning the use of tools in a craft new to him. The second kind of imitation Royce describes as the voluntary reproduction of external objects. He cites as examples drawing, painting, modeling, and certain types of building.[7] The latter are examples of what Royce calls "intelligent functions," whereas reproducing sounds or a child's strutting as though he were a soldier he calls "motor functions."

[4] *Ibid.*, p. 25.   [5] *Ibid.*, p. 36.   [6] *Ibid.*, lecture 1, pp. 67–68.
[7] "Preliminary Report on Imitation," *Psychological Review* 2:221 (May 1895).

But Royce is not content to stress the role of the imitative functions in human learning. He finds them to be indispensable to all our mental and, as we shall see, our moral development. He goes so far as to offer a definition of man in terms of his imitative tendencies.

Whatever else man is, he is above all an imitative being. His whole social life is a system of imitations. His morality is a doctrine concerning what ought to be imitated. His art is more than half an explicit imitation of the beautiful aspects of things. His science is an elaborate imitation of the conceivable structure of things.[8]

With imitation so broadly conceived, Royce is aware that a more careful analysis of the concept of imitation is needed in order to point out its scope and limitations. To this analysis we now turn.

2. The Nature and Scope of Imitation

As we have seen, Royce believes that the concept of imitation must be allowed to range over both what he calls motor and what he calls intelligent functions. Royce finds further evidence for the prevalence of imitative activity in the frequently observed contagion of virtue and vice, as for example in epidemics of crime or suicide; in the irresistible sway of fashion; in such familiar social phenomena as commercial panics, mob behavior, fads, reform movements, and national conversions; and in standards of artistic appreciation and taste.[9] Moreover, self-consciousness begins in an imitative process by assimilating abilities, patterns of behavior, vocational ideals, and the like from a vast store of models which society places at the disposal of the child. Even the adult ego consists largely of one's social position, one's rights, and

---

[8] H.U.A., folio 64, lecture 4, p. 3.
[9] "The Imitative Functions, and Their Place in Human Nature," *Century Magazine* 48:138 (May 1894).

one's aptitudes—all of them learned for the most part through imitation. Finally, as we shall see in the next section, Royce attributes the development of the individual's social and moral conscience as well to imitative processes. Reluctantly, Royce seems to conclude that Gabriel Tarde's dictum, "La société, c'est l'imitation," is somewhat extreme and in need of qualifications.

The scope of the imitative processes being so vast, Royce finds it no easy matter to give imitation a cogent and workable definition. It is proper to ask first of all how imitation originates. "Does man learn to imitate because he is brought up in a social environment; or, on the contrary, is he capable of life in a social environment only because he is first, by nature and instinct, an imitative animal?" [10] Is it more feasible to regard imitation as an instinctive or as an acquired response? Royce has a predilection for the former, without wishing to exclude the latter. He presents three theories of imitation current in his own day.[11]

The first, attributed to Sully and Alexander Bain among others, holds that imitation is an acquired response. Two examples are offered. A mockingbird accidentally copies a sound, finds it attractive, and repeats it until it becomes habitual. A child is warned to avoid a certain action; the parent describes it so vividly that the fascinated child imitates the proscribed action instead of obeying the moral precept.[12]

The second theory, attributed to Wundt, holds imitation to be an original and instinctive process. Similarly constituted creatures tend, Royce says in summary of this view,

---

[10] *Ibid.*   [11] H.U.A., folio 64, lecture 5, pp. 42–76.
[12] By way of illustration, Royce makes a "personal confession." In Gore Hall Library certain parties were lighting matches in dark alcoves. A sign was posted forbidding this, and threatening appropriate punishments. Royce had never dreamt of lighting matches there; but now he begged the authorities to remove the sign, for within a week he'd have a compulsion to light matches in every dark corner.

"to have the same instinctive association of outward emotional expression and inner mood, so that your expression produces my mood." Your weeping makes me sad. I find myself imitating the gestures of a passionate speaker. Royce objects that this theory is too extreme, that by itself it cannot explain all imitation, that the observations upon which it is based are very inexact, and that none of us imitate the same models in the same way. Nevertheless, he thinks that it expresses a part of the truth. Frequently, we

meet for the first time with people undergoing some great experience of passionate joy or sorrow such as we ourselves have not yet experienced . . . It is fair to say that at such times we at least seem to ourselves to get, by sympathy, both a real insight into these other minds, and a really novel experience of life for ourselves.

If such processes do occur, Royce adds, an original instinct to imitate would have to be posited to explain them.

Royce finds it necessary to supplement these two theories of imitation with a third, that of Professor J. Mark Baldwin, a contemporary pioneer in child psychology. What the first two theories fail to explain is the element of selection, or preference of certain models over others, that is involved in most imitative behavior. Baldwin's theory posits an "ideal factor" as constituting the original spur to imitation. "This ideal factor," Royce summarizes, "is the presence before us of personally interesting models whose activities we desire to imitate decidedly in advance of knowing how we shall imitate them." Once again Royce is quick to grasp the moral implications of such a theory. It is in the presence of these social models, who attract us instinctively, that we first encounter "the stimulating half-suggestion . . . of the higher ideal, towards which we strive." Royce is particularly inclined to Baldwin's theory because the ideal factor it stresses tends to remain effective as the individual matures. "Thus it is that infants learn to draw. Thus they learn their games.

Thus too, grown up, they learn about their calling, and about their world."

The importance of the "ideal factor" at the basis of Royce's theory of imitation should not be underestimated. As I understand him, Royce is rejecting the view that individual moral character is developed entirely through social training. The child's extraordinary responsiveness to the moral stimuli in his social environment suggests that he has innate in him a quasi-moral disposition or capacity from the very outset. Why, it must be asked, is the child disposed to imitate certain of his elders more than others? The answer Royce suggests, albeit unclearly, is that certain of his elders, more than others, seem to the child to embody his own imaginative projections of himself into idealized situations and relations. At a fairly early age the child becomes vaguely conscious of wanting to be something more than he is. While he is dependent upon his elders for concrete models of what this "something more" might be, the original impetus toward imitating them must be a conative tendency within the child himself.

At this point the reader may very well wonder whether Royce has forgotten his own rather vehement attacks on "moral sense" and "moral feeling" theories in *The Religious Aspect of Philosophy*. But I think a distinction is in order. Royce did not object to theories claiming an innate moral conscience or innate moral feelings like sympathy or benevolence so much on the grounds that there are no such innate capacities. His objection was rather that even if such innate capacities do exist, they cannot be supposed of themselves to justify moral distinctions or to establish moral principles. Royce's own postulation of an innate idealizing tendency amounts to no more than an attempt to explain, as best he can, the individual's general native capacity for response to moral suggestions. The idealizing tendency is not a moral faculty in the sense that it somehow cognizes, intuits, or feels what is morally right or wrong, good or evil. Nor is it an other-regarding impulse whose expression or cultivation assures a high degree of moral conduct. Nor, finally, does Royce argue that just because there *is* (psychologically) an idealizing tendency in all of us, we *ought* (morally) to work for its satisfaction. The presence of such a disposition can at most account in part for the psychological moving appeal of moral ideals and moral principles. It cannot justify their moral binding force.

In one significant respect, however, Royce finds Baldwin's theory of imitation to be too narrow. Baldwin defines the act of imitation as a mere repetition of its own stimulus. According to Royce, this definition overlooks an essential element found in all acts of conscious imitation: namely, the awareness of the contrasts as well as the resemblances between any imitative act and its model. The most obvious contrast brought to light in every imitative act is that the imitator experiences his series of imitative motor processes as being relatively controllable, plastic, and reproducible at will, whereas the perceived series imitated clearly is none of these things.[13] In most cases this contrast is as interesting and instructive to the imitator as is the intended resemblance, for it provides one of the earliest and most indispensable stimuli to the imitator's self-consciousness. It is precisely through the relative success or failure of his imitative acts that the imitator first learns to estimate his capacities and his limitations.

It follows that there need not be any one established or even desired degree of closeness in the resemblance between the original and its "copy." Children at play want their imitations to be unlike as well as like their models, for it is in this manner that a certain measure of personal originality finds expression. This "tendency to deliberate idealization of our imitations, to deliberate deviations from the literal," is

[13] "Preliminary Report on Imitation," p. 223.

found not only in childhood play but in adult art as well. For art is to a large measure symbolic interpretation through acts of imitation in which all but the deliberately chosen aspects of things are neglected.

Royce seeks further to illuminate Baldwin's "ideal factor" by relating it to an analysis of the functioning of personal authority. His observations here are strikingly prophetic of more recent sociological analysis, especially Max Weber's concept of charisma. In another unpublished lecture of the same year, 1893, Royce argues that the individual expresses his preference in imitating his fellow men "in so far as he finds the society of certain amongst them fascinating, the personality of these his beloved guides impressive, their companionship indispensable, their approval satisfying, their institutions majestic, their faiths soul-compelling." [14] Since imitation is natural, authority need not be oppressive. Even more striking are the following two passages, designed to discover further what "the charm of authority" (Royce's own phrase) is.

It isn't so much the command as the gentle, perhaps the imperturbably obstinate, perhaps the graciously enthusiastic assurance that the thing is certain to happen, which arouses to an effective manifestation of those ideo-motor processes to which one appeals when one makes commands.

And, what

makes the leaders of men generally authoritative? Are not such leaders of men irresistible, because they believe and continually show by their bearing, not that they mean to put their feet on our necks, but that they are sure that this good thing will be done, and that we can be depended upon to help do it? [15]

[14] "The Two-Fold Nature of Knowledge: Imitative and Reflective," prepared for the Chicago World's Fair Congress, August 24, 1893; folio 62, p. 49.
[15] H.U.A., folio 64, lecture 5, pp. 24–25. Royce retells a legend about Caesar. When his army reached the banks of the Rhine, his men were frightened of the German barbarians to the point of mutiny. Reminding them of

Imitative preference, then, can be accounted for at least in part by the immediate charismatic attraction exerted by some members of the individual's society.

Having described at length the different kinds of imitative functions and even conducted a survey and several laboratory experiments to corroborate his theories,[16] Royce at last attempts a schematic summary of his findings. He divides imitative processes into three general and to some extent overlapping classes: (1) elementary and instinctual imitations of the actions of our fellow men; (2) subsequently acquired tendencies to reproduce or to picture things in our physical environment; and (3) consciously idealized, playfully falsified, and symbolically abbreviated imitations of the interesting aspects of things. In the third case especially we find what is perhaps the origin of self-consciousness, the contrast between what is me and what is not me.

Royce is aware that the vast scope which he has assigned to the imitative functions threatens to imply that we must call *all* conscious processes forms of imitation.

If imitation occurs wherever there are relatively inner or organic experiences—e.g., images or trains of images which, in some respect, resemble certain relatively external or perceptive experiences—then where can we name an experience involving any images whatever, or any organic adjustment, which will not have something imitative about it? [17]

The answer can be found, Royce believes, in the particular sort of motor adjustment characteristic of imitative behavior. He defines an act of imitation as

a more or less conscious motor adjustment that tends to set off a series of given experiences by furnishing from within the con-

---

the tradition of Roman courage, he then added that he really does not care whether the rest of his army follows him or not, for he *knows* that his beloved tenth legion will. That, apparently, did the trick. They all followed him into battle.

[16] Summarized in "Preliminary Report on Imitation," pp. 230–235.

[17] *Ibid.*, p. 226.

scious counterpart of some one or more of the aspects of the first series—a counterpart which is both like and unlike the original, and whose contrast is therefore often as instructive as its similarity.

This definition, Royce thinks, adequately covers the three classes of imitative behavior which he has specified. But he adds two criteria to distinguish a genuine act of imitation on the part of conscious human beings from mere acts of blind reduplication. The first requires that "the consciousness of the imitator be as truly a consciousness of his adjustment as it is a consciousness of his model." Infantile behavior is thereby excluded. The second is that the model must always be a complex series of facts, never a simple sensation like a color. Thus, in contrast to Baldwin, Royce urges that every act of imitation properly so called be regarded as an act of "reinforcing, emphasizing, signalizing, clarifying," and not merely repeating, its complex stimulus.

Several years later, in *The World and the Individual*,[18] Royce further maintains that imitation is a basic source of the continuity of our social experience. For

an act of imitation . . . is essentially the construction of something that lies, in a technical sense, *between* the acts of my model, and what were formerly my own acts . . . [For] *I never merely repeat his act.* Imitation is a kind of experimental origination, a trial of a new plan, the initiation of a trial series of acts . . . The result is . . . that the original, and puzzling, diversity between the imitator and the model has, by the interposition of the imitative act between these prior courses of action, come to appear as a *diversity of stages in the same series.* The triad, formed of the three terms,—(1) the original activities of the imitative being, (2) the activities of the model, and (3) the imitative act itself,—is now a triad of connected members whereof the third lies between the two others. The finite world has hereby won a new consciousness of the unity of its own life.

[18] (New York, 1899), II, 311–312. There is an unmistakable foreshadowing of Royce's later doctrine of interpretation here.

3. *Imitation and the Moral Life*

A well-developed moral philosophy generally begins with an investigation into the structure of human personality and of the social context in which it develops, including a study of such matters as the nature of human desire and human motivation, the relation between reason and the passions, and the capacity for voluntary decision. Royce's previous failure to undertake such an investigation was in part responsible, I believe, for the vagueness, the looseness, and the lack of plausibility of his early doctrines of moral insight and moral harmony. Thus in *The Religious Aspect of Philosophy* Royce never adequately explained, among other things, why men are in general predisposed to adopt a moral attitude toward the conflict of interests and purposes that is a part of their everyday experience.

Now Royce's theory of imitation may be regarded as the first step in his attempt to provide what was lacking in his earlier moral philosophy. Although this is not the place for a thorough appraisal of Royce's doctrine of imitation as a psychological theory, I do believe that it has considerable plausibility, and that recent psychological inquiry tends, if anything, to confirm rather than refute it.[19] Our primary con-

[19] Royce's theory strikingly anticipates the somewhat more extreme Freudian theory of "identification." Professor R. B. Brandt, in discussing Freud, defines identification as "the tendency of a person, under certain emotional conditions, to imitate, consciously or unconsciously, the whole personality of another—including behavior, attitudes, and values." (*Ethical Theory* [Englewood Cliffs, N.J., 1959], p. 140. Cf. especially Freud's *Group Psychology and the Analysis of the Ego* [New York, 1949].) In the light of Royce's doctrine, Brandt's remark that Freud offered "the *novel* proposal that the development of a conscience is part of a wholesale incorporation of the qualities of other persons," may be open to challenge. (Brandt, p. 141, italics added.) However, Royce did not believe, as Freud apparently did, that the individual's mature moral conscience is *wholly* the product of a process of "introjecting" social norms, standards, and models.

To be sure, Royce's hesitant predilection for an innatist theory of imitative behavior conflicts with the tendency of most modern "association"

cern is with the implications of Royce's theory of imitation for his moral philosophy.

In the first place, then, let us consider the moral significance of the role of imitation in the learning process. At its more conscious stages the learning process is for the most part a matter of gaining proficiency in the understanding and use of general concepts. Now Royce has argued with considerable persuasiveness that general concepts are learned largely through imitation. This applies, of course, to moral concepts as well. If we wish to inculcate in our children a sense of moral responsibility, we must first teach them the meaning and use of moral concepts. Royce insists that moral concepts are learned most effectively through repeated imitative behavior of social models. Thus, "if you want to teach one what justice is, you teach him either to behave justly, or in the more technical and legal cases, to administer or to apply just criteria or standards to cases." [20]

If Royce's theory is correct, the central importance of imitation in moral learning helps to account for the presence, in most societies, of a fundamental similarity of moral standards, moral sentiments, and moral behavior. Moreover, as Royce has attempted to show, the imitative processes carry over into maturity. They continue to play an important role in the formation of the adult's entire system of beliefs. On Royce's view, the distinguishing characteristic of a belief is a certain psychological "set," or the readiness to act in a certain determinate manner. Since even in adults these psychological "sets" are largely the result of imitative processes, the

---

and "reinforcement" theorists to regard the imitative processes as acquired through learning (cf. Neal Miller and John Dollard, *Social Learning and Imitation* [New Haven, 1941] especially Appendix II). But even if the latter view could be substantiated beyond question, Royce's emphasis on the "contrast-effect" in conscious imitative behavior illuminates an important aspect of the subject which more recent theorists have tended to overlook.

[20] "Social Factors in the Development of the Individual Mind" (1898), folio 70, lecture 6, p. 19.

persistence of a community of moral beliefs under normal conditions is assured. Here we have in its broadest implication Royce's conception of the plasticity of the individual in the hands of his social environment.

In the second place, Royce stresses the role of the imitative processes in the formation of the individual's "social" conscience:

Our social morality . . . is in one direction dependent upon our regard for the will, the interest, the precepts, or the welfare of our fellows. Now such regard is, in its turn, dependent upon our power, by imitation, to experience and to comprehend the suggested will, interest, authority, and desires of those about us. So, then, without imitativeness, no chance for the development of the social conscience.[21]

Thus Royce's analysis of imitative behavior provides a dependable basis for at least the minimum of interpersonal responsiveness presupposed by any sound ethical theory.

This responsiveness, however, does not of itself guarantee what most of us would regard as genuinely moral behavior. For if, as one of his critics has suggested, Royce regards the individual's conscience as the "mere 'resultant of forces' playing upon us from without,"[22] it is difficult to see how we could have the degree of personal autonomy necessary for us to be held morally responsible at all. Moreover, there is no guarantee that the social pressures to which we so pliably conform are always *moral* pressures. If this were Royce's full conception of moral conscience, then, in a hypothetical society of evil men, the devil's conscience would indeed approve of the devil's acts, and nothing could be done about it.

However, Royce does not in fact regard conscience as the "mere resultant of forces playing upon us from without"

[21] "The Imitative Functions, and Their Place in Human Nature," p. 141.
[22] Cotton, *Royce on the Human Self*, p. 50. I do not think Cotton sufficiently appreciates Royce's emphasis on the role of self-consciousness and the need for contrast in human imitative processes.

—principally because he does not regard human imitation
itself in this manner. For on Royce's view, as we have seen,
no human act of conscious imitation is a mere repetition of
its stimulus. From the very first the imitator confronts his
model with his own irreducible element of originality, of
personal uniqueness of interest and ability, so that the resulting act of imitation is always a novel occurrence and not
merely a copy. It will be recalled that Royce expressed a
preference for Baldwin's theory of imitation because of the
"ideal factor" it emphasized. This theory maintained that the
imitative instinct involved at its core the desire to emulate
impressive and fascinating (charismatic) social models.
Royce came to regard this "ideal factor," present already in
childhood, as the matrix of the individual's distinctively
moral conscience.

It seems to me that in the tendency of children to idealize their
social comrades and to deal with a somewhat fantastic social
order you have the motives that must be and are of very great
importance for the later development of one's conception of conscience.[23]

For in this process, the child "learns to conceive himself not
as he merely and literally is, but as he more ideally might
be." [24] But in his interpretation of Baldwin's theory Royce
had gone beyond it by insisting that the ideal factor expresses
as much the desire that one's imitation contrast with its
model as the desire that it resemble its model. As a result,
Royce is able to hold that the individual's *moral* conscience,
so far from being the mere product of social pressures, is
inevitably the expression of a unique personality with its
own unique point of view. Moral conscience, to be sure, is
not innate. Society teaches me to form a conscience as much

[23] "Social Factors in the Development of the Individual Mind," folio 69,
lecture 3, p. 35.
[24] "Some Aspects of Social Psychology," Cambridge Conferences (Spring
1898), folio 70, lecture 6, pp. 7–8.

as it teaches me to form concepts or beliefs. But the conscience that I eventually come to possess is my own.

Thus Royce, through his psychological investigation of the imitative processes, has come a long way toward providing a universal *source* for the moving appeal of ethical ideals and values. For he has discovered their source in the individual's primitive instinctual structure. In the instinctive impulse to imitate charismatic personalities Royce has uncovered one of the potential affective bases on which any moral appeal must ultimately rest, since the alleged validity of moral values is irrelevant to their persuasiveness unless the agent feels a genuine concern for them. Moreover, he has provided a plausible, empirically oriented, and naturalistic explanation of the origin of the individual's social conscience. Finally, by insisting upon the presence of an element of originality in every imitative process, Royce has preserved the moral autonomy of the individual in the very face of the weighty social pressures to conform which confront him. In so doing, Royce has at least begun to explain how the scope of moral endeavor may come to range beyond the mere conventional morals and mores of a particular social group. A fuller explanation is forthcoming in the next two chapters.

Chapter Four

REFLECTION

IN the previous chapter we saw how Royce's analysis of the imitative processes led him to the conclusion that most of the early content of the individual's consciousness is supplied by his social environment. In the present chapter we shall be concerned with Royce's thesis that the individual's mature self-consciousness, his reflective awareness and estimation of himself, is just as strongly conditioned by his relations to his fellow men. We shall examine in turn Royce's view of what is involved in the formation of self-consciousness, his analysis of the notion of "self" in its several senses, his conception of the freedom and responsibility of the self, and his view of how we come to know other minds or selves.

1. The Origins of Self-Consciousness

As might be expected, Royce discovers the first indication of self-awareness in the imitative behavior of the child. We saw that for Royce one of the essential characteristics of the process of imitation is the contrast, not merely the resemblance, between any act of imitation and its model. In imitative processes, the child is aware, however dimly, of two sets of mental contents. The first set includes his perceptions of his model's actions and his representations of what these actions may mean. The second set includes his own imitative actions and the feelings associated with them. The child experiences the former set as being relatively unexpected, unrelated to his awareness of his own body, and uncontrollable; the latter is closely connected with his bodily sensations and appears to him to be more or less under his own control. It is these differences that force upon the child his first primitive awareness of the psychological contrast between ego and non-ego. "And it is in this contrast that the source of true self-consciousness lies."[1] Royce insists again and again that contrast is the matrix of awareness, and that social contrast is the matrix of self-awareness. At those times when other persons tend to fade out of our conscious field, such as when we are absorbed in some strenuous activity, self-consciousness tends to dim as well. On the other hand, our self-consciousness is most acutely aroused by the approval or the criticism of our fellows.

Consistently with this theory of self-consciousness, Royce argues that even our moments of solitary reflection and meditation are controlled by the habits that we have acquired in social intercourse. We bring home with us the memory of social triumphs and failures, of those who admired us and those who humiliated us. Even what most of us take, in the moments when we are alone with ourselves, to be the inner voice of conscience is for the most part merely "a well-knit system of socially acquired habits of estimating acts." The conclusion is warranted, Royce believes, that

the normal inner life of reflection, of conscience, of meditation . . . is simply . . . an imitation, a brief abstract and epitome, of our literal social life. We have no habits of self-consciousness which are not derived from social habits, counterparts thereof. Where the analogy of our relations to our fellows ceases, reflection ceases also.[2]

But the imitative processes lead the individual inevitably to reflective self-consciousness in another and, for the purposes of our analysis, more important way. The vast plural-

[1] "Some Observations on the Anomalies of Self-Consciousness" (1894), in *Studies of Good and Evil* (New York, 1898), pp. 184f.
[2] *Ibid.*, pp. 192–194.

ity of diverse social models, and the evident impossibility of imitating them all at once, forces the maturing individual to select among them. Unfortunately, Royce does not make explicit in his analysis what he regards as the principles upon which this choice is made. His insistence upon the "ideal factor" that provides one of the initial spurs to childhood imitation suggests that a principle of selectivity is operative even prior to the development of a capacity for conscious choice. The child is simply drawn to imitate those of his fellow men whose personalities attract and fascinate him the most. This principle of sheer charismatic attraction undoubtedly carries over into maturity as well. But one would suppose that something more is needed to explain the reflective choices of an adult.

At any rate, Royce's conception of social relations clearly indicates, first, that such choices must somehow be made, and second, that in making them the individual is inevitably brought to self-consciousness, to a reflective awareness of the contrast between the world about him and something which he calls his "self."

Royce devoted considerable effort to an analysis of the notion of self—an analysis that was to play, as we shall see in Part III, a profound role in his moral philosophy. To this analysis we now turn.

2. The Notion of Self

Whatever may have been the extent of Hegel's influence on Royce (a subject much debated among Royce scholars), on one point at least this influence is constantly visible. Royce, with Hegel, insisted throughout his life on the limited and fragmentary character of the "given" in human experience. Royce's early ventures into theory of knowledge led him, after some difficulties, to specify the "given" as the momentary, present datum of consciousness.[3] But, according to Royce, this datum in and by itself is unintelligible. It must be attended to, reflected upon, and, as we shall see presently, interpreted in terms of other given and constructed mental content before we can properly be said to "know" anything. This process entails what Royce described as a transcending of the present moment through a constructive act of "temporal extension" in which we "acknowledge" a past and "anticipate" a future.[4] The immediate must be mediated: Royce accepted this Hegelian dictum wholeheartedly.

Royce's denigration of the given carried over into his psychology as well. A psychological inventory of the contents of the idea of "self" or ego must indeed begin with what is immediately apprehended. But the given "self" turns out upon introspection to be no more than a "very ill defined mass of internal sensations" [5]—fragmentary, nonrecurrent, and virtually inexpressible. Throughout his life Royce maintained that we have no direct experience of "selfhood" in any significant sense, that is, as a permanent identical being, a substance, a soul, or an active principle. Is the reference of the term "self" to be confined, then, to this given mass of chaotic inner sensations? Royce answered with a qualified no. There are at least two "derived" forms of self-knowledge, both of them obtained through reflection.

The first is my knowledge of myself as subject, as thinker of thoughts. This subject, Royce insists, is the presupposition of all reflective thinking. That much Royce is determined to defend against skeptical onslaughts. He engages in a polemic with Hume on this point. In one of the best-known

[3] See, in particular, "On Purpose in Thought" (1880), in *Fugitive Essays*, ed. J. Loewenberg (Cambridge, Mass., 1920), and Professor Loewenberg's introduction to this volume.

[4] "Tests of Right and Wrong" (1880), in *Fugitive Essays*, p. 200.

[5] H.U.A., folio 65, lecture 8, p. 49.

passages of the *Treatise*, Hume insists that self-reflection discovers no unified "I," but only some particular sense content.
Royce comments:

"I enter," then, that is, I observe, I watch, I find, I know. But,
adds Hume, *what* I know is always some content of consciousness, some impression or idea. Yes indeed; but to say this is explicitly to say that, when I know this content as immediate, my
knowing itself is not the content known, but just precisely the
knowing thereof. *That* I know, this truth is itself more than the
content known. And so Hume, in the very act of asserting that
the known is, as such, merely content, and never other than content, mere ideas, and never a peculiar thing, called a Self . . .
implies, yes in the words: "when I enter . . . I stumble upon,
I catch,"—he explicitly asserts, that the knower *is*, and is more
than the content known. I as Subject of knowledge, am indeed
never the known content; but that is the very proof that the Self
is not, and cannot be reduced to, the series of states that it knows.[6]

Royce was as critical as Hume himself, however, of the
various efforts made by philosophers and psychologists alike
to give *content* to this "I" as pure subject or knower.

I have no immediate knowledge or inner experience of myself
as Subject . . . Nor do I have such mediate or derived knowledge of myself as pure Subject as I have of the objects of the
physical world. The Self as physical object is, on the contrary,
merely the body, the sum total of its deeds and works . . . Thus
neither in the inner nor in the outer world do I ever find an
object that can properly be called the identical Subject, the
Knower . . .[7]

To the "psychological partisans of the self of the 'inner
sense,'" Royce offers a rejoinder borrowed from De Morgan,
to the effect that "I am wiser than to hold a candle in order
to look down my own throat." To the defenders of a "felt

---

[6] "The Two-Fold Nature of Knowledge: Imitative and Reflective," folio
62, pp. 25–27. The Hume passage under discussion may be found in *A
Treatise of Human Nature*, ed. L. A. Selby-Bigge (Oxford, 1902), bk. I, pt.
iv, sec. 6, p. 252.
[7] H.U.A., folio 62, pp. 32–33.

intuition" of the "activity" of a self in the process of knowing, sensing, and so forth, Royce replies that such concomi-
tant psychological facts, even if discernible, do not define a
self. "If," Royce says sarcastically,

> whenever one tried to attend, or to think, one always . . . heard
> the same sweet music, or saw, in internal vision, rainbow colors,
> some psychologists would doubtless be found asserting that the
> knowing subject is directly known not only as active, but also as
> sweet voiced and bright colored.[8]

The second form of derived self-knowledge or self-reflection reveals what Royce calls the self as object, or the "empirical ego." This he defines as "the sum total of all the conscious deeds and plans and activities of this organism of
mine, coupled with all the things that I regard as forming an
essential part of this my activity." [9] "The Empirical Ego is
the whole man at work." It can be expanded indefinitely to
include my entire past and future, my social position, my
country, at times even my walking stick. Royce had the "empirical ego" especially in mind when he argued, as we saw
above, that the presence of myself to myself as an object of
reflection originates and develops almost wholly within the
context of my social relations with others. Thus "a child is
taught to be self-conscious just as he is taught everything
else, by the social order that brings him up." [10] Were he to
grow up in a completely nonhuman environment, "there is
nothing to indicate that he would become as self-conscious
as is now a fairly educated cat."

We have now examined Royce's analysis of the notion of
the "self" in two senses. The first, the "I" as logical subject,

[8] *Ibid.,* p. 43.
[9] H.U.A., folio 65, lecture 8, p. 62. For a similar analysis of the "empirical
self," see William James, *Principles of Psychology* (New York, 1890), chs.
ix and x.
[10] "Self-Consciousness, Social Consciousness, and Nature," in *Studies of
Good and Evil,* p. 208.

was defended by Royce as the necessary presupposition of all introspective reflection. However, it is of itself a bare abstraction devoid of empirical content, and not, strictly speaking, an object of knowledge at all. The second, the "empirical ego," is a loosely connected mass of internal sensations, physical activities, and, above all, socially derived standards of self-appraisal. As Royce summarizes, I am to begin with merely

this individual in contrast with what my fellows at large require of me, think of me, express to me, find admirable or intolerable in my character, my conduct, or my conscious state . . . But so far my idea of myself has only a chance unity, and an imperfect organization.[11]

The content of the "empirical ego" is as such too varying and fragmentary, its boundaries too shifting, to provide what we commonly regard as a genuine sense of personal identity.

Royce's conclusion is that some further, internal principle of organization is required to account for the experience of mature selfhood. It is to be found, he believes, in the individual's adoption of a personal ideal or life purpose. "If I really know what, on the whole, I mean to be, the chaotic succession of empirical states of my ego which varying experience brings to me, will not break up my deeper unity." [12] The process whereby the individual comes to have a life purpose of his own has been partially described already. A passage from *The World and the Individual* expresses it more fully:

Now what literal social life thus trains us to observe, the inner psychological processes of memory and imagination enable us indefinitely to extend and to diversify. The child soon carries over his plays into more or less ideal realms, lives in the company of imaginary persons, and thus, idealizing his social relations,

---

[11] "Some Aspects of Social Psychology," folio 70, lecture 6, pp. 14f.
[12] *The Conception of God* (New York, 1897), "Supplementary Essay," p. 283.

idealizes also the type of his self-consciousness. In my inner life, I in the end learn ideally to repeat, to vary, to reorganize, and to epitomize in countless ways, the situations which I first learned to observe and estimate in literal social situations. Hereby the contrast between Ego and Alter, no longer confined to the relations between my literal neighbor and myself, can be refined into the conscious contrasts between present and past Self, between my self-critical and my naïve Self, between my higher and lower Self, or between my conscience and my impulses . . . And thus my experience of myself gets a certain provisional unity.[13]

The significance of Royce's conception of the self in terms of a life plan or purpose should not be underestimated. According to Royce, the self in its most distinctive sense, that is, the sense we have in mind when we think of the human individual as a person in his own right, is to be understood not as the individual's innate possession, not as a datum given in his consciousness, but rather as an achievement of which he is capable, a task which he has yet to accomplish. Prior to his choice of a unifying life plan or ideal, he does not, strictly speaking, exist as a person at all. Royce writes:

it is never the case that the Self first exists, and then afterwards freely chooses his ideal. On the contrary, the Self exists only as the conscious chooser . . . of this ideal. The Self finds itself only as having already begun to choose, never as now first choosing. It knows itself only as the being with this ideal.[14]

It is only through his adoption of a life purpose that the individual is able to attain a sense of continuing self-identity. For it is his commitment to such a purpose that alone brings into significant relation his momentary self-awareness with what he was before and with what he is still to become.

The deeper implication of this doctrine is that selfhood in its most meaningful sense must be defined in what are essen-

---

[13] *The World and the Individual*, 2 vols. (New York, 1899), II, 265.
[14] *The Conception of God*, p. 295.

tially voluntaristic and moral terms. Royce makes this implication explicit when he refers to the notion of selfhood as an
"ethical category" or a "teleological category." [15] His meaning is most clearly conveyed in the following passage:

> The term "person" . . . can mean only the moral individual,
> i.e. the individual viewed as meaning or aiming towards an ideal
> . . . for only the moral individual, as a life lived in relation to a
> plan, a finite totality of experience viewed as meaning for itself
> a struggle towards conformity to an ideal, has, in the finite world,
> at once an all-pervading unity, despite the unessential accidents
> of disease and of sense, and a single clear contrast, in its whole-
> ness, to the rest of the universe of experience.[16]

The uniqueness of the moral individual is further assured by
the fact that his life plan or ideal is essentially the object of
his own exclusive interest. No one else chooses precisely this
ideal for his own, and no one else is able to fulfill it in quite
the same way.

Thus Royce conceives the acquisition of personality, that
is, of moral individuality, as involving a complex process of
mutual interaction between social conditioning and individual self-expression. His best description of this process occurs in his unpublished writings.

> My doctrine starts from the obvious fact that a moral individ-
> ual, a person with rights and duties, is not born, but is made. He
> is the product of a long process of social adjustment and of inner
> consciousness . . . His moral freedom, his private judgment, his
> rights,—all these are not original but acquired characters of his
> personality. His conscience is not the root nor yet the source, it
> is rather the result, the flower, of his moral life. He is not born
> self-conscious; nor yet, at birth, is he free, or dutiful, or conscien-
> tious. He wins these qualities, if at all, then only through the aid
> of a long social training. On the other hand, no social training

---

[15] *The World and the Individual,* II, 275; *The Conception of God,* p. 267.

[16] *Ibid.,* p. 292. Royce points out that the individual's life plan or ideal
need not be a morally worthy one. An evil life plan is still a life plan, and
as such affords the basis of unity involved in the experience of selfhood.
(Cf. pp. 288–289.)

can make a moral personality unless, at each step of the process, the embryonic moral individual himself cooperates in the process, —becomes, as they say, self-active, takes over the moral motives and makes them his own,—wins individuality through somehow coming into a voluntarily chosen unity with his social world.[17]

We might say that there is a three-step process leading to the achievement of selfhood. The child first comes equipped with a basic impulse or tendency to strive toward ideal goals, vague and unformulated though these may be at the outset. Next, through social processes of imitation and contrast, these ideals receive some measure of content and conscious formulation. Finally, the mature individual, confronted with the problem of choosing among and reconciling a plurality of these conflicting socially inculcated goals and ideals, comes to define a unique ideal or life plan for himself. This life plan affords the individual a conception of a potential existence which contrasts with and serves as a standard for criticizing his empirically observable "self" as it exists here and now. A man's sense of selfhood, Royce observes, is fundamentally based upon the contrast "between all his life and strivings, and his conscientious ideal of the perfect life. A man's conscientious ideal gives him all the more unity and permanence by virtue of its very remoteness." [18] Royce adds that most of us experience an even sharper contrast between what we are and what we could have been.

You never know a man's self-consciousness, until you learn something of this graveyard of perished ideal selves which his experience has filled for him, and which his memory has adorned with often very fantastic inscriptions.[19]

Royce's investigation of the notion of selfhood led him at last to the conclusion that the self in its most significant sense—as a life lived according to a plan—is not properly an

[17] Pittsburgh lectures on the doctrine of loyalty (1908), folio 82, lecture 1, pp. 13–14.
[18] "Some Aspects of Social Psychology," folio 70, lecture 6, p. 15.
[19] The Conception of God, p. 284.

object either of intuitive or conceptual knowledge as these are commonly understood. The self is not a datum given in a moment of consciousness; hence, it is not an object of knowledge "by acquaintance." But neither is the self adequately comprehended in its uniqueness through one or more abstract general ideas; hence one's "knowledge about" one's self tends to remain peripheral to what is its most essential characteristic.

Your own true self simply does not just now exist to be known. It belongs to the past and to the future, as well as to the present; and your whole life is needed to embody and to live out what it means.[20]

In the last years of his life Royce, under the influence of C. S. Peirce, developed a doctrine of "interpretation" as a third type of knowledge distinct both from intuitive perception and abstract conception. He came to believe that interpretation, in so far as it is by its very nature a self-perpetuating rather than a terminating cognitive process, is alone able to comprehend a continuing and developing phenomenon such as human selfhood. We shall examine this doctrine in the next chapter. Our immediate concern is further to specify, if possible, the sense in which, according to Royce, the self may be said to be responsible and free in its activity.

3. The Freedom and Responsibility of the Self

During most of his philosophical career, Royce confronted the problem of man's freedom, and thus the problem of man's responsibility as a moral agent, from two more or less distinct points of view. As a metaphysician, Royce attempted to preserve in some significant sense the freedom and responsibility of the finite individual in spite of his "inclusion,"

[20] Extension Course on Ethics (circa 1915), folio 94, lecture 5, p. 16.

as part or aspect, in an Absolute Consciousness or Will.[21] In conformity with our intention, in this study, to treat Royce's ethics as far as possible independently of his absolute idealism, and in conformity as well with Royce's determination to conduct ethical inquiry so far as possible independently of metaphysical presuppositions,[22] we shall forego discussion of the problem at issue from the point of view of Royce's metaphysics.

However, Royce approached the question of man's freedom and responsibility from the point of view of the moral psychologist as well. From this vantage point Royce's problem is couched in quite different terms. He feels that he must somehow account for an element of personal initiative and self-determination on the part of the human person in spite of the far-reaching extent to which what he is and how he acts are conditioned, even determined, by his social environment. This Royce attempts to do through development of a psychological concept greatly in vogue in his own day, that of "attention."

As early as 1882, Royce argued that the first step taken by the mind in transforming fleeting sense impressions into what we call knowledge is an active process of attention. Attention, Royce claimed, "is the same activity that, in more developed shape, we commonly call will. We attend to one thing rather than another, because we will to do so, and our will is here the elementary impulse to know." [23] Attention intensifies the impressions upon which it fixes, brings them to clearer consciousness, and in most cases qualitatively modifies the object attended to. "Attention constantly tends

---

[21] Very briefly stated, Royce's argument is that the very fact of my inclusion in an Absolute Will must be understood to mean that my own unique will is included in the Divine Will as one of *its* purposes. Thus, I am free in the sense that I am a unique embodiment of the Will of the Absolute (cf. *The World and the Individual*, II, 330ff.). Most of Royce's critics have found this argument unconvincing.

[22] See Chapter One.

[23] "How Beliefs are Made" (1882), in *Fugitive Essays*, p. 354.

to make our consciousness more definite and less complex; that is, less confused, and more united." This, according to the young Royce, is the "law of attention," and it largely determines "what we are to know and what we are to believe." [24]

Some twenty years later, in *Outlines of Psychology*,[25] Royce gave his fullest account of the doctrine of attention. He defined attention most broadly as "the process of furthering our current interest in an experience." As we attend to the objects of our special interest, these grow clearer in our minds, become more definite, and are brought into sharper "relief" against their backgrounds. Three sorts of physiological processes accompany the act of attending: (1) motor adjustments occur in our sense organs, bringing them into better relation with the object of our interest; (2) a brain "set" which tends to favor cerebral habits most useful in comprehending the sort of objects in which we are interested comes into prominence; (3) correspondingly, a brain "set" tending to inhibit movements and habits that would interfere with or distract from the satisfaction of the pervading interest comes into play.

Royce makes no special effort to explain on what basis we select particular objects of attention. He does, however, believe that there is a residue of "self-activity" involved in attentive selection which cannot be accounted for completely in terms of habits formed under the influence of environmental conditioning.[26] This residue he describes as "restless persistence." Even in a young child we observe a tendency to persist "in a great number of its still unadaptive move-

---

[24] *Ibid.*, pp. 356–357. Royce wishes to underscore the power of selective attention to shape our beliefs about external reality. He warns that "in every case where we fancy ourselves sure of a simple law of Nature, we must remember that a good deal of the fancied simplicity may be due, not to Nature, but to the ineradicable prejudice of our own minds in favor of regularity and simplicity."

[25] (New York, 1906), pp. 261–264.

[26] *Outlines of Psychology*, pp. 299ff.

ments, in a great number of its still useless actions, despite their inefficacy." [27] We witness here a "predisposition to endless experiment and to the trying of various relations with the environment" resulting in actions for which the child's previous training had not prepared it. This is most noticeable in childhood play.

Just because the play activities are carried out at a time when they are not necessary to the preservation of the organism, they receive a free and manifold development . . . [28]

In adults, this restlessness is expressed in the disposition to persevere, to keep searching elsewhere—anywhere—for a chance solution to a balky problem.

Thus, Royce is led to believe that he can account at least for the element of "spontaneity" we feel is present in our ability to break from the fixed pattern of our socially acquired habits. His thesis is that

the restless over-activity of the organism in carrying out its instinctive processes, or in seeking opportunity for the establishment of new functions, is the principal condition of every significant form of mental initiative.[29]

Neither social conditioning nor special instincts can fully account for

the power of the organism to persist in seeking for new adjustments, whether the environment at first suggests them or not, to persist in struggling toward its wholly unknown goal, whether there is any apparent opportunity for reaching such a goal or not. Such persistence is the one initiative that the organism can offer to the world.[30]

Now this restlessness, this capacity for initiative, reaches its highest manifestation in our processes of selective attention. Royce therefore endeavors to reinterpret the notion of

[27] *Ibid.*, p. 307.   [28] *Ibid.*, p. 324.
[29] *Ibid.*, p. 318, quotation appears in italics.
[30] *Ibid.*, p. 325, quotation appears in italics.

voluntary action, of willing, in terms of selective attention. Willing has to do with the guidance of conduct. When we guide our conduct, we focus on the furthering of those desires or tendencies to action whose realization we conceive as essential to our over-all well-being. But so to focus is, in a word, to attend. "And such attentive preference of one course of conduct, or of one tendency or desire, as against all others present to our minds at any one time, is called a voluntary act." From a psychological point of view, therefore, we may define willing as "the attentive furthering of our interest in one act or desire as against another." [31]

Concluding his psychological account of volition, Royce distinguishes between acts of will that are *original* and those that are *originative*. He argues that we cannot consciously and directly will any new act, but only those acts we have already learned how to perform. We can indeed decide on courses of action involving new experiences and unforeseen consequences for us: getting married, taking our first trip abroad, adopting a new career, and so forth. But all that we can consciously and directly will in these cases are such familiar actions as saying yes, buying the ticket, signing our name, and the like. Choice, therefore, is an *unoriginal* power. Yet it may be and often is *originative* in the sense that deliberately doing an appropriate series of such familiar things may "begin a new life for the doer." [32]

[31] *Ibid.*, p. 368, both quotations appear in italics. For a similar identification of the act of choice with the concentration of attention, compare J. H. Muirhead's well-known analysis of the voluntary action of rising from a chair and going over to the fireplace. Muirhead singles out the step of fixing attention on one object of desire to the exclusion of others as the act of choice, decision, or resolution strictly speaking. (*The Elements of Ethics* [London, 1892], pp. 46–47.)

I might remark that Royce's argument seems to hinge on the alleged psychological impossibility of divorcing thought from action. "To think of any sort of activity, therefore, already implies a tendency to this form of activity. And actually to will a given act is *to think attentively of that act to the exclusion or neglect of the representation or imagining of any and all other acts.*" (*Outlines of Psychology*, p. 369, Royce's italics.)

[32] *Ibid.*, p. 371.

While this psychological account of human freedom is, I submit, suggestive, surprisingly "modern," and by no means implausible, it is neither complete nor entirely satisfactory. For in a sense, Royce's account of attention both explains and presupposes human freedom. It is an empirically oriented psychological theory which is designed to characterize the *activity* of willing in a relatively nonmysterious, nonmetaphysical way. Yet attention clearly presupposes the fact of a prior free choice, in terms of an original power to attend or not to attend freely. In other words, the theory of attention helps to explain *how* we choose, although it cannot tell us why it is *that* we choose or where this power of ours originally came from. Thus a wholesale reduction of volition to the process of attention would be questionable both on psychological and on philosophical grounds. But any criticism of Royce's various ventures into psychology sufficiently extended to be worthwhile would take us beyond the bounds of the present inquiry. Much more to the point is the question how such an account of volition might afford psychological grounds for holding that men can be held morally responsible for their actions and decisions.

To this question Royce addressed himself in *The World and the Individual.* There he makes a distinction between the inevitable formal limitation of our capacity for attentive response, inherent in our natures as finite individuals, and the manner in which we exercise and develop, or inhibit and constrict, the capacity which we do have.[33] For the limitation inherent in our nature we are not responsible. Human awareness as we know it is irrevocably confined to a limited time span, to a "specious present" preventing us from attending to more than a few of the happenings around us at any one time.[34] We are responsible, however, for what we do or

[33] *The World and the Individual,* II, 57ff.
[34] Royce even goes so far as to define human finitude as our inability to attend successfully to more than a "very few of the details of the universe" at any given moment.

neglect to do with the capacity that is ours. Within the limited field of my awareness I am free either consciously to cultivate my powers of response or deliberately to narrow my attentive concerns. If I do the former, Royce insists, I am fulfilling one of my fundamental obligations as a moral agent. If I do the latter—if I manifest what Royce calls "a viciously acquired naïveté" [35]—I do something that is *morally* wrong.

This doctrine already commits Royce to the essentially self-realizationist ethical theory he was to develop more fully in his later writings. Professor Paul Ramsey has pointed out that, in characterizing the use we make of our attentive powers as a question of our moral attitude, Royce is in effect describing our ability to determine ourselves in act.[36] To a significant extent we are free to construct our characters through an intensive development of our capacities for response. When we do so to the best of our ability, we are acting morally. When, through laziness, through indifference, or through sheer perversity, we fail to do so, we are acting immorally. For each of us as a rational human being, an expanded range of responsiveness is a positive moral good. Each of us upon reflection considers himself obligated to enlarge his field of human concern as much as he is able.

In our everyday experience, Royce observes, we feel a sense of guilt or sin most keenly when we deliberately ignore an ideal to which we have previously committed ourselves. "To sin is *consciously to choose to forget,* through a narrowing of the field of attention, an Ought that one already recognizes." [37] That constitutes what Royce later called a de-

[35] *Ibid.,* p. 358. Royce's interpretation of responsibility in terms of responsiveness seems to me to be both a more plausible and a more insightful thesis than his over-all reformulation of volition in terms of attention. It anticipates, moreover, a similar orientation in the ethics of the contemporary philosopher Martin Buber.

[36] "The Idealistic View of Moral Evil: Josiah Royce and Bernard Bosanquet," *Philosophy and Phenomenological Research* 6:573 (1945–1946).

[37] *The World and the Individual,* II, 359. Italics in text.

liberate act of self-betrayal, an act of moral treason.[38]

We might summarize Royce's doctrine by saying that if the human person is to be held free enough to be regarded as morally accountable for his action and character, he must have in a significant measure the capacity of self-determination. From a psychological point of view, this capacity is best accounted for in terms of his power, within his over-all human limitations, to enlarge or to constrict his attentiveness and responsiveness to what happens around him, and above all to the ideals and obligations he has already accepted as his own. It is largely in this way that he succeeds or fails to achieve mature selfhood.

We turn now to the question of how we come to know other minds or selves.

4. Other Minds

According to Royce, self-consciousness is for the most part a social product. It originates and develops within the context of a polar tension between "ego" and "alter." The question naturally arises how we gain access to other minds. The traditional "analogy" theory, a mixture of psychology and epistemology, has it that I have a certain feeling, say a, and express this physically by way of phenomena x, y, z. When I observe another man expressing himself in similar physical ways, x_1, y_1, z_1, I infer that these expressions are occasioned by the same or a similar mental state, a_1, as my own. This theory Royce finds inadequate. It is based on the assumption that our knowledge of others is derived from our knowledge of ourselves. To Royce, the facts reveal that it is mostly the other way around. In the first place, Royce reminds us, "my idea of myself, as empirical Ego, is on the whole a social product, due, strangely enough, to my ideas of other peo-

[38] The Problem of Christianity, 2 vols. (New York, 1913), I, 245–248, 263, 266.

ple . . . I believe, and in believing conceive myself as demanding the approval of good judges. I esteem myself, and in doing so conceive myself as esteemed by others." [39] In the second place, the phenomena of imitation which Royce has described convinced him that children learn, however dimly, of the existence of other minds long before they have attained the self-consciousness needed to make the analogy between their own mental states and those of others. In the third place, the analogy theory fails to account for the freshness, the novelty experienced in encountering other minds.

Where I am *merely* reminded by what a man says of my own past ideas, I am likely to conceive these expressions of his as expressions of my own ideas, rather than his . . . Hence my comprehension of my fellow's ideas as his cannot be derived from a mere reasoning by analogy . . . On the contrary, my fellow's acts are most likely to attract my attention, when I do not recognize them as like mine.[40]

Royce's own theory is that "we believe in another mind, the mind of our fellow, primarily because another mind is a permanent and often unfailing source of ideas, of information about the world, of knowledge, of new plans, in short of meanings." Royce insists that interpersonal communication is a matter of ideas rather than of feelings. Feelings as such are too inaccessible, too indescribable, to be communicated. The relations among them, and between them and other mental states, however, are within the province of ideas and therefore are communicable.

[39] "The External World and the Social Consciousness," *Philosophical Review* 3:532 (September 1894).
[40] "The Social Factors of the Human Intellect" (circa 1897), folio 68, lecture 2, p. 12. A more recent writer, Philip Wheelwright, seems to agree with Royce on this point. Professor Wheelwright points out that we come to know (and respect) another mind "not solely, not perhaps even mainly, by its likeness to us, but by the new thoughts and new imaginings to which its many-sided communication prompts us." (*The Way of Philosophy*, rev. ed. [New York, 1954], p. 273.)

Not our experiences, but the relations between our experiences are the common matters of social communication . . . Even sympathy with another's feelings has to be on the whole of this ideal sort. We comprehend another's feelings in so far as we learn to share and to apprehend his attitude toward the objects which arouse his feelings, the sense of his inner life, the way in which one of his feelings is linked with another feeling, resembles it or differs from it, harmonizes with it, or opposes it. And this is true of the most intuitive . . . sympathy.[41]

Royce has no intention of repudiating the analogy theory altogether. He merely wishes to stress—consistently with his notion that individual self-consciousness is a phenomenon derived from social processes of imitation and learning— that our awareness of other minds begins with their impingement on us rather than with inferences from ourselves to them. What usually happens, on Royce's view, is this. Someone else experiences certain phenomena, say feelings *a* and *b*. He talks to me about them—for the most part seeking to convey to me an idea of how they are related. As I begin to understand him, I bring experiences of my own, say feelings *c* and *d*, into similar relation. Only then *may* I make an analogy between my experiences and his. I may conclude that my experiences *c* and *d* are in significant respects like his experiences *a* and *b*. But this conclusion, Royce warns, is always doubtful and subject to subsequent modification.

In his last years Royce offered a somewhat fuller explanation of the complex process of interpersonal communication by way of his theory of interpretation. We shall return to the problem of other minds, therefore, in the next chapter.

5. Reflection and the Moral Life

At the end of the preceding chapter we discussed the role of imitation in the individual's acquisition of moral concepts and in the formation of his social conscience. Royce's doc-

[41] H.U.A., folio 68, lecture 2, p. 14.

trine of reflection is at least in part a further effort to explain, from a psychological point of view, how the individual comes to maturity as a moral agent.

The broader implication of Royce's doctrine of reflection has already been indicated. It is that for Royce the notion of selfhood in its most significant sense must be conceived in what are essentially moral terms. The individual person establishes a continuing identity for himself only when he adopts a life purpose or plan. On the basis of his commitment to such a purpose he is able meaningfully to connect his momentary awareness of himself with what he was and what he will become. To "know" such a person is to know to what he is committed. To appraise his character is to esteem him for living up to his commitments, or to disapprove of him for failing to do so.

This implication is, of course, present in what Royce has to say about our awareness of others as well. We know them best when we know their commitments. It is the novelty, the difference of their life plan from ours, that first attracts us to them and makes us aware of them as persons in their own right. And it is in our encounters with them that we feel the urgency first of adopting and later of criticizing, modifying, and expanding our own life plans. Thus, whenever two or more men encounter one another as persons, the moral life is a going concern.

Perhaps the outstanding characteristic of Royce's analysis of self-consciousness is the extent to which he finds it dependent, both for its origin and for its growth, upon the society of one's fellow men. What I take myself to be is, to begin with, largely a matter of what others think of me. The moral implication is clear: self-evaluation takes its rise, even if it does not end there, in society's estimation of my individual worth. Thus, according to Royce, the imitative individual's instinctual receptivity to the moral ideals prevalent in his society is augmented by the dependence of his rational and reflective judgments of himself upon the judgments of his fellow men. In this manner Royce expands his genetic explanation of the existence of a community of moral sentiments, standards, and ideals.

But as we have seen, while self-appraisal begins in virtually full subjection to what others think of me, it cannot end there. Royce is emphatic on this point. The very multiplication of social pressures to conform to various ideals of personal life and to accept divergent standards of moral excellence makes it imperative that the individual choose a life plan and a system of moral standards of his own. Such choice is the necessary condition of the individual's attaining a sense of mature selfhood, of personal identity that transcends the amorphous and fragmented character of what Royce has described as the "empirical ego." Moreover, the principle of choice involved in the individual's adoption of a life plan of his own must derive somehow from within himself.

Now as we saw in section 3 earlier, Royce's account of this principle of choice may not be entirely satisfactory. The best explanation he is able to offer is by way of his concept of attention. Within the psychological limitations of my powers of awareness, I am free to respond or not to respond to what lies in my conscious field through attending or refusing to attend to it. Thus to a significant extent I am able to construct my moral character by the manner in which I develop my powers of response.

Royce's doctrine of attention, indeed, is more an explanation of how the individual is free to cultivate or to undermine a personal moral commitment he has already made, than it is an explanation of how this commitment is made in the first place. The latter, and surely more difficult, question is no doubt partially answered in Royce's doctrine of imitation. But it is only in his later theories of loyalty and of the community that a full explanation is to be found. For the moment, it should be pointed out that Royce's doctrine of attention does constitute an interesting and not implausible psychological theory compatible with our common-sense ascription of moral responsibility. We may not fully understand how an individual comes to have a moral life purpose of his own. But if and when he has one, we are justified in ascribing to him moral responsibility for the manner in which he cultivates or betrays this purpose.

One further result of Royce's investigations in social psychology deserves notice. With his theory of the fundamentally social origin of self-awareness, Royce is afforded a further critical perspective on the egoism-altruism controversy. He now perceives that one of the classic formulations of the problem of ethics—how to convert the instinctually, that is, the naturally egoistic individual to altruistic concerns—rests on a psychological mistake.

This whole customary popular and philosophical opposition between a man's self-consciousness, as if it were something primitive and lonely, and his social consciousness, as if it were acquired, apart from his self-consciousness, through intercourse with his fellows, is false to human nature. As a fact, a man becomes self-conscious only in the most intimate connection with the growth of his social consciousness. These two forms of consciousness are not separable and opposed regions of a man's life; they are thoroughly interdependent. I am dependent on my fellows, not only physically, but to the very core of my selfhood, not only for what, physically speaking, I am, but for what I take myself to be.[42]

It is the habits and states of self-consciousness, not of social consciousness, that are secondary and derived.[43]

Royce now concludes that "the ethical problem is not:

[42] "Self-Consciousness, Social Consciousness, and Nature," in *Studies of Good and Evil*, p. 201.
[43] Cf. "The External World and the Social Consciousness," *Philosophical Review* 3:533: "Imitation is the primary, originality the secondary, submission the earlier, rebellion the later, authority is the natural, reflective independence the derived element, in the social and cognitive life of man."

Shall I aim to preserve social relations? but: What social relations shall I aim to preserve?"[44] Both egoism and altruism, he maintains,

are very complex and derivative motives, due to a considerable previous training of our social instincts. Our primal instincts themselves, as we inherit them, are very largely social, but they are neither egoistic nor altruistic. They are just instincts.[45]

Royce concedes that our "original" instincts favor self-preservation, but reaffirms that the sort of self-consciousness required to make the egoism-altruism conflict possible in the first place develops only long after acting on instinct has given way to purposive, rational behavior.[46] He reminds us that even our self-assertiveness, our need to contrast ourselves with our fellow men, is not opposed to the impulse to imitate them, but on the contrary presupposes that impulse for its effectiveness.

The normal relation between the two is that we constantly use our imitativeness to give us opportunities for self-assertion. Having followed a given model, I can make use of the power thus acquired to display myself in the presence of other fellow-beings —to distinguish myself by my skill in a given act.[47]

Thus Royce's psychological investigations led him to the view that the isolated, instinctually egoistic, and fundamentally a-social individual is a fiction. Man is by nature a social animal; his self-assertive tendencies are phenomena deriving from and not prior to the social environment in which he finds himself. For Royce, therefore, the meaningful area of moral controversy centers not in how to make men socially responsive and responsible, but in what forms of social re-

[44] "Self-Consciousness, Social Consciousness, and Nature," in *Studies of Good and Evil*, p. 203.
[45] "Social Factors in the Development of the Individual Mind," folio 69, lecture 2, p. 30.
[46] H.U.A., folio 69, lecture 3, pp. 4–5.
[47] *Ibid.*, p. 22.

sponsiveness and responsibility are best for them. Royce's very insistence upon man's pervasive sociability led him to be exceptionally wary of the dangerous tendency of some moral philosophers to suggest that what is social behavior is *ipso facto* moral behavior. We shall return to this point in a later chapter.

Chapter Five

INTERPRETATION

WITH the doctrines of imitation and reflection just described, Royce has done much toward offering a plausible account of the formation of the individual human personality and the processes of interpersonal communication. To a large extent Royce's theory of imitation explains how we learn to act and to think, while his theory of reflection affords considerable understanding of how we express our individuality. Nevertheless, Royce did not complete the psychological and epistemological substructure of his mature ethical theory until the end of his life when, under the influence of C. S. Peirce, he presented his theory of interpretation. This theory came to perform a number of crucial tasks in Royce's over-all philosophical system. It enabled him to clarify how the individual comes to attain a sense of continuing personal identity. It provided a more adequate explanation of the process of interpersonal communication. It afforded for his ethical theory a more concrete statement of the goals of social and moral endeavor. And, finally, it played a decisive role in the revision which his metaphysics underwent toward the end of his philosophical career.

This being the case, it will be impossible to discuss the full scope of Royce's theory of interpretation in the present chapter. Royce treated interpretation primarily as an epistemological concept. Our present focus, accordingly, will be epistemological. We shall first of all examine Royce's claim that ordinary cognitive processes of perception and conception must be supplemented by a third distinct type of process, interpretation, if we are to account for much of the knowledge we actually possess. Thereafter, the nature and structure of interpretation will be discussed. This will be followed by a closer look at the role of interpretation in three major areas of human concern: the attempt to determine our own selfhood, the attempt to communicate with and to know our fellow men, and the attempt to determine the nature of the external world as a realm of publicly accessible and verifiable objects of experience.

1. The Need for Interpretation

Royce's doctrine of interpretation is primarily designed to overcome what he regards as certain inadequacies in traditional theories of knowledge. These, according to Royce, have tended to be "dualistic" in nature, limiting the possible types of distinct cognitive processes to perception and conception. By perception Royce understands knowledge by direct acquaintance or immediate sense apprehension. By conception Royce understands the ability to have "knowledge about" abstract universals such as numbers and relations, or complex objects involving such universals.[1] Frequently, as in the Platonic stress on the conception of essences and in the Bergsonian emphasis on intuitive perception, one or the other of these cognitive processes is given preeminence. But in most theories of knowledge, Royce observes, human knowing is regarded as somehow involving a synthesis of these two modes of cognition.

Now it is Royce's contention that these dualistic theories are unable adequately to account for the knowledge that we actually have (1) of ourselves as persons, (2) of other

[1] The Problem of Christianity, 2 vols. (New York, 1913), II, 122; cf. the essay "Mind," in Encyclopedia of Religion and Ethics, ed. James Hastings (New York, 1916), pp. 649–657. Royce's doctrine of interpretation is most fully presented in these two works.

men as persons, and (3) of the external world as a realm of publicly verifiable objects. We saw in Chapter Four that for Royce the notion I may come to have of my own selfhood, of my uniqueness and individuality as bearer of a life plan or purpose, is not a matter of immediately perceiving inner physiological or psychological states, nor is it a matter of forming an abstract conception of myself as knower, substantial unity, and so on. In regard to our fellow men, it is generally admitted that we have no direct acquaintance with their inner psychological states. But in addition, Royce contends, no abstract conception of our fellow men is able to account for our knowledge of them as persons, that is, as bearers of unique life plans and purposes in their own right. Finally, Royce believes, our knowledge of the external world as a domain of publicly accessible and verifiable objects cannot exhaustively be accounted for in terms either of our own percepts (which each of us alone can verify), or of our abstract conceptions (which remain on the level of generality having to do merely with types of objects), or of combinations of both.

Royce therefore proposes a third form of cognitive process, distinct from and in addition to perception and conception, which he terms "interpretation." Before we examine in greater detail Royce's view of the role of interpretation in our knowledge of ourselves, other men, and the external world, it would be useful to summarize his theory of the nature and structure of interpretation in general.

2. The Nature and Structure of Interpretation

Royce begins his discussion of interpretation by calling attention to several obvious and everyday uses of the term. "When a stranger in a foreign land desires the services of an interpreter, when a philologist offers his rendering of a text, when a judge construes a statute, some kind of interpretation is in question."[2] These three activities have at least this much in common, that in each instance a three-term relation is involved: someone interprets something to someone else. Thus in the philological example, a translator (A) interprets an author or a text (B) to a potential reader (C). A further feature of the triadic relation in question is that it is essentially nonsymmetrical. In any single process of interpretation, one of the terms is the interpreter, a second the object to be interpreted, and the third the interpretee, that is, the one to whom the interpretation is addressed. A process of interpretation, therefore, not only involves a three-term relation, but it brings these three terms into a determinate order.

Royce refers to the object that is to be interpreted as a *sign*. His attempt to define what he means by a sign, however, is not wholly satisfactory. In its broadest sense a sign, for Royce, is simply an object that calls for interpretation. In order to define the notion of a sign more specifically, Royce tells us that it is essentially

either a mind or a quasi-mind,—an object that fulfills the functions of a mind. Thus, a word, a clockface, a weathervane, or a gesture is a sign. Our reason for calling it such is two-fold. It expresses a mind, and it calls for interpretation through some other mind, which shall act as mediator between the sign, or between the maker of the sign, and some one to whom the sign is to be read.[3]

However, that definition in turn is somewhat too narrow for Royce's own purposes. Peirce, from whom Royce, as he generously acknowledged, learned the "doctrine of signs," held that any object of *thought*, as distinct from an object of immediate perception or instantaneous intuition, is by its very nature a sign, that is, a *problematic* object requiring a process of interpretation by reference to other signs before it can be understood.[4] Briefly, Peirce held that all significant

[2] *The Problem of Christianity*, II, 109.   [3] *Ibid.*, p. 283.
[4] *The Collected Papers of Charles Sanders Peirce*, ed. Charles Hartshorne

human knowledge is mediated rather than immediate knowledge; that is, between any given object and a mind whose object it is, there is interposed a sign (usually a number of signs) representing that object to that mind. Royce's repeated insistence that virtually all our knowledge requires cognitive processes of interpretation, in addition to perception and conception, indicates that he was in basic agreement with Peirce's dictum that "all thought is in signs."

Royce, moreover, agrees with Peirce that every sign is capable of evoking an endless series of further signs. Royce writes:

> Since an interpretation of a sign is, in its turn, the expression of the interpreter's mind, it constitutes a new sign, which again calls for interpretation; and so on without end; unless the process is arbitrarily interrupted.[5]

Another reason for this contention is that any given sign admits of alternative interpretations and is therefore subject to further development, in many different ways, through being combined and compared with other signs. It follows, as Professor W. B. Gallie has pointed out, that in general "there can be no such thing as *the* (one and only) sign of a given object, and no such thing as *the* (one and only) interpretant of a given sign."[6] Signs, in short, are elements within a system of signs: their meanings cannot be grasped or communicated apart from their relations to other signs within that system.

Herewith both Peirce and Royce wish to emphasize not only that our knowledge of any given object is never, or at

---

and Paul Weiss, 8 vols. (Cambridge, Mass., 1931–1960), 5.253: "To say, therefore, that thought cannot happen in an instant, but requires a time, is but another way of saying that every thought must be interpreted in another, or that all thought is in signs." (Cf. 5.285.)

[5] *The Problem of Christianity*, II, 283. Cf. Peirce, *Collected Papers*, 1.541, 2.42, 2.92, 5.284. Cf. also John Smith, *Royce's Social Infinite* (New York, 1950), p. 88, for a symbolic formulation of interpretation as a self-perpetuating process.

[6] *Peirce and Pragmatism* (London, 1952), p. 125.

least rarely, complete, but that our competence in understanding and using the signs that purportedly refer to it is a matter of degree, of more or less successful approximation. Inasmuch as most of our problematic objects of knowledge are "public" objects, that is, objects about which we seek to communicate with one another and whose existence and nature we seek to verify in common, Royce specifies as a further characteristic of interpretative processes that they are by their very nature *social*. The metaphor of conversation appropriately suggests the manner in which interpretative processes are generated and developed.[7]

But if interpretative processes are by their very nature self-perpetuating, the question naturally arises as to what ends they serve. Here Royce is compelled to speak in broad, general terms. He takes it as an incontrovertible fact of human experience that each one of us as a rational individual struggles to achieve a level of coherent knowledge or insight which in our private experience as such we are unable to attain. Throughout his life Royce defined human rationality in essentially purposive terms, as the quest for an orderly and integrated experience, organized from the vantage point of some sort of "conspectus" that is denied any one of us at any one time. In *The Religious Aspect of Philosophy* and in *The World and the Individual*, Royce resorted to the concept of an Absolute Knower or Consciousness which embodies this higher conspectus. It is, of course, this familiar doctrine, so generally identified with Royce's philosophy as a whole, that has led to his being classified as an absolute idealist.

Now in his later work Royce's view of the motive of rational human endeavor remains unaltered. It is still described as the quest for "a larger insight,"[8] for "a larger

[7] *The Problem of Christianity*, II, 159.
[8] *The Sources of Religious Insight* (New York, 1912), p. 85.

unity of consciousness . . . a conspectus," [9] for "a connected, a reasonable, a comprehensible system of ideal activities and meanings," [10] in short, for "wholeness." [11] But Royce's conception of the agency that embodies this broader conspectus is significantly changed. In place of the Absolute Consciousness which embraces, or contains, or, as some of Royce's critics have charged, swallows finite individuals, we now find the "Community of Interpretation," consisting solely of the activities and interrelations of these same finite individuals. This basic shift is part of a general metaphysical reorientation in Royce's later philosophy, a matter to which we shall return briefly in the Appendix.

For the present, it should be pointed out that interpretative activity subserves highly general and remote ends that may equally well be characterized as logical and as ethical ideals. On the one hand, Royce, once again in concert with Peirce, understood the quest for rationality and coherence to be ultimately a moral quest. It is one of the ends, perhaps the most important end, definitive of the striving for self-possession or self-realization. And self-realization is, in turn, the central concept of Royce's later ethical theory, as we shall see presently. On the other hand, Royce, like Peirce, regarded logic as a normative science—not only in the sense that it determines certain standards of valid thinking, but in the sense that its ultimate purpose or ideal, the furthering of rationality, coherence, and clarity in human discourse, is an ethical one.

If we then ask how we are to determine whether or not a certain line of interpretative activity is leading us toward the ends we seek, only a tentative answer is possible. Inquiry

[9] *The Problem of Christianity,* II, 188; cf. *The Philosophy of Loyalty* (New York, 1908), p. 339.
[10] "Mind," p. 654.
[11] "Error and Truth," in *Royce's Logical Essays,* ed. Daniel S. Robinson (Dubuque, Iowa, 1951), p. 111.

directed toward the adequate interpretation of our own selves, of our fellow men, and of the external world cannot be said to reach its goal in any one particular interpretative process. Thus we are dependent upon the "leadings" that we encounter in the course of inquiry. As our signs are gradually rendered more precise, more consistent with one another, and more coherent with our experience as a whole, we have some justification in supposing that we are approaching nearer to our ultimate goals. But it is only if and when we attain these far-off goals that we shall know with certainty how we reached them. Meanwhile, we must rely on our capacity, in concert, to criticize and to correct the particular interpretations of signs that we make.

In the light of what has just been said, Royce's motives in distinguishing between cognitive processes of perception and conception on the one side and interpretative processes on the other should be somewhat clearer. Whereas perception and conception as such involve dyadic relations between, respectively, perceiver and immediate datum and conceiver and abstract universal, interpretation involves a triadic relation of interpreter, sign to be interpreted, and interpretee. Whereas perception and conception are as such what Royce calls "self-limiting" processes, that is, processes that naturally terminate in isolated objects perceived and distinct universals defined, an interpretative process is by its very nature self-perpetuating unless arbitrarily interrupted. The resultant interpretation of any given sign becomes in its turn a sign requiring further interpretation. Whereas perception tends to be "lonesome" in its restriction to isolated perceivers, and conception tends to be "sterile" in its confinement to determining abstract objects of thought,[12] interpretation is by its very nature a social process, the ever-expanding and endlessly rewarding "conversation" among many inquirers. Finally, interpretation has as its comprehensive goal the in-

[12] *The Problem of Christianity*, II, 149–151.

tegration of the objects of perception and conception into a coherent, all-encompassing body of knowledge in which the community of all interpreters could ultimately find satisfaction.

We may now consider in greater detail Royce's conception of the role of interpretation in the quest for selfhood, in interpersonal communication, and in the determination of publicly accessible objects of experience.

3. Interpretation in the Quest for Selfhood

In the light of his earlier analysis of the concept of self, Royce in his last years reached the position that one's own selfhood is cognitively accessible to one, if at all, only through processes of interpretation. We recall his insistence that we have no intuitive knowledge of ourselves as "selves" in any significant sense of the term. Royce conceded that I have perceptual acquaintance with certain physical and emotional states occurring in or attendant upon my own physical organism. He conceded further, and debated the point with Hume, that I have a purely formal conception of myself as the logical subject of the thoughts I think. But Royce insisted that a continuing notion of "who" I am is contingent upon my ability to "extend" myself temporally and to give my life a meaning in terms of a purpose, ideal, or life plan.

Royce now maintains that neither perceptual nor conceptual processes are adequate to define such a life plan. Rather, it is a process of interpretation that alone makes it possible for an individual to acquire a life plan.

When such interpretation goes on within the mind of an individual man, it constitutes the very process whereby, as is sometimes said, he "finds himself," "comes to himself," "directs himself," or "gets his bearings . . ." [13]

[13] "Mind," p. 652.

Royce contends that acts of conscious reflection involve tri-adic relations in spite of the fact that a single personality is involved. When at any given time I consider a task in which I am engaged, an obligation which I feel, or an ideal which I am attempting to realize, I interpret myself to myself.[14] What usually happens in situations like this, Royce urges, is that my present "self" (which seeks to fulfill its task, obliga-tion, or ideal), interprets my past "self" (which set for my-self that task, incurred that obligation, or formulated that ideal), to my future "self" (which is to accomplish the task, meet the obligation, or realize the ideal in question).[15]

When an individual thus attempts the "ideal self-exten-sion" without which, according to Royce, he cannot give his life a coherent meaning, he manifests "the will to be self-possessed."[16] The process of self-interpretation involved in the effort to attain self-possession or self-realization is, of course, inherently without limit, until it is arbitrarily inter-rupted by the individual's death. But its ideal end, could it ever be attained, would be that interpretation of himself in which the individual were aware of having realized all of his potentialities and deeper aspirations. Once again, as we see, Royce is refusing to separate logical from ethical ideals in the structure of human ends. In the final analysis, Royce insists, my will to interpret may be taken as identical with my will to be self-possessed.

4. Interpretation in Interpersonal Communication

In the previous chapter we saw that Royce's psychological investigations had led him to question, already in the 1890's,

---

[14] *The Problem of Christianity*, II, 40ff., 63ff.   [15] *Ibid.*, pp. 42, 111.
[16] *Ibid.*, p. 193. The reader should recall Royce's contention (Chapter Four, section 2) that selfhood is essentially a moral category. Thus there can, in effect, be no real distinction between knowing oneself and "becom-ing oneself." Royce is now maintaining that selfhood literally *is* the result of a process of self-interpretation.

the traditional account of our knowledge of other minds. It was granted by the familiar analogy theory there described that we have no direct perceptual acquaintance with the inner mental states of our fellows. This theory maintained that our mental states are accompanied by certain physical expressions. When we observe similar physical expressions in the behavior of our fellow men, we infer that mental states like our own must then and there be present in their otherwise inaccessible minds. Royce found this theory wanting on two main counts. In the first place, the learning process in childhood indicates that we frequently come to know the ideas of our fellow men even before we know our own. Secondly, the impact that the ideas of others have on us is due in large measure to their freshness or novelty. The analogy theory, however, would allow access only to ideas in others with which we were already familiar. In an effort to develop a more adequate theory of interpersonal communication, Royce then suggested that what we somehow communicate to one another are ideas about the relations among our mental states, rather than those states themselves. But Royce was not yet in a position to make this suggestion clear.

By 1913 Royce had come to believe that the postulation of a third fundamental cognitive process, interpretation, is necessary to explain interpersonal communication. In the essay "Mind" he gives the following example. Suppose I hear a man cry "Fire!":

the sort of knowledge which takes place in my mind when I hear and understand this cry essentially depends on this fact: I regard my fellow's cry as a sign or expression of the fact either that he himself sees a fire or that he believes that there is a fire, or that, at the very least, he intends me to understand him as asserting that there is a fire, or as taking an interest of his own in what he calls a fire. Thus, while I cannot understand my fellow's cry unless I hear it, unless I have at least some perceptual knowledge, and while I equally shall not have a "knowledge about" the nature of fire, and so a "knowledge about" the object to which the cry refers, unless I am possessed of something which tends to be conceptual knowledge of his object, my knowledge of my fellow's meaning, my "grasping of his idea," consists neither in the percept of the sign nor in a concept of its object which the sign arouses, but in my *interpretation* of the sign as an indication of an idea which is distinct from any idea of mine, and which I refer to a mind not my own, or in some wise distinct from mine.[17]

The point that Royce is attempting to make here may be somewhat obscured by the cumbersome style in which he expresses it. When a neighbor shouts "Fire!" he is trying to communicate a matter of some urgency. Suppose I hear him but do not see either him or the fire. My perceptual knowledge of the situation is quickly exhausted in my hearing his voice, and in my more or less reflexive tendency to have certain vivid images of fires come to mind from my own previous experience. My conceptual knowledge includes some general idea I have of my neighbor, involving perhaps his tendency to panic in crises, and the like. It includes also a general idea of fire, invoking no doubt certain behavioral responses I am inclined to make in the presence of fire.[18] But in spite of the perceptual and conceptual knowledge which I have at my disposal in this situation, I am likely to be at a loss as to what to do. What I lack is an interpretation of the relation between my neighbor's shout and the event to which this shout purportedly refers. This interpretation can be elicited through a process of questioning him.

An objection might occur to the reader at this point. Royce has claimed that interpretative processes are by their very nature self-perpetuating, that they are terminated, if at all, only by external and arbitrary interruptions such as death or social separation. But the situation just analyzed would hardly seem to call for a potentially endless series of

---

[17] "Mind," p. 650.
[18] Here Royce's earlier analysis of general ideas, summarized in Chapter Two, might be borne in mind.

interpretations. In *The Problem of Christianity* Royce offers another example of the need for interpretation, in which the term "sign" may be taken quite literally. A traveler who cannot read will fail to grasp the *meaning* of a road sign unless it is read, that is, interpreted, to him.[19] But surely this even simpler example by no means involves a potentially limitless sequence of interpretations. Once the traveler has had the sign interpreted for him (this should not take long if, by hypothesis, he has a mind), the matter is at an end.

It would seem, then, that Royce's claim is somewhat exaggerated. Not all interpretative processes are (or need be) self-perpetuating. Nevertheless many of the more significant ones are. If we grant that when men attempt to communicate they are frequently motivated by the desire to "get to know one another" and, if we accept Royce's view as to the inherent limitations of perception and conception, then his claim that interpretative processes are by nature indefinitely recurrent seems more justified. The following passage seems to me to put forth Royce's claim most plausibly.

In literal conversation our neighbour utters words which already express to us ideas. These ideas so contrast with our own present ideas that, while we find the new ideas intelligible, and, therefore, view them as expressions of a mind, we do not fully know what they mean. Hence, in general, our neighbour having addressed us, we in reply ask him, more or less incidentally or persistently, whether or not this is what he means—i.e., we give him back our interpretation of his meaning, in order to see whether this interpretation elicits a new expression which is in substantial agreement with the expression which we expected from him.[20]

Royce adds that this conversational method may be described, in the language of pragmatism, as the formation of "working hypotheses." But, since these hypotheses refer to states of mind, they are "never conceivably capable of direct

---

[19] *The Problem of Christianity*, II, 287.   [20] "Mind," p. 654.

verification." If another's mind is, as Royce maintains, opaque to perceptual and conceptual processes, neither percepts nor concepts will adequately verify interpretative processes with respect to it. Royce remarks that "the metaphor of conversation . . . furnishes the best means of indicating wherein consists the relative, but never immediate, verifiability of the truth of an interpretation." [21]

Thus in interpersonal communication the best to be hoped for, perhaps, is an approximation to the kind of coherence of meaning and unity of purpose that may be achieved in the case of self-interpretation. As Royce puts it:

> Our interpretation of our neighbour satisfies our demands, precisely in so far as our interpretations, which are never complete, and which always call for new expressions and further interpretations, lead to a conversation which remains, on the whole, essentially "coherent," despite its endless novelties and unexpected accidents.[22]

This being the case, we may conclude that one important goal of interpersonal communication—one man's understanding of another in the broadest sense—is at best only partially achieved at any one time. And even then it is defeasible.

5. Interpretation in the Determination of Publicly Accessible Objects of Experience

The third major area of human concern which Royce sees as requiring cognitive processes of interpretation is the effort to obtain communicable knowledge of our physical environment. Long before he explicitly formulated his theory of interpretation, Royce had argued the thesis that our consciousness of the external world is deeply influenced by cer-

[21] Ibid.   [22] Ibid.

tain social motives. In Chapter Three we examined Royce's attempt to offer a psychological account of the origin of our general ideas through an analysis of the imitative processes. By the late 1890's Royce had taken the bolder step of trying to explain psychologically the origin of the very categories of thought that help determine our general ideas. He declared his intention of explaining "human reason as a social product, and its whole equipment of fundamental truths, as an expression of deep, but still human social needs." Among these fundamental truths or ideas Royce finds four paramount:

(1) That we "live in a natural world which has an independent existence of its own, apart from our purposes";

(2) "That this independent world antedates our own existence, and will survive any of us";

(3) "That the facts of this world are subject to necessary laws of causation, so that given certain antecedents, certain results must follow";

(4) "That the things of the world have some definite constitution, in so much that the changes which occur in the world are due to the changing relations amongst permanent things." [23]

These ideas, Royce believes, are almost universally held to be necessary and true. Yet they cannot be confirmed by observation. Nor can their truth be ascertained merely by an analysis of their meaning. How, then, do we come by them? Royce examines and rejects two traditional views, the first claiming that they are innate, the second that they are the result of individual experience. Against the first Royce argues that we have inherited organic tendencies and capacities, but no innate ideas; "the mind apart from training shows no signs of innate ideas." [24] Against the second view

[23] "The Social Factors of the Human Intellect" (circa 1897), folio 68, lecture 4, pp. 12–13.
[24] *Ibid.*, p. 9.

Royce simply maintains that such ideas are beyond the range of individual experience. Royce also rejects a contemporary theory, that of Herbert Spencer, which seeks to compromise between these older theories. Spencer would have it that these ideas are somehow residual from the experiences of the human race as a whole, and are built into the inherited organization of the individual's nervous system. For the race, then, these ideas are due to experience. For the individual, they are due to hereditary assurances. Royce fails to discover any evidence for such a supposed inheritance. He points instead to the mass of evidence on the other side, indicating that the child must first be taught the language and habits of civilization.

Royce's own view is that two factors, both social, determine the universality and the conviction of certainty with which these ideas are held. The first is that the social conditions of rationality itself necessitate these ideas or categories. The second is that they are due to the very conditions under which our social consciousness is formed and transmitted.[25] What Royce means by these factors will become clear in the sequel.

He finds, moreover, that two characteristics are shared by all four of the fundamental categories he has listed: (1) they all "imply that the facts of the world are in some way independent of human caprice, human wishes"; (2) they all "require us to view the world as . . . conforming to exact law, embodying precise rules." The need for exactness is, according to Royce, one of the basic motives of social organization. Any cooperative social enterprise requires of its participants a measure of exactness and precision in behavior. Such behavior is necessarily rule-bound. These rules impose limitations upon individual caprice. Through repeated conformity to these rules, the conception of an "ob-

[25] *Ibid.*, p. 11.

jective" natural and moral world, independent of anyone's personal whim, gradually takes root.

Royce gives as examples the origin of time-keeping and of precision in commercial relations. The passage on time-keeping is worth quoting at length.

In order to determine time, man was led to take account of whatever natural fact, the object of common observation and report, would serve to determine time agreements. To fix in this way upon the facts of the calendar, early implied for men the belief in some sort of natural law. The law of the time-keepers was probably the first observed law of nature which had a really exact character, a really mathematical definiteness. Yet the observation of such laws depended entirely upon obvious social motives. Time agreements had to be obtained for social purposes; since man had to require man to be more or less punctual, in order that common actions should be entered upon. Yet time-keeping was the beginning and the source of astronomical science and of its vast conceptions of a world order.[26]

In much the same way the social requirement of weighing and measuring in commercial transactions was a decisive force in the development of the physical sciences, with their orientation toward natural phenomena admitting of precise measurement.

Finally, Royce urges, these social motives to precision and calculation led to the very conception of reality which our culture has come to accept. In a lengthy passage that strikingly illustrates to what extent later nineteenth-century social psychology has come to dominate his thinking, Royce argues that there is a reciprocal interaction between social behavior and our social conception of the nature of reality.

For the process upon which man enters here works as it were both ways. It first affects his view of his own life, by defining for him contracts which he otherwise could not make at all. For unless he could weigh and measure in this exact way, he could

[26] *Ibid.*, pp. 18–19.

not make such elaborate contracts, he could not develop such abstract ideas, he could not enter upon such elaborate social business. On the other hand, man comes to conceive that the natural objects which enable him thus to define his contracts, have a peculiar reality, a peculiar independence of his caprices, a peculiar definiteness of nature which now exalts them, in grade of mere physical reality, above other natural objects. The things that you can measure and weigh come to be conceived as peculiarly exemplary parts of the real world, so that one gradually gets the idea that natural objects are real, are independent of us, and are existent apart from our wishes, just in proportion as they are exact, definable, measurable. In terms of this standard man henceforth conceives reality, so that in the end, after a long process of this discipline, he at last today believes it *a priori* necessary that real natural objects, in so far as they are real, should be subject to quantitatively exact laws. The vague regions of our experience, where you cannot weigh and measure, where exact definition, and the rigidity originally demanded of commercial contracts, cannot be realized, come thus to be regarded as parts of nature which we do not well understand . . . or as relatively unreal and intangible phenomena, the product of illusions.[27]

In a generally neglected essay entitled "The External World and the Social Consciousness," Royce presented the conclusions to which his psychological investigations had led him. He contrasted our private, more or less chaotic experience of things with the public, more or less well-ordered realm of objects about which we communicate in our daily activities and in science.

By an external thing we mean an object of experience which is, or may be, a common object for as many observers as you please. An object, however, can be known to be common only in so far as our personal experiences of this object prove, upon appeal to our fellows, to be verifiable in a measure sufficient to satisfy the demands of our socially critical self-scrutiny upon the level that this fashion of self-scrutiny happens in any case to have attained.[28]

[27] *Ibid.*, p. 22.
[28] *Philosophical Review* 3:518–519 (September 1894).

Thus, for instance,

as only the definably localizable in space can be independently
verified and agreed upon by a number of socially communicating
beings, and as only what we all agree upon can stand the social
test of externality, the principle that what is for all must, if in
space at all, occupy a definite place, and have definite size and
boundaries, becomes a relatively *a priori* principle for the things
of the verifiable external world.

All of us at one time or another have seen a rainbow. A
rainbow, then, would seem to pass the "test of social community." But we have come to realize that no two of us ever
see a rainbow in precisely the same place. This, Royce argued, leads us to conclude that a rainbow as we see it is not
a real physical thing at all, but "a show thing, based upon
physical realities, whose nature becomes a topic for further
investigation." [29]

Royce concluded from this analysis that some of the traditionally proposed criteria of externality, such as vividness,
resistance to our will, or even Mill's permanent possibilities
of sensation, are inadequate. Pains can be extremely vivid;
emotionally influenced muscular constrictions thwart us no
end; sleepiness can be a permanent possibility of sensation.
Instead, it is the test of social community or public verifiability that is the true *differentia* of what we are accustomed
to call the external world. Royce went so far as to say that
we develop our "representative" theory of knowledge, that
we come to "establish the idea of a *tertium quid,* the external
object as it is for itself," [30] only when we come to regard an
object no longer as yours or mine but as *our* object.

This perspective on our notions of the external world is
maintained, although in somewhat modified form, in Royce's
theory of interpretation twenty years later. When two mature individuals attempt to share an experience, they do not

[29] *Ibid.,* p. 520.   [30] *Ibid.,* p. 542.

so much imitate each other's responses to things as they attempt to interpret to one another, through the medium of conversation, what they see, feel, and think in regard to such objects. Continuing to insist that our belief in an external physical world is a belief in a domain whose objects can be experienced in common by many observers, Royce in *The Problem of Christianity* offers as example two men rowing in a boat. Each of the men experiences the boat, the oars, and the water on which he rows for himself. Yet each believes that both of them are experiencing the same boat, oars, and water. What is the warrant for such a belief? Royce answers that this belief necessitates a triadic, interpretative cognitive process.

Each rower verifies his own idea of the boat. Neither of them as an individual, verifies the other's idea of this boat. Each of them, as interpreter, either of himself or of the other man, believes that their two individual experiences have a common object. Neither can (merely as this individual) verify this idea. Neither could, as an individual, ever verify his belief in the interpretation, even although they two should row in the same boat together until doomsday.

If the common interpretation is true, then the two oarsmen actually form a community of interpretation, and are even now believing what would seem to be true if, and only if, this community of interpretation were actually to reach its goal.[31]

Royce regards this example as typical of everyday experience. He admits that in situations like this we may remain unaware of the principles underlying our common-sense opinions about natural facts. We are less inclined to remain thus unaware, Royce believes, when we reflect on the established processes of discovery and confirmation in science. When an individual scientist makes a discovery about the physical world, this discovery is not yet a scientific fact; "it is a scientific discovery only in case it can become, through

[31] *The Problem of Christianity*, II, 240–246.

further confirmation, the property and experience of the community of scientific observers." [32] The process whereby confirmation of an individual's discovery is achieved is, Royce contends, an instance of interpretation. The structure of interpretation in the scientific community is once again triadic, determinate, and nonsymmetrical.

The scientific community consists, at the least, of the original discoverer, of his interpreter, and of the critical worker who tests or controls the discoverer's observations by means of new experiments devised for that purpose. [33]

Interpretation plays an even more vital and striking role in the *formation* of scientific hypotheses. Royce, once again indebted to Peirce, makes the arresting claim that "every instance of conscious and explicit comparison involves an elementary form of interpretation." [34] Comparison at first glance seems only to require consciousness of familiar dyadic relations such as likeness and difference. But ask the question "What constitutes the difference between A and B?" or "*Wherein* does A resemble B?" and it becomes evident that a mediating or third term is needed to *interpret* the perceived or conceived relation. More complicated instances of this interpretative process may be exemplified by the most creative aspect of science—the formation of hypotheses. When Darwin was confronted with the problem of explaining the relation between individual variation and survival, he apparently resorted to the Malthusian principle of natural selection as the mediating "third" to interpret these two facts. Royce considers the more striking instances of forming such hypotheses as the work of genius. "The really creative insight has come from those who first compared and then mediated, who could first see two great ideas at once, and

[32] *Ibid.*, p. 231. [33] *Ibid.*, p. 249.
[34] *Ibid.*, pp. 169ff. Peirce, *Collected Papers*, 1.553.

then find the new third idea which mediated between them, and illumined." [35]

The extent of Royce's claim here, it should be noted, is that his analysis of social processes establishes at most only *one* important source of our conception of a world of natural laws. Royce is urging that men's concerted efforts to cope with their physical environment necessitate their applying to it a priori certain categories such as independent existence, causality, temporal continuity, definite spatial location, exactly determinable structure, and the possibility of "public" verification—quite apart from the more "metaphysical" question as to whether the external world embodies these characteristics in and of itself. Moreover, Royce is not even pretending to offer here a complete psychological inventory of the contents of the human mind. Such an inventory might conceivably reveal that the individual perceives or cognizes an external world of ordered relations and necessary connections independently of processes of social training and socially motivated activities. Even were this to be the case, however, Royce's "social" psychology might constitute a plausible supplement to such an "individual" psychology.

Nevertheless, Royce does attempt a broad metaphysical generalization of his and Peirce's theory of interpretation at the conclusion of his discussion.

We all of us believe that there is any real world at all, simply because we find ourselves in a situation in which, because of the fragmentary and dissatisfying conflicts, antitheses, and problems of our present ideas, an interpretation of this situation is needed, but is not now known to us. *By the "real world" we mean simply the "true interpretation" of this our problematic situation.*[36]

[35] *The Problem of Christianity*, II, 192. See Professor John Smith's expanded statement of the Darwin example in *Royce's Social Infinite*, pp. 99–100.
[36] *The Problem of Christianity*, II, 264f. Italics in text.

This definition of the "real world" leads Royce to conceive of it as a progressive "Community of Interpretation" in the broadest sense of the term. For according to him "an interpretation is real only if the appropriate community is real, and it is true only if that community reaches its goal." [37]

This conception of reality as "an essentially social universe" consisting of signs and "an infinite series of acts of interpretation," [38] represents the final formulation of Royce's metaphysical idealism. It is this "social universe," conceived as a vast Community of Interpretation, that replaces Royce's earlier "Absolute." Later we shall need to examine this doctrine further, and contrast it with Royce's earlier versions of his idealism. Here it has merely been outlined so that the presentation of Royce's ethical theory may be completed. For Royce contends that man owes his ultimate moral commitment to just such a universal "Community of Interpretation."

To summarize Royce's theory of interpretation, we might attempt a more schematic outline of its main features.

(1) All men have an ineluctable need for rationality, coherence, and continuity in their own lives and in their environment as a whole, both physical and social.

(2) We have little or no direct, intuitive knowledge of objects, whether these objects are our own "selves" as subsistent personalities, the minds of our fellow men as intelligible to us, or the things in our external environment as "public" objects.

(3) Moreover, our cognitive acts of perception and con-

---

[37] *Ibid.*, p. 269. Recall Royce's definition of reality as a "system of signs." Inasmuch as (a) what is being interpreted, (b) the interpretation itself, and (c) the community of interpretation are all signs or groups of signs, it follows that reality *is* a "Community of Interpretation" in which all three are essentially ("internally") interrelated.

[38] *Ibid.*, pp. 296–297. For hints of a strikingly similar view, cf. Peirce, *Collected Papers*, 5.448.

ception are too limited by nature to afford us the kind of coherent experience we demand. Every meaningful act of comparison already requires a cognitive process essentially different from perception and conception—a process which Royce calls interpretation.

(4) Interpretation in its simplest form involves a triadic relation consisting of an interpreter, a sign or meaning as object to be interpreted, and an interpretee.

(5) The goal of any process of interpretation is a full and coherent understanding of the problematic situation being interpreted. In some of these situations the goal is a limited one, requiring perhaps only a single act of interpretation. In others, the goal can only be conceived as an ideal limit that can at best be approximated by an endless series of interpretative processes on the part of a vast number of mutually cooperative investigators.

(6) A community of interpretation exists whenever the triadic relation just described exists, regardless of whether it takes the form of self-interpretation, interpretation of another mind, or interpretation of physical objects.

(7) The external world becomes intelligible to us only as we gradually come to transform its manifold and more or less discrete objects into a domain of signs susceptible to a process of orderly and continuous interpretation. What we mean by "the real world" may be represented in terms of a progressive, world-wide "Community of Interpretation." The goal of this Community, admittedly a remote ideal, is a complete, final, and "true" interpretation that would render the experience of mankind fully coherent.

6. Interpretation and the Moral Life

In bringing this discussion of Royce's psychological and epistemological theories to a close, a brief comment on the relevance of these doctrines to Royce's ethical theory is in order. The basic problem which Royce's ethical theory, both in its early and its mature form, was designed to solve is that of providing a plausible and defensible answer to theoretical moral skepticism. On Royce's analysis, this skepticism is in large part the result of the persistent failure of moral philosophers to resolve the antinomy between what he called "ethical realism" and "ethical idealism," or, in its alternative formulation, between moral objectivity and moral autonomy.

Our ordinary moral consciousness makes two central demands which are not easily reconciled. On the one hand, it requires that moral values have a validity, and moral obligations a binding force, for the moral agent independently of his private caprice or whim. On the other hand, it requires that the human person make his moral commitments voluntarily, that is, that his moral life be more than a matter of his reacting passively to the pressures of his social environment. Ultimately, his moral values must be of his own choosing, and his moral obligations self-imposed. Royce, therefore, felt that his success as a moral philosopher depended upon his ability to reconcile two seemingly conflicting yet equally essential axioms of any sound ethical theory—moral objectivity and moral autonomy—without sacrificing one for the sake of the other.

Now it is evident that the doctrines of imitation, reflection, and interpretation examined in the last three chapters do not as such resolve the problem of Royce's ethical theory. Nevertheless, they are relevant to his ethical theory in at least two important ways. In the first place, a doctrine of man in relation to society provides an understanding of the context in which the moral life is lived—a context no plausible ethical theory can afford to ignore. In the second place, such a doctrine provides an understanding of man's capacities and limitations as a potential moral agent.

Thus Royce's doctrine of imitation is designed to explain in part how moral concepts are first learned and how the individual's social and moral conscience is originally formed. It accounts to some extent for the existence of common moral principles and sentiments and of interpersonal moral responsiveness. At the same time, by stressing an irreducible factor of initiative and originality involved in human imitative processes, it suggests the origin of the socially dependent individual's sense of personal identity and uniqueness.

Royce's doctrine of reflection in turn provides a better understanding of how the individual comes gradually to achieve a sense of selfhood and to recognize his fellow men as "selves" in their own right. His capacity for moral autonomy is assured by his ability to formulate for himself a life plan which, although it is socially inspired, is of necessity personal and uniquely his own.

The present chapter was concerned with Royce's later theory of interpretation. One of the most significant aspects of this theory is the analysis of the very notion of objectivity which it involves. It is Royce's contention that the determining criterion of objectivity in human experience is "publicity." By this Royce means that before we allow real, external, or objective existence to be ascribed to any alleged object of anyone's experience, it must meet certain socially accepted standards of common accessibility and verifiability. The standards in question, such as locatability in space, continuity in time, determinability of structure, and susceptibility to causal investigation, when taken together, represent a conceptual scheme which, in our quest for knowledge and truth, we bring to our experience. With this conceptual scheme at our disposal, we attain access, through endless processes of interpretation, to a realm of common experience infinitely larger in scope and more coherent in structure than that available to a single isolated individual.

To be sure, certain basic human interests determine the nature of our conceptual scheme and the purposes of our interpretative activity. Thus an irreducible element of subjectivity marks the manner in which we confront our external environment. Nevertheless, these interests and the interpretative processes by which we pursue them are so universal and so well-established that they render our concerted quest for knowledge and truth as "objective" and as "impersonal" as circumstances permit.

Now Royce's account of the criteria of objectivity governing our interpretation of the external world suggests the possibility that analogous criteria of objectivity govern the realm of moral discourse. That is to say, the standards and rules governing moral argumentation and moral judgment may closely resemble, at least in form, those governing theoretical and scientific reasoning and judgment. In point of fact Royce does, with several qualifications, develop this implication in his later ethical theory, as we shall see in Part III.

Just as Royce's analysis of objectivity in interpretative processes in general affords fruitful suggestions about the nature and criteria of moral objectivity, his account of the role of interpretation in the attainment of individual selfhood sheds further light on the nature of moral autonomy. Royce has insisted that the achievement of selfhood involves the individual's determination of a personal life plan. This life plan is formulated through what has been described as a process of self-interpretation. Royce, as we shall see presently, maintained the view that the individual's responsibility as a moral agent is to be defined in terms of this process of self-interpretation. With certain qualifications, the individual may be held morally accountable by his fellow men only for those moral commitments which, as a result of this process, he has voluntarily taken upon himself.

Finally, Royce's theory of interpretation enables him to explain what his earlier, somewhat behavioristically oriented theory of learning was unable to explain: namely, how we are able to gain access to the "inner" lives of our fellow men.

The conversational aspect of interpretation described above makes possible not only interpersonal communication in general, but that special form of communication involved in our efforts to judge one another morally. Since interpersonal moral judgment is concerned principally with motives, and since personal motives are preeminently a part of an individual's "inner" life, the significance of Royce's theory of interpretation as affording access to these motives can hardly be overestimated.

It has been urged that a well-constructed ethical theory should be preceded by an investigation of human nature. Accordingly we have presented Royce's investigation in the form of a more or less schematic reconstruction of a body of psychological and epistemological data which he presented and the theoretical generalizations which he ventured in regard to them. Taken together, Royce's theories of imitation, reflection, and interpretation provide a relatively coherent and thoroughgoing account of man's life in society. The outstanding features of this account are Royce's analyses of how men learn, how they communicate with one another, how they develop a sense of personal identity, and how they come to have experiences in common. If these analyses can be said to be characterized by any one dominant theme, it would be the depth with which and the extent to which the individual human being is implicated in the life of his society. As Royce himself maintained:

Man is first a social animal, and then gradually may become a moral being. If he were not social, no such moral obligations as he now recognizes could have any meaning for him . . . In a world where telepathy was universal and adequate, there would be no lying; and in that world truth-telling would be no more a virtue than breathing is a virtue in our world. Or again, if we always necessarily forgot all our promises, there could be no duty to keep them.[39]

[39] From the introduction to a series of lectures delivered in 1907 in an undergraduate ethics course at Yale; folio 77, p. 28.

While an extensive criticism of Royce's account of the social context in which the moral life takes rise would take us beyond the scope of this essay, one final remark is in order. This account can, I believe, be fairly said to stand or fall on its own merits. Neither its three major categories—imitation, reflection, and interpretation—nor its naturalistic, empirically oriented, descriptivist tenor derive from a philosophical *parti pris*. Nor, moreover, do the social psychologists and philosophers to whom this account is variously indebted—Durkheim, Sully, Tarde, Wundt, Baldwin, Peirce, James, and a host of others—represent a unified school with shared metaphysical presuppositions. Indeed, Royce's dialectical conception of the relation between the individual and society, between Ego and Alter, has certain characteristics of the Hegelian methodology so fashionable in the nineteenth century. But again, Hegel's dialectical method as a tool of social analysis does not of itself commit its user to Hegelian metaphysics.

Thus the cogency and the plausibility of Royce's mature ethical theory is in part dependent upon the merits of a certain extra-ethical body of data and doctrines underlying it. But the latter is not, as some of Royce's commentators have supposed, the absolute idealism for which he is best known.

PART III

THE STRUCTURE OF ROYCE'S
MATURE ETHICAL THEORY

Chapter Six

THE MORAL ATTITUDE

SHORTLY after the turn of the century, Royce began to reformulate the ethical theory he had begun in *The Religious Aspect of Philosophy*. This reformulation occupied the center of his attention during the last decade of his life. Unfortunately, there is no really systematic presentation of this later ethical theory in any of Royce's writings. It is scattered throughout several published works and a number of unpublished papers and lectures. Moreover, the published works, notably *The Philosophy of Loyalty* (1908) and *The Problem of Christianity* (1913), emphasize the substantive or normative aspects of this theory, whereas the more analytical or, in contemporary parlance, metaethical aspects are dispersed for the most part in the relatively inaccessible unpublished writings. It is thus understandable but regrettable that the latter material has received such scant attention from Royce's commentators and critics.[1]

The following three chapters, therefore, attempt a more or less schematic reconstruction of Royce's later ethical theory, drawing heavily upon his unpublished writings. A careful study of these documents reveals that the later Royce developed a multidimensional approach to such key ethical problems as the nature of value, of obligation, of moral principles, and of moral reasoning. This multidimensional analysis, while couched in the terminology of another philosophical

[1] For a list of Royce's unpublished papers, including those having to do with ethics, see the bibliography in J. Harry Cotton's *Royce on the Human Self* (Cambridge, Mass., 1954), pp. 306–308. For a fuller list, see J. Loewenberg's bibliography in *Philosophical Review* 26:578–582 (September 1917).

era, strikingly anticipates certain tendencies in recent discussion, notably in the writings of Stephen Toulmin and H. D. Aiken.[2]

The next three chapters are devoted, each in turn, to one of the phases of ethical inquiry undertaken by the later Royce. For want of better terms, these phases shall be designated the "precritical," the "self-realizational," and the "communal," respectively. What is meant by these terms will become clearer in the context. Briefly, the precritical phase involves the effort to define a formally moral attitude, and to elucidate certain regulative principles of moral discourse, prior to a critical determination of the grounds of moral value and moral obligation as such. The self-realizational phase represents the attempt to define moral goodness and moral obligation by reference to the principle of self-realization, conceived as the ultimate criterion of value for the individual moral agent. The communal phase marks the attempt to exhibit the principle of self-realization in its social context, that is, it seeks to integrate a critical conception of the individual's moral well-being with that of the social order as a whole. Although Royce conceives of these phases as overlapping to some extent, he finds that distinctive forms of moral argumentation and justification are appropriate to each of them.

It is worthy of mention at the outset that Royce's later ethical theory is formulated quite as independently of his metaphysical idealism as was the earlier ethics in *The Religious Aspect of Philosophy*. The extra-ethical doctrines and investigations upon which it may be said to depend in any way have already been presented in Part II. There is one point, indeed, at which Royce's ethics and metaphysics appear to meet. As the highest normative principle of moral

[2] For Toulmin, see *An Examination of the Place of Reason in Ethics* (London, 1953). For Aiken, see especially "The Levels of Moral Discourse," *Ethics* 62:235–248 (July 1952), and "Moral Reasoning," *Ethics* 64:24–37 (October 1953).

conduct, Royce proposes devotion to a universal "Community of Interpretation." There are good grounds for believing that toward the end of his life Royce replaced the idealistic "Absolute" with the "Community" in his metaphysical system. Whether or not this interpretation is correct, the doctrine of the Community, as Royce formulates it, is in any case more compatible with the autonomy and genuine moral responsibility of the individual person than was the earlier "block universe" Absolute. These issues, somewhat peripheral to the central doctrines of Royce's mature ethical theory, are discussed briefly in the Appendix.

1. Precritical Value Predication

Moral philosophy began once again to occupy the center of Royce's attention when in 1907 he gave a series of lectures at the University of Illinois in Urbana,[3] followed shortly afterward by the publication of *The Philosophy of Loyalty*. The opening passages of the Urbana lectures indicate that Royce's conception of the nature of moral philosophy has remained essentially unchanged. Once again, as in *The Religious Aspect of Philosophy*, Royce maintains the view that there is a legitimate domain of philosophical ethics not reducible to a mere psychological description of human behavior and attitudes. Royce characterizes the reductionist view as holding that

the only proper business of any doctrine of values must be just the treatment of men's opinions about good and evil, about right and wrong . . . as coolly and disinterestedly as any science treats its own facts. The theory of values would simply describe,

---

[3] Four unpublished lectures, contained in folio 76 in the Widener Library Archives at Harvard. Some pages of the last two lectures are missing. Royce refers to these lectures in the preface to *The Philosophy of Loyalty* (New York, 1908). Since the quotations from Royce in this chapter are all from the first of the Urbana lectures, entitled "The Problem of Ethics" (folio 76), separate citations will not be given.

classify, and reduce if possible to psychological laws, these opinions.

Although Royce grants the legitimacy of such an enterprise, he insists "that there is also a place for a reasoned and philosophical account of the true values which persons ought to attach to themselves, to their conduct, and to their world." Royce believes that "the effort to reach some sort of rational insight into the true value of things," difficult as this might be, is nevertheless an ineradicable tendency of human nature; and indeed, "upon the accomplishment of this task reasonable living depends."

Nothing points up the difficulty of this task so sharply as the radical subjectivity of value predications in their most elementary form. To Royce it is obvious that

things have value from the point of view of persons. A person is a being with a will of his own. It is because of his will that, for him, values exist at all. The world of values and the world of wills are logically inseparable . . . A person in a fact-world is like a light in a room. Facts without persons are empty of significance, as the dark room is empty of visible meaning.

Were there but one person who constituted the "light of the world," and had he but one desire, problems of objectivity vs. subjectivity, reality vs. appearance in regard to value would hardly arise. But in fact there are many persons with many desires, and in our experience these desires conflict not only as between several of us but within the consciousness of any one of us as well.

This being the case, are there any criteria by which we can determine, intrapersonally as well as interpersonally, which of several conflicting desires or purposes is worthiest of being satisfied or fulfilled? More broadly stated the question concerns the relation, if any, that exists between what is in fact desired or valued and what is morally desirable or valuable. At first glance, Royce's answer to the question is equivocal. Suppose, Royce says, that I am attempting to resolve a conflict over values with another man. I may begin by pointing out to my opponent "the truth, that his values and my values stand in the first place on an equal level." For "if his valuation can furnish a reason why something is worth doing, my valuation furnishes me just as genuine a reason why something else may be worth doing." But what sort of a reason is this? Royce continues:

I am simply insisting on the truth that whoever wills anything in this world defines thereby a value, a something that is declared to be worth doing. I am drawing a conclusion, so far, that what in an impersonal sense, is objectively worth doing, depends as much and of course as little upon his private valuation as upon mine.

This somewhat obscure passage is likely to puzzle the reader. For it seems to suggest two quite different, perhaps even contradictory theses. The first sentence suggests that the mere fact that someone desires something is sufficient to confer value upon it. The second sentence suggests that the mere fact that someone desires something is not a sufficient condition for its being regarded as valuable. It might be supposed that the difficulty is due to Royce's having confused two senses of "valuing." By valuing something we may mean prizing or esteeming it; but we may also mean appraising or estimating it.[4] Thus the passage might have been clearer had Royce said that for me to regard anything as subjectively valuable, that is, valuable from my private perspective, it is sufficient that I prize or esteem it; whereas for me to regard anything as objectively valuable, that is, as valuable from any reasonable perspective, it is necessary that I appraise or estimate on other than subjective grounds.

But this interpretation has two serious defects. The first is that it raises precisely the question at issue, namely, whether

---

[4] A common enough distinction. See, for instance, John Dewey, "Theory of Valuation," *International Encyclopedia of Unified Science*, II, no. 4 (Chicago, 1952), pp. 5–6.

there are any objective standards for the appraisal of any-thing as valuable beyond the fact that it is indeed prized or valued by someone. The second is that this interpretation does not render accurately what Royce wishes to say. In order to see why, let us pursue Royce's argument further.

What actually happens when we ascribe conflicting values to anything?

There are two men, A and B. A wants something, it may be an apple or a life, a piece of property or a revolution, success, or the expression of a private hatred. B wants something which cannot be obtained unless A's purpose is defeated. Both A and B thus set different values upon the same acts or things. Now the truth is that these values equally belong to the world of values. If we want to find out what the true value of the thing or of the act is, we must take account of both of these valuations. So far as they merely exist they furnish equal reasons for viewing the act or the thing in a given way as possessed of value, it being presupposed of course that A and B do not notably differ in intensity or vigor.

Again Royce's language is somewhat obscure. His point might be restated as follows. Person A turns up in a world as yet devoid of values. He desires something, say x, which thereby acquires a property for him, namely value y, which it did not have before. Person B enters and, among other things, also attaches a value, although a different one, y_1, to x. What Royce calls a "world of values" is in the process of being created. A complete description of object x would now include the value properties that A, B, C, etc., have ascribed to it—that for instance x pleases A (y), hurts B (y_1), bores C (y_2), and so forth.

Assuming that this is a fair statement of Royce's argu-ment, it is designed to establish two things. First, anyone who wishes to take cognizance of such a "world of values" and who wishes to describe it fully, must take into account all valuations made by anyone, since on Royce's view it is persons who confer value in the first place. If this sounds like a task absurdly beyond the powers of any one individual, so be it. Royce is not arguing that one can or should take all valuations made by anyone into account. What he is saying is that since individual desires or interests ("wills") alone *initially* confer value on things, the only way to find out what things are in fact *initially* worth is to find out what these various desires and interests are. As we shall see presently, Royce, while insisting that all valuation begins from the point of view of private desires and interests, does not mean to suggest that all valuation ends there.

The second point that Royce's argument is designed to establish is that all such valuations have a *prima facie* legitimate claim to being considered on an equal basis—*because*, other things (intensity, vigor, earnestness, and so on) being equal, *there is as yet no principle for arbitrating among them.* The real point of the troublesome passage on page 137 above seems to be, therefore, that at the elementary stages of our valuational activity there simply are no grounds for claiming that anything is valuable or desirable other than the mere fact that it is valued or desired by someone.

It would seem, then, that Royce is defending a variety of what since his time has come to be known as an "interest theory of value," that is, the theory holding that value in general is to be defined as any object of interest. Royce is saying, in effect, that any human being who desires or wills anything confers, by the very fact that he does so, a value upon that thing.

Is this meant to imply that Royce is equating what is desired with what is desirable, what is valued with what is valuable? I believe that in one very limited sense Royce does mean to equate these. He expresses this limited sense when he remarks that "my will *seems to me* something *elementary and obviously worth* carrying out." [5]

But notice the qualifications that the underlined words

[5] Italics added.

suggest. (1) The quoted passage does not equate being desired with *being* desirable, but only with *seeming* desirable. Thus what seems to me desirable at the first moment that I desire it may turn out upon further reflection or experience not to be desirable after all. (2) The quoted passage does not equate being desired by me with being desirable *in general*, that is, for everybody, but only with seeming desirable for *me*. While there may be good reason to require that others take my desires into account when making value appraisals, they need hardly share my desires in order to do so.[6] (3) Most important of all, the quoted passage does not specify the sense in which we are to understand the term "worth." It does not specify that my will is in all instances *morally* worth carrying out. On the contrary, the qualifying adverbs "elementally" and "obviously" suggest that the close connection between what is desired and what is desirable is possible, even unavoidable, *only* at what we may now intelligibly call a "precritical" stage of value predication—a stage to which the term "moral" is properly applied only in an extended sense. Neither in this passage nor in any other passage in these lectures does Royce state or even suggest that "desired" and "valued" are to be equated with "*morally* desirable" and "*morally* valuable." The principal reason for this, as we shall see in what follows, is that Royce's multidimensional ethical theory commits him to a fundamental distinction between value in general and moral value.

On this interpretation, Royce has shown that at the precritical stage of value predication there is as yet no basis for distinguishing between reflective and unreflective, reasoned and arbitrary value judgments. In the absence of such distinctions, no *moral* point of view, properly speaking, is possible. Precritical valuations are nonmoral just because they

---

[6] The suggestion to the contrary in *The Religious Aspect of Philosophy*, which was criticized in Chapter Two, pp. 54–55, is nowhere repeated in Royce's later writings.

are all equally "subjective" (private). The only "objective" point of view one can adopt toward them is that of the neutral observer—to describe each of them accurately, to list them as fully as possible, and to concede that *prima facie* each has as great, or as small, a claim to validity as any other—a point of view more appropriate to the psychologist and anthropologist than to the moral philosopher.

2. The Moral Attitude

The remarks made at the end of the last section suggest that while Royce is prepared to define value in general as any object of any desire or interest, he is not prepared to define *moral* value in this manner. Royce's argument thus far might be restated as follows. It is the primary function of a theory to interpret and explain a certain group of data. A general theory of value has for its primary data the entire realm of human desires, specifically with regard to the values that men attach to the objects of their desires. Roughly speaking, value in general may be defined as any object of anyone's concern. But not every human concern is necessarily a moral concern. Nor is the object of every human desire necessarily and permanently found to be desirable, even by the one who initially desires it. It seems plausible, therefore, to suppose that moral value must somehow be distinguished from value in general.

Thus we might say that Royce is attempting to delimit the area of moral value as a subclass of value in general, while at the same time seeking to preserve a distinctive meaning for the term "moral" in order that it shall qualify "value" in a significant way. Moral value *qua value* bears a necessary relation to human desire or interest, while the reference of moral value *qua moral* is limited to objects of a particular kind of interest whose characteristics remain to be determined.

The particular kind of interest in question may best be understood by examining Royce's conception of the kind of value dispute that occurs at the elementary or precritical stage of value predication. It should be borne in mind that at this stage there are as yet no commonly accepted ethical principles to which one could make appeal in order to justify one's own value predications or to influence another to modify his. The characteristic use of terms such as "good" and "right" at this stage, Royce finds, is to express or describe first-personal attitudes. "When I hold that a given course of conduct is the right one . . . I inevitably express, in the first place, my own point of view. I inevitably state my personal appreciation of some situation in which conflict is involved." At this stage when I say that Jones has good intentions or that it is wrong for Smith to lie, the only apparent warrant I have for these assertions is that I happen to approve of Jones' intensions or to dislike lying. When I find my opponent disagreeing with me, the initial efforts I make to get him to adopt my attitudes are likely to be somewhat primitive: physical and psychological coercion (such as used in child-rearing) or emotional suasion. But at this point valuational utterances, regardless of whether they function expressively, descriptively, or incitively, are as yet devoid of supporting reasons.

More than one moral philosopher, especially in recent times, has maintained that this situation is characteristic of the moral life as a whole. Since there are no objective standards of value or of conduct, disagreements in moral attitude cannot be resolved by rational means. One such moral philosopher was Arthur Balfour, whose view was presented in Chapter Two. Royce mentions him again at this point, twenty years after he first attempted to answer Balfour's skepticism. How, Balfour had asked, is it possible to argue with a man whose personal moral code requires that he shoot me from behind a hedge at every opportunity? Or if it be a question of moral custom, how reason with a head-hunter? These moral commitments—if that is what they are —are ultimate and no appeal beyond them is possible.

Royce still regards the skeptical conclusion as premature. He grants the absurdity of attempting to argue with a convinced ambusher or headhunter at the moment of action. But suppose a temporary state of truce for the purposes of discussion were achieved. "Is there any reason which, from my point of view, I can still give to my enemy for my assertion that his opinion is wrong, and that my opinion is right?" There at least seem to be such reasons, for history instructs us that attitudinal stalemates are not in fact inevitable.

Reason has actually played its part in bringing about the discouragement of killing. Men's opposing systems of moral opinion have not proved wholly impervious to genuinely novel but thoughtful considerations,—considerations which were somewhat external to the systems themselves, and which therefore tended to reform these systems. There is, then, at last a chance that there are principles which my enemy has not explicitly accepted, but which I can reasonably bring him to accept . . .[7]

Rational argument is of course useless against passion. It could appeal only to a "decidedly rational being." But Royce has, after all, given abundant evidence, as we saw in Part II, for the contention that men in society are generally disposed to be rational. Rationality being presupposed, however, a principle such as the Golden Rule, presented simply in the form of a plea for consistency, may well have an effect on one's antagonist. Royce suggests the following model argument:

Can you recognize me as a man sufficiently to begin an argument with me, unless you recognize that my life has the same kind of value that your life has, namely, the value of somebody who thinks and wills and lives, in essentially the same way in which you think and will and live?

[7] The reader may notice that Royce's tone is more cautious, more probing than it was in The Religious Aspect of Philosophy.

The distinctive feature of this model argument is that it does not attempt directly to give a reason why one man's value commitments should be preferred to another's. Rather, it is asking its hearer to adopt a certain attitude toward value-attitudes in general. Otherwise put: it urges the adoption of a more or less formal, second-order interest in interests themselves. Royce's point is that this second-order interest—this determination to confront value disputes reasonably and impartially, to seek their resolution on the basis of some "higher ground," and to respect the disputants as persons who have a *prima facie* claim to recognition is formally constitutive of the *moral* attitude as such.

Royce's contention, then, is that however much disagreement there may exist between man and man over substantive moral principles and the ends or goals these substantive principles reflect, the very domain of moral activity is marked out by certain procedural principles or rules the rejection of which would be tantamount to a rejection of morality itself. The concept of moral value, as distinct from value in general, has reference in the first instance to these procedural or regulative principles. Some further discussion of them is necessary.

3. Procedural Moral Principles

At several points in this chapter the expression "precritical stage of value predication" has been used. This was designed to underscore Royce's conviction that initially we attach value to the objects of any and all of our desires, without subjecting the latter to critical appraisal and control in terms of more ultimate ends or purposes. This situation remains essentially unchanged even when, in the face of interpersonal and intrapersonal conflicts of desire, we adopt what in the previous section has been called a moral attitude. For the procedural principles constitutive of this moral attitude cannot of themselves rank values or resolve value-disputes. They do not favor one substantive end over another. They merely legislate a certain formal mode of behavior which men are to adopt when they deliberate and argue about questions of value and conduct. By doing so, however, these principles represent the first step in transforming, as a more recent writer has put it, "the chaos of warring codes into a reasonably well ordered universe." [8] In *The Religious Aspect of Philosophy* Royce explicitly defended one such regulative principle, namely, harmony. Two decades later, in the Urbana lectures, he distinguishes at least four procedural principles: reasonableness, impartiality, respect for persons, and harmony. Let us examine these briefly in turn.

a. Reasonableness

It will be recalled from our previous discussion that Royce considers the resolution of conflicts over values to be impossible unless the antagonists are first of all willing to be reasonable. Consider once again the model argument quoted above. Its immediate purpose is not to get my interlocutor to change his values or to adopt mine, but rather to bring him to a better reflective understanding of the predicament in which we find ourselves. Royce is not claiming that if my opponent accepts my argument our conflict will be resolved. To be sure, I am stating certain alleged facts about the nature of value in general, which I wish him to consider. But even if he assents to these alleged facts, he has as yet been given no reason why he should pursue my interests or redirect his own.

Royce does claim, however, that when I argue in this manner I am manifesting a certain attitude of reasonableness toward conflicting values which is commendable in it-

[8] Robert M. MacIver, "The Deep Beauty of the Golden Rule," in *Moral Principles of Action*, ed. Ruth Anshen (New York, 1952), p. 43. MacIver actually defends only one such rule, the Golden Rule. But his line of argument in favor of this principle is strikingly similar to Royce's.

self. Moreover I am urging my antagonist to adopt a similar attitude. If he does adopt this attitude, then as far as he and I are concerned a new dimension of critical reflection upon values is opened up. For the first time we commit ourselves to the attempt to offer reasons for our respective value predications, to listen to each other's reasons, and to seek nonviolent ways of reconciling our differences. We now recognize the intrinsic desirability of broadening our critical perspectives, expanding our moral vision, and placing ourselves in new relation with one another. In short, we are extending to the realm of values the same deep interest in reason and order that we manifest toward the physical world.

Considerations of this kind are what we have in mind when, during more heated moral controversies, we simply ask one another to "be more reasonable." It is possible to be reasonable without being moral. But it is not possible to be genuinely moral without being reasonable.

b. Impartiality

Impartiality is, in Royce's view, a second essential defining characteristic of the moral attitude. Royce has already been quoted extensively as saying that virtually the only reasonable, "objective" conclusion we can reach in regard to value conflicts is that any and all valuations by whomsoever made stand initially on a par. The following passage contains perhaps the clearest statement of Royce's view of impartiality in the moral life.

Things get value from the point of view of persons. [But] all personal estimates, if made with equal vigor, and if insisted upon with equal earnestness, stand upon precisely an equal rational footing. And to say this is to report a truth about the world of values,—an objective truth. This truth is there whether anyone recognizes it or not. My valuation is subjective; it depends upon my personal point of view. My opponent's valuation is subjective; it depends upon his personality and his plans. But the fact that both are valuations determines values which whether we personally recognize them or not are as real in the world of one of us, as they are in the world of the other; and the truth that these valuations of ours are facts in the same world of values . . . is objective, it exists apart from either of us, apart from both of us. A fair judge, if we could find one to whom to appeal our case, would recognize this truth, and would recognize it disinterestedly.

The close connection that Royce draws here between impartiality and objectivity should not go unnoticed. In the domain of values, to be impartial or to be objective is equally to be open to and cognizant of the desires of others. As Royce puts it, if the first rule of scientific inquiry is: "Be objective; consider the facts as they are," the first rule of an inquiry into value is: "View every valuation from the point of view of the one who makes that valuation. Put yourself in his place." [9] The possibility of objectivity in the moral domain does not presuppose the universal acceptance of certain ends of action or certain substantive principles of conduct. It merely presupposes the willingness of moral agents to appraise values and norms from points of view other than and in addition to their own. To do that, they need to evaluate impartially, but not unanimously.

c. Respect for Persons

To many moral philosophers, the principle of respect for persons is virtually a self-evident principle of moral consciousness. It is commonly expressed in the maxim, "Treat persons as ends and not merely as means to your own private advantage." Royce clearly subscribes to this maxim, although whether or not he considers this or any other moral

[9] This analogy, as Royce is well aware, should not be pressed too far. Objectivity and impartiality do not have quite the same connotations in the moral realm as they have in the realm of scientific inquiry. In both domains these terms are used to prescribe the discounting of personal preference and prejudice. But being objective and impartial in regard to other persons involves a degree of responsiveness and sensitivity to their peculiar value-orientations far in excess of that generally required *vis-à-vis* scientific objects.

principle to be self-evident is not so clear. In any case, it is evident from his discussion in the Urbana lectures that he regards respect for persons as a fundamental procedural principle of moral reflection and conduct. While Royce's remark that "my will seems to me something elementally and obviously worth carrying out" has been interpreted as having validity only at a precritical stage of value predication, requiring careful qualification subsequently from the point of view of a critical appraisal of desires and interests, the remark is even then defensible only if a principle like respect for persons is presupposed.

In his later view Royce seems to hold that this principle is on a par with the other procedural principles such as reasonableness and impartiality, that it is closely related to them, and that it has the same origin as they do: in men's critical reflection upon the situation confronting them in regard to elementary value predications. Initially, each man's sole "warrant" for the valuations he makes is that he has made them. When conflicts arise, each initially confronts the other as an autonomous, self-legislating agent whose own desires and interests are sovereign. Their very willingness to argue with one another and to seek a reasonable solution to their conflict presupposes that they recognize one another as persons each in his own right, each with a legitimate *prima facie* claim to having his interests respected and fulfilled. The paradox, and perhaps the tragedy, of the moral life is that this mutual recognition is at once acknowledged and withheld whenever interpersonal conflict over values manifests itself in its more violent forms.

d. Harmony

The last principle that Royce singles out for discussion as being constitutive of the moral attitude in general is harmony. We recall that in *The Religious Aspect of Philosophy* Royce defended the acceptance of the principle of harmony as offering virtually our only hope of overcoming "the chaos of warring values." Royce so dignified the principle of harmony because of the peculiar relation in which it stands toward those warring values. Harmony, Royce maintained, is not simply one more contending value. It is not, strictly speaking, a contending value at all. Rather, it is a formal ideal or a procedural principle prescribing the maximum reconciliation of all conflicting values at a minimum cost in terms of compromise or redirection for each of them.

In his discussion of the principle of harmony in the Urbana lectures, Royce once again draws an analogy between the rules governing scientific inquiry and those governing inquiry into values. A second elementary principle of scientific inquiry is: "Look for the laws that bind the facts together." The corresponding ethical principle of procedure is: "See whether some lawful plan of action can be discerned whereby the conflicting valuations with which men begin can be harmonized." Clearly, on this view, harmony is an ideal of action only in a purely formal sense. As a procedural principle, harmony does not favor this or that substantive value. Nor, for that matter, does it specify the manner in which contending values are to be scaled or reconciled.

It is noteworthy that Royce is no longer as adverse as he was in *The Religious Aspect of Philosophy* to offering factual considerations in support of ethical principles. Our elementary predicament in regard to values is such that, other things being equal, the harmonization of conflicting interests necessarily results in more value being realized than is the case when conflict persists. In Royce's own words:

If matters can be so arranged that A's will and B's will can cooperate with each other and help each other, instead of hindering each other, then the new and transformed situation possesses more objective value than the old situation. That is, a state of things in which A's will cooperates with B's will is better, other things being equal, than the situation in which A's will conflicts with B's will. And this again is an objective truth about the world of values . . .

For the conflict, if it occurs, can end at best in the success of only one of us. The peace, and the consequent cooperation of both of us, would by hypothesis accomplish what we are both seeking. And this would be an objectively valuable result, and would possess at least the value which both of us give to our own distinct purposes.[10]

Several remarks about this passage are in order. (1) Royce's claim for the objectively greater value inherent in a harmonized situation must be understood in its proper context. At this point we are still in the precritical phase of value predication. Only in the first instance does each object of interest have the same putative claim to being as worthy of attainment as any other. Subsequent investigation may reveal that certain objects of interest are morally worthy of being attained while others are not, or at least are less so. The very attempt to harmonize all value claims will no doubt reveal certain objects of interest as intrinsically unworthy of being attained—but on the basis, now, not of the principle of harmony itself, but of other, substantive principles. (2) That much having been said, I think that we may understand Royce's notion of "more value" quite simply in a quasi-quantitative sense. In the precritical phase of value predication, before other standards of value appraisal have been developed, each interest may be said to count as one and no more than one. The "quantum" of putative value-to-be-achieved in the world at any one time is simply the sum total of all interest claims. Thus, it follows logically that the greater number of interests harmoniously satisfied, the greater amount of value actually achieved. (3) Nevertheless, Royce does not go on to argue that the "more inclusive"

[10] Once again the reader's indulgence is asked for Royce's quaint language. I do not believe that there are any mysterious metaphysical implications lurking in the phrase "cooperation of wills" that do not lurk in the phrase "harmonization of interests."

interest is *ipso facto morally* preferable to the "less inclusive" interest.[11] There are, to repeat, no moral standards as yet for appraising interests as such. Every interest carries with it a putative value claim. But the claim that its satisfaction is morally valuable must still be justified. Hence, only those interests that are inclusive of or conducive to the harmonization of morally worthy interests would be morally preferable to those that are not.

The principle of harmony, then, occupies a status similar to those of reasonableness, impartiality, and respect for persons. All four are procedural or regulative principles constitutive of the moral attitude formally conceived as a demand for order in the moral life. We turn next to the question of their justification.

4. *The Problem of Justification*

Procedural principles such as the ones just discussed serve to govern in a formal manner the very processes of moral discourse themselves. Strictly speaking, therefore, no *moral* justification of these principles is possible. Within the context of moral argumentation, we legitimately may, and frequently do, appeal explicitly or implicitly to these principles when our antagonists refuse to state and defend their value judgments reasonably, when they manifest unwillingness to consider valuational points of view other than their own, when they withhold recognition of their interlocutors as human beings having *prima facie* the same dignity and intrinsic worth as voluntary agents which they claim for themselves, and when they stubbornly refuse even to seek ways to reconcile value disputes. But should our antagonists question these principles themselves, there are no other, "higher" procedural moral principles which we could cite as reasons

[11] Cf. Ralph Barton Perry, *General Theory of Value* (Cambridge, Mass., 1926), *passim*.

for adhering to them. Nor, of course, could we appeal to substantive moral principles, such as the Utilitarian principle of the greatest happiness for the greatest number. Principles prescribing methodological procedures to be used in the formation and defense of any and all value judgments cannot be justified in turn by principles prescribing or enumerating particular ends of action. Procedural principles have logical priority both within the structure of an ethical theory and within the structure of moral discourse, even though in the latter they may not be genetically prior.

This does not, however, preclude the possibility of reinforcing adherence to procedural ethical principles by appeal to nonmoral considerations. It is obvious to anyone with a modicum of enlightened self-interest that his systematic refusal to treat others as persons in their own right will sooner or later redound to his own disadvantage. Royce makes a similar prudential appeal to self-interest when he observes that failure to harmonize conflict over values "can end at best in the success of only one of us." At worst, but not uncommonly, such failure ends in mutual frustration.

A question related to the problem of justification, but having more strictly to do with psychological motivation, may arise in this context. Does not the acceptance of at least some of the procedural principles under discussion presuppose the existence in men of certain affective dispositions? Reasonableness and impartiality, to be sure, are more likely to be interfered with than strengthened by the presence of passions. But do not the willingness to respect others and to seek harmony presuppose some measure of benevolence or sympathy? Royce's reply, while not fully developed, is nevertheless illuminating. An affection such as sympathy may be a psychologically necessary condition prior to insight; and without insight, the value predications of others may never be brought home to us. But that would not make the value predications of others any less real objectively speaking, or any less deserving of our attention and consideration.

Royce's point is that men are not made of whole cloth. Our intellectual recognition of certain procedural ethical principles may be accompanied by an affective inability or disinclination to adopt them in our daily lives or to apply them in earnest. The point may be made more broadly by saying that universality of acceptance is not a necessary condition for objectivity in the domain of morals. Objectivity is possible in moral discourse whenever there are rules, recognized by parties to normative disputes, by reference to which they are able to appraise and to correct moral judgments.

Nevertheless, it is incumbent upon Royce to show that all or most men are in fact capable of adopting the moral attitude in the manner defined. Otherwise the possibility of a genuine moral order is jeopardized. While this problem is somewhat peripheral to ethical theory narrowly conceived, it is clear that Royce's solution to it may be found in his analysis of human personality structure as presented in Part II. Men are disposed toward reasonableness and impartiality, toward respect for persons and harmonization of conflict on the interpersonal moral plane because these dispositions have already become second nature to them through their reflective attempts to achieve a sense of selfhood. Each individual's effort to establish a coherent and continuing personal identity already requires that he adopt toward his own warring and ephemeral desires essentially the same second-order attitudes that he is subsequently asked to manifest toward the conflicting interests of other men.

The tendency to carry over into the sphere of interpersonal relations the same attitudes we adopt toward ourselves is reinforced by the nature of our imitative impulses. The pervasiveness of these impulses reveals that our own mature interests are initially formed and subsequently modified largely through our attraction to the interests of persons around us. Thus the enlargement of our concern for the interests of others which is implied in the moral attitude is a natural outgrowth of elementary and universal impulses.

Finally, perhaps the most important natural stimulus toward the cultivation of the moral interest is found in the interpretative processes. Interpretation is the cognitive process *par excellence* of man as a reasonable and social animal. It is through interpretation that the individual integrates his own interests into a life plan. It is through interpretation that he learns to understand the interests and concerns of his fellow men. It is through interpretation that he and his fellows define a world of objects experienced in common and together formulate ends of social action. Each of these forms of interpretative activity fosters by its very nature attitudes of rationality, disinterestedness, conciliatoriness, and mutual respect among the interpreters.

5. Appraisal

Before commenting on the doctrines just presented, a brief summary might be in order. The structure of Royce's mature ethical theory is characterized by a multidimensional analysis of judgments of value and conduct, the establishment of moral principles, and the forms taken by moral argumentation and deliberation. The first part of this analysis deals with what has been termed a precritical phase of value predication. In this phase putative values are brought into being by more or less indiscriminate first-personal ascriptions of value to any object of any interest. In the absence of standards of normative appraisal, the realm of values thus formed is fundamentally unstable and chaotic, since the uncontrolled proliferation of objects of interests results in apparently unresolvable conflicts.

In the face of this situation, reflective men are naturally disposed to adopt a second-order interest in the harmonious satisfaction of first-order interests themselves. This second-order interest, heralding men's first effort to adopt a moral attitude, is marked by the adoption of certain procedural principles pertaining to moral appraisal and argument in general. Royce distinguishes four such principles: reasonableness, impartiality, respect for persons, and harmony. The recognition of these principles as objectively valid and binding on all men constitutes their initial effort to bring order into the moral domain.

The procedural principles, inasmuch as they are regulative of moral discourse as such, cannot be given independent moral justification. Nevertheless, they strongly commend themselves to enlightened self-interest, and their acceptance is psychologically motivated by forces working deep in man's nature as a social being.

Considered as an elucidation of the "inner logic" of the development of the moral consciousness, rather than as a genetic account of its origin,[12] Royce's first phase of ethical inquiry seems to me both sound and attractive. In support of this opinion, I should like to make a brief comment on each of the four major topics discussed in this chapter.

My first comment has to do with Royce's analysis of our initial conception of value. According to Royce, men ascribe value in the first instance to any object of any interest they happen to have. Tentatively, Royce thereupon offers an "interest theory" of value. But the indiscriminate ascription of value to any object of any interest results, as Royce shows, in personal and interpersonal frustration and conflict. Correspondingly, although Royce does not make this explicit, an interest theory of value results in paradox. As a recent critic of the interest theory has put it, the paradox is that of

ascribing value to something intrinsically in virtue of a relation between it and something else. If intrinsic value is attributed to

[12] There is every reason to suppose that Royce intended his theory to be about the former and not the latter.

objects of satisfaction or interest, then according to the usual view of the matter, it is the object itself which is thought of as possessing the value, even though, as Perry puts it, it is interest which "confers" the value upon the object. But it is both offensive and confusing to say that objects are intrinsically valuable, i.e., in their own right, and yet that they are so only because something else bestows value upon them.[13]

Now whether Royce himself regards the interest theory as ultimately unsatisfactory for this reason or for some other reason, I do not know. But it is clear that he does regard it as unsatisfactory. An adequate appraisal of value requires much more than an indiscriminate acceptance either of interests *per se* or of their objects *per se* as bearers of value, or, for that matter, of the relation between them as the determinant of value. To suppose otherwise would be to blur hopelessly the distinction, upon which Royce is throughout so insistent, between desired and desirable, between what is valued and what is valuable. As Royce goes on to argue, the formation of a *moral* interest or attitude is tantamount to the recognition that the desirability of any interest, as well as of any object of interest, is subject to appropriate processes of criticism and evaluation. Thus, Royce, while he is appreciative of the initial attractiveness of an interest theory of value, carefully restricts its plausibility and range of application to a precritical phase of value predication.

My second comment is in regard to Royce's account of the moral attitude. There is, it seems to me, a profound wisdom in Royce's explication of the *moral* attitude or interest in procedural rather than in substantive terms. By so doing, Royce remains faithful to his insight, first expressed in *The Religious Aspect of Philosophy*, into the nature of human value commitments. Men manifest their autonomy, their re-

[13] H. D. Aiken, "Evaluation and Obligation" (1950), in *Readings in Ethical Theory*, ed. W. Sellars and J. Hospers (New York, 1952), pp. 523–524. Professor Aiken in this article defends a "satisfaction" theory of value.

sponsibility, and their integrity as individual persons most decisively in their projection of ends of action or, as Royce liked to call them, life plans. If a man's value commitments are not in some sense ultimate and unique, *his* values and not another's, we tend to regard him as immature, as incomplete, as not yet "come into his own."

For the moral philosopher, the consequence of this realization is (or should be) the recognition that in the end the highest moral authority for the vindication and rejection of values must lie with the individual person himself. The moral philosopher, if he is wise, will forego the futile attempt to formulate ethical principles that pretend to prescribe values for all men or to decide between their conflicting valuations. He will, if he is true to his calling, disdain the arrogant dogmatism of building into his conception of what it is to be moral the substantive values or ends of action to which he (or his group) happens to be committed.[14]

It is to Royce's credit, then, that he keeps his conception of the moral attitude free of substantive moral content. The moral attitude, for Royce, is a manner of reflecting critically upon one's own value commitments and of responding reasonably to the value commitments of others. It represents a determination not so much to reconcile conflicting values as such—in the final analysis this is impossible—but rather to "humanize" and "rationalize" the forms in which such conflicts occur. The procedural principles representative of the moral attitude are neutral with respect to conflicting ends of action. Their primary function is to control the manner in which men seek to impose their own ends and values upon one another. Only on such a view of the moral attitude, I submit, does it make sense to say that morality is a well-nigh universal human concern.

My third comment is somewhat more critical in tenor. It

[14] Once again see MacIver in *Moral Principles of Action*, for a discerning statement of this view.

bears upon the four procedural principles which Royce has distinguished. While I believe that he has made a sound beginning in singling out for discussion what are among the more important and most universally recognized of these principles, his analysis of them is far from complete. Thus it might be objected that justice and the avoidance of unnecessary human suffering have the same status as the principles Royce advances, and deserve to be included among them. Perhaps Royce thought that impartiality involves an implicit commitment to the principle of justice, and that the willingness to seek harmonization of conflict implies acceptance of the principle of least suffering. But he does not make this clear. His list of principles, then, is in any case incomplete, although it may be said in his defense that a complete list valid for all men in all societies is difficult if not impossible to give.

More serious, perhaps, is the question whether conflict among procedural principles themselves is possible and, if so, what could be done about it. Royce does not consider this problem at all. Yet it is not difficult to imagine situations in which these principles might counsel contradictory modes of behavior. If respect for persons is thought to extend to fulfilling the last wishes of the deceased, their survivors may find themselves performing obligations that are anything but reasonable in the eyes of the living. If impartiality is thought to entail a rigid enforcement of justice whereas harmony is thought to embrace benevolence and the minimization of suffering, a creditor or juror may well wonder at what point the quality of mercy must be restrained. It would seem, in any case, that there is more than one procedural principle and that they are not reducible to one another. If so, moral tragedies and unresolvable moral dilemmas must be recognized as genuine possibilities in human experience. Royce, who in another context recognizes this as vividly as did Hegel in his reading of Sophocles' *Antigone*,[15] might at least have indicated his awareness of the problem in the present context as well.

Finally, it should be observed that Royce's lifelong dissatisfaction with the skeptical position represented by Arthur Balfour can now be set in a clearer light. Royce's position, briefly stated, is this. On the one hand, an individual's value predications may be said to be ultimate only in the sense that his uniqueness as an autonomous and responsible moral agent requires that in the last instance he and he alone be the final judge of what is truly valuable for him. On the other hand, the existence of procedural principles governing personal moral deliberation and interpersonal moral relations ensures that no value predication need be ultimate in the sense of being arbitrary, "purely subjective," or impervious to standards of critical reappraisal and re-evaluation. To ask for a justification on moral grounds of these standards themselves is to ask for an impossibility. Nevertheless, the refusal to accept these standards is equivalent to a refusal to be moral at all. If Balfour's skepticism amounts to saying that not all men are moral and that to those who are not it cannot be proved that they ought to be, Royce would heartily agree. But if Balfour's skepticism is intended to show that the domain of morals is intrinsically and necessarily beset with chaos and arbitrariness, Royce has taken the first step in formulating a plausible ethical theory to the contrary.

---

[15] For Royce, see his discussion of General Lee's conflict of loyalties during the Civil War (*The Philosophy of Loyalty*, pp. 183ff). For Hegel, see *The Phenomenology of Mind*, 2 ed. rev. (London, 1949), pp. 491ff.

Chapter Seven

SELF-REALIZATION

IN the previous chapter we examined the first phase of Royce's later attempt to reconstruct his ethical theory. The chaotic and uncritical nature of value ascriptions men are initially disposed to make led Royce to set aside for the moment the task of discovering and defending substantive principles of moral value and moral obligation in favor of eliciting first of all certain formal, procedural rules recognized by the moral consciousness as governing the domain of moral inquiry and activity in general. These rules—Royce distinguished four of them: reasonableness, disinterestedness, respect for persons, and willingness to seek the harmonization of value conflicts—together constitute what we termed the moral attitude. Royce regarded the adoption of this attitude as logically the first step taken in the effort to bring order and coherence into the realm of values and conduct.

But the procedural principles constitutive of the moral attitude do not serve to determine what is good or what ought to be done to attain the good. Thus the all-important task of showing how, if at all, men may bring a dimension of critical reflection to bear upon substantive ethical questions remains to be accomplished.

In embarking on this task, Royce takes as his starting point the doctrine of the human self which we examined in Part II. It is Royce's conviction that critical appraisal of values and conduct takes rise within the context of the individual's efforts to order his own desires and interests toward their greatest possible harmonious satisfaction. This conviction leads Royce to adopt a form of what is traditionally known as self-realization theory in ethics.

The present chapter is divided into two sections. The first is concerned with Royce's concept of value and its relation to the concept of self-realization. The second section is an attempt to reconstruct Royce's theory of the nature and ground of moral obligation in the light of his principle of self-realization. In so far as Royce's theory of obligation is not fully formulated in his ethical writings, I shall take the liberty of piecing it together in what I take to be its most plausible form. In so doing, I shall draw heavily on Royce's explicitly stated views concerning moral deliberation and interpersonal moral judgment.

It should be remarked at the outset that with the development of his self-realizational theories of value and obligation, Royce's mature ethical theory is by no means complete. A third phase of ethical inquiry is opened up by Royce's final and possibly most significant contribution to substantive ethical theory: the doctrine of loyalty to an unlimited "Community of Interpretation" as constituting the ultimate commitment men can make in their effort most fully to realize their moral capacities as human beings. This doctrine will be examined in the following chapter.

1. Self-Realization and Value

At the end of his discussion of the moral attitude in the Urbana lectures, Royce acknowledges that he has so far barely begun the task of giving a "reasoned and philosophical account" of moral values and moral conduct. The "very abstract" and thereby "impractical" procedural principles he has so far formulated are by themselves incapable of determining, ranking, or harmonizing values. Yet it is a familiar fact of our moral experience that we do somehow determine, rank, and, on occasion, harmonize conflicting values both intrapersonally and interpersonally by appeal to some substantive standards or norms. A critical elucidation of the nature and ground of this appeal is Royce's present concern.

a. The Locus of Value

One of the most difficult problems confronting any critical theory of value is that of determining the *locus* of value. Most moral philosophers, Royce included, have agreed that a world devoid of sentient beings could not possibly possess any value. It is tempting to conclude that all values must inhere in states of consciousness. This is in fact the conclusion of the ethical idealist, who maintains that values are created by the desires or wills of human beings. But although the existence of sentient beings is a necessary condition of the existence of value, it does not follow that their states of consciousness by themselves are the sufficient condition for the determination of value. Indeed, the "subjectivist" conception of value does violence to much of human experience. Some of our most deeply cherished values—the beauty of a sunset, the love of another person, the truth of a scientific theory, the goodness of an act of self-sacrifice—are discovered and responded to rather than invented or created. Accordingly, the ethical realist has been tempted to suppose that values inhere in the nature of things independently of anyone's consciousness of them. But such an extreme "objectivist" view finds it difficult to specify what meaning the notion of value could have in a universe in which there were no one to appreciate values.

Now we recall that Royce regarded the antinomy of ethical realism and ethical idealism as a conflict of one-sided positions. Neither view in its extreme form adequately accounts for the moral life. In regard to the question of value specifically, it is as unsatisfactory to hold that values inhere exclusively in states of consciousness as it is to maintain that they reside exclusively in states of affairs external to consciousness. Royce found this conflict of one-sided perspectives to recur in the precritical "interest" theory of value which, as we saw in the last chapter, oscillates between locating value now in the desiring consciousness, now in the object desired, and again somehow in the relation between them. A more adequate theory of value would seem to be one holding that values are properly predicated of complex situations having both states of consciousness and their objects as parts. In such situations sentient beings and the objects of their interest and striving "conspire," as it were, to create the values that the former alone are capable of recognizing. On such a view, it is strictly speaking incorrect to say either that desire creates value or that preexistent values compel desire. The relation between desire and value is not a causal one at all. Rather it is one of reciprocity or mutual implication—characteristically the relation of parts of an organic whole.

But it is one thing to determine the *locus* of value and quite another thing to specify a *criterion* of value. For the latter, Royce has recourse to the analysis of human personality structure presented in Part II.

b. A Criterion of Value

Royce's investigation of the notion of "self" led him to conclude that at first glance this concept is meaningful in only two senses.[1] The "I" in one sense, namely, as logical subject, must be posited as the necessary presupposition of all conscious reflection. But of itself this logical "I" is a bare abstraction, empty of empirical content. The "I" in a second sense, namely, as "empirical ego," turns out upon inspection to be a loosely connected mass of internal sensations, physical activities, and socially, that is, externally derived plans of action and standards of self-criticism. But the "empirical

[1] See Chapter Four, section 2.

ego" thus understood is too centrifugal in nature, its contents too varying and fragmentary, its boundaries too shifting, to afford what we commonly regard as a genuine sense of personal identity.

Royce therefore found it necessary to discover some other, internal principle of unity and organization to account for our experience of mature selfhood. He claimed to find such a principle in the mature individual's tendency to make a voluntary commitment to an overarching personal ideal or to adopt a life plan. The "self," Royce argued, may then be understood in a third sense, distinct from both the logical and the empirical ego. With the adoption of a life plan, the mature individual may speak significantly of his "more permanent," "higher," "ideal" self, his "self as a whole," in contrast with his momentary, lower, impulsive, fragmentary self.

In this third sense the self is properly regarded not as given but as an achievement, not as an inborn possession but as a task to be accomplished. It is for this reason that Royce speaks of selfhood in its most significant sense as an ethical category. The individual person's continuing identity is made possible only through his adoption of a life purpose. For it is the commitment to such a purpose that meaningfully connects an individual's momentary awareness of himself with what he was before and what he will become. To know a man is to know his commitments; to judge him is to esteem him for the extent to which he lives up to his commitments, or to criticize him for his failure to do so. A passage in *The World and the Individual* perhaps best expresses Royce's view of the distinctively moral connotation attached to the notion of selfhood:

If we ask a man to observe once for all what he now is, we call attention to various empirical accidents of his life,—to his bodily presence, to his organic sensations, to his name, to his social status, and to his memories of the past. But none of these are of any uniquely determined significance; and not thus can we show a man what he is. But when, in vexation at the moral ineffectiveness of a man, we significantly use the imperative mood and say, "Whatever you know or do not know about yourself, at all events *be somebody*,"—we lay stress upon what is, after all, the essential point. What we mean by our words is the exhortation: "Have a plan; give unity to your aims; intend something definite by your life; set before yourself one ideal." We conceive, in such cases, that the self is definable in terms of purpose, of continuity of life-plan, and of voluntary subordination of chance experience to a persistently emphasized ideal.[2]

Now it is Royce's contention that with the projection of an idealized self conceived as a life purpose, the individual comes into possession of a norm or standard by which he henceforth makes personal value appraisals. In terms of his life plan he is afforded an autonomous critical vantage point from which to appraise the multiplicity of his impulses, desires, and interests and to order them toward the perfection of his self as a whole. Henceforth, whenever he experiences a conflict between what he conceives as good for his self as a whole and what he conceives as good for some partial or momentary aspect of his self, he is conscious of an obligation to pursue the former and a feeling of guilt or remorse whenever he fails to do so. This consciousness of obligation is the form in which the individual first manifests a moral consciousness, distinct from and frequently in sharp conflict with his consciousness of various desires.

Thus, as a more recent proponent of a view similar to Royce's has put it, while the individual's moral consciousness derives all of its contents from the ends of desire, the moral consciousness is in no way reducible to the desiring consciousness.[3] Over and above his conflicting desires or interests there arises in the individual a higher-order interest

[2] *The World and the Individual*, 2 vols. (New York, 1899), II, 288f. Cf. pp. 269, 277.
[3] C. A. Campbell, *Moral Intuition and the Principle of Self-Realization*, reprinted from *Proceedings of the British Academy* 34:19, 24 (1948).

in resolving conflict and harmonizing competing desires. In the first instance this higher-order interest is self-directed, that is, it is specifically concerned with achieving and maintaining order within the individual's own self. In and through the exercise of this interest, the individual manifests his capacity, as a rational and purposive being, to detach or disassociate himself from his immediate drives and desires. The possession and intensive development of this capacity is a necessary condition of the individual's achievement of the status of moral agent.

But it is not, of course, a sufficient condition. An individual can hardly be said to be a moral agent when his reflective interests are oriented exclusively toward the perfection of his own self. It is only when these second-order interests freely turn outward, toward other persons and toward the world at large, that moral agency in the full sense of the term is achieved. This turning outward is accomplished under the influence of what Royce described as moral insight in *The Religious Aspect of Philosophy*.[4] Once the individual is able to perceive and to appreciate the reality of his fellow men as fully as his own, he is able in principle to overcome the "illusion of selfishness" characteristic of the morally blind. Responsive to the interests and needs of others as fully as he is to his own, open to the objective demands of the situations in which he finds himself, the individual then manifests to the fullest the moral attitude in its four-fold character. The will representative of his self as a whole is then a disinterested will to the good, capable of overcoming the biased distinction between value-for-him and value-for-another. In short, his quest for self-realization takes on the form of promoting the greatest possible good wherever and whenever the opportunity presents itself.

As Royce defines genuine selfhood, then, it is an ideal structure that cannot be understood in subjectivistic or ego-

---

[4] See Chapter Two, section 2.

istic terms. The value that is realized in the process of self-realization is not the intrinsic value of the self as such, but rather the value of what stands over against the self, in which the self is necessarily implicated. The conclusion that Royce draws from his analysis of the self is that nothing short of a fully embodied, objective "realm of values" will satisfy the moral demands of the mature individual's self as a whole.

Royce now maintains that self-realization, thus understood, affords in principle an adequate criterion of value. For the moral demands of the ideal self as a whole, while they are deeply personal in their origin and nature, nevertheless have as their essential reference an objective moral world-order in which the actual self is always only a part, never the whole. In the domain of value, therefore, the criterion of self-realization provides a solution to the idealist-realist antinomy: it is the standard of value of an autonomous moral agent whose ideal moral requirements are nevertheless objectively oriented.

c. Some Objections Considered

In order to shed further light on Royce's self-realizational criterion of value, it might be helpful to consider certain objections that have been brought to bear against self-realization theories in general. For these objections have sometimes been thought to invalidate at the outset any and all forms of self-realization theory. Two objections in particular have been made to this effect. The first is that self-realization theory entails psychological and ethical egoism. The second is that self-realization theory involves logically fallacious reasoning from nonmoral premises to moral conclusions. Inasmuch as these criticisms appear to have contributed to the relative decline of self-realization theory in the Anglo-Saxon philosophical community after the turn of the century, it is important that they be answered if Royce's doctrine is to retain anything more than historical interest.

(1) The charge of ethical egoism has been levelled against self-realization theory largely on the basis of its conception of desire. Self-realizationists, Royce included, have commonly held that all conscious desire is desire for some conceived personal good. Critics of this doctrine, notable among them H. A. Prichard,[5] have interpreted this to mean that all desire is desire for some prospective state of the self. Were this what the self-realizationist really intended to say, he would quite obviously be committed to a theory of psychological egoism. But psychological egoism would be incompatible with, or at least would render extremely implausible, the sort of ethical altruism generally supposed to be a requirement of the moral consciousness, and advocated by the self-realizationists themselves.

In spite of certain misleading locutions in the writings of self-realizationists, I consider the egoistic interpretation of them to be a mistake. What has led the critics astray is a special psychological feature of the phenomenon of desiring to which self-realizationists wish to call attention. Human desire, as contrasted with mere animal impulse, is necessarily self-referential. That is to say, in desire I am conscious of the object as *my* object, something that *I* want. But there is no reason to suppose that the objects of my conscious desires are always, or even usually, states of myself. It is entirely possible, in fact quite common, for *your* well-being to become something that I want.

What the self-realizationist wishes to emphasize is that any voluntary, deliberate, responsible act on the part of a human agent is prompted by his self-conscious awareness of something that *he* wants—but not necessarily something he wants merely for *his own* sake, or private advantage. Properly speaking, the difference between the egoist and the altruist is not that the former aims at self-satisfaction

[5] *Moral Obligation* (New York, 1950), pp. 71ff.

whereas the latter does not. Rather, it is that the former tends to *find* self-satisfaction in one class of objects—namely, those that will further his private advantage or provide him with personal pleasure—while the latter tends to *find* self-satisfaction in a different class of objects—namely, those that will give others pleasure or contribute to their well-being. In each case there is dissatisfaction with some state of affairs, accompanied by a will to alter that state of affairs with an eye to removing the source of the dissatisfaction. But it is only when one's effort to remove one's dissatisfaction knowingly involves placing personal advantage over the welfare of others that the desire in question can be called egoistic.[6]

Since, therefore, the self-realizationist is by no means committed to psychological egoism, there is no reason why his theory need involve ethical egoism. On the contrary, as Professor Campbell has urged, there is in the self-realizationist view a presumption that, in as much as the ends of desire are not predominantly egoistic, the moral end, derived from reflection upon the ends of desire, will not be egoistic either.[7]

(2) A second and much more serious criticism, most clearly formulated by the English intuitionist G. E. Moore, is directed at the way in which the self-realizationist allegedly justifies his conception of moral goodness. Beginning with a metaphysical assertion concerning the existence of a certain "supersensible reality" which he calls the "true self," the self-realizationist, as Moore understands him, proceeds forthwith to the conclusion that the "true self" is intrinsically good. But reasoning of this sort, according to Moore, involves an attempt to argue directly from a nonmoral premise to a moral conclusion—an obvious logical fallacy.[8]

Now I do not believe that Royce's particular form of self-

[6] Cf. C. A. Campbell, pp. 17ff.   [7] *Ibid.*, p. 22.
[8] *Principia Ethica* (Cambridge, Eng., 1960), pp. 113-114.

realization theory is susceptible to this criticism. In the first place, the "higher" or "ideal" self to which Royce appeals is not a metaphysical or "supersensible" reality. It is an ideal organization of natural desires, a life plan capable of providing the natural man with abiding satisfaction. As Royce understands it, the moral agent is in principle capable of envisioning his ideal self without benefit of metaphysical speculation.

In the second place, Royce never argues from the existence or reality of this ideal self to its goodness. In fact, he expressly repudiated such arguments as being invalid in *The Religious Aspect of Philosophy*, where he attacked the Stoic's doctrine on grounds very similar to Moore's. What Royce does claim is that men form their ethical conceptions through critical reflection upon their own deepest interests and needs. Now reflection on one's own deepest interests and needs, Royce contends, involves a reference, at least implicitly, to the demands of one's "higher self." Thus a full understanding of the criteria of good and evil, right and wrong, requires an understanding of the nature of the higher self. But from this it does not follow that Royce *infers* what is good from assertions about the nature of the self. It is more accurate to say that he regards a proposition of the form: "The realization of his higher self is a moral end for the individual," not as a conclusion logically derived from assertions about the nature of the self, but as a proposition believed to be self-evident once we understand the nature of the higher self. A proposition of this sort is what Moore calls a universal synthetic proposition. It neither asserts the identity of the higher self with the morally good, nor does it involve an inference from the former to the latter. As a universal synthetic proposition, it may well be susceptible to other sorts of criticism—for instance, that it is false to our moral experience or that it involves an epistemologically suspect intuition claim—but not to the charge of logical fallacy.

2. Self-Realization and Obligation

We turn now to the question of the nature and ground of moral obligation. Unfortunately, Royce's theory of obligation is not fully formulated. Most of what he has to say about obligation may be found in his analyses of moral deliberation and interpersonal moral judgment. After examining these, therefore, I shall attempt to reconstruct the remainder of Royce's obligation theory in what I take to be its most plausible form.

a. Moral Deliberation

As might be expected, Royce conceives of the process of moral deliberation in self-realizationist terms. Recalling the account of the self discussed in Part II, Royce maintains in the Urbana lectures that moral deliberation is for the most part a matter of harmonizing impulses and desires of the moment with one's consciousness of the deeper, more permanent, and more comprehensive interests of one's self as a whole. This harmonizing process presupposes, of course, the individual's ability to "extend" the time span of his consciousness of self backward into the past and forward into the future. Without a rational consideration of my past intentions and my future aims, I would lack the basis for making intelligent decisions in regard to present conduct. Royce describes the decision-making process in a striking metaphor. Here and now I tend to choose that act

that is, so to speak, aligned between my past intention and my future goal,—just as one who sets stakes in a garden border aligns a middle stake between two already set . . . I value a present act as right or wrong, for my purposes, according as this act is or is not on the line, so to speak, which leads from my past intention towards my future goal.[9]

[9] Urbana lectures, folio 76, lecture 1, p. 53.

On this view the individual in the first instance determines the rightness or wrongness of his present actions by reference to his more lasting and comprehensive aims. In an undated notebook, Royce refers to the "aligning" process just described and adds:

> This makes right *relative* to purpose and goal. Remove goal and activity either vain or else now unfinished. Remove past purpose, and activity now impulsive, but not reasonable. Given all three and alignment is possible . . . Right is my present act by relation to purposes which imply it and of goals to which it implies an approach.[10]

And in the Urbana lectures Royce writes:

> Ethical values . . . belong to single acts in so far as we judge that these acts do or do not conform to an already accepted purpose. In order that my life should possess an ethical value for me, I must then possess purposes, or ideals, which I have accepted as mine. In the light of these ideals I must myself judge my own individual acts . . . In general, then, it is the already accepted purpose that makes an act, when viewed in the light of this purpose, right or wrong.[11]

While this is only the beginning of Royce's account of moral deliberation, several features in regard to it should be noted. In the first place, Royce, along with self-realization-ists in general, seems thus far committed to a teleological as opposed to a deontological view of moral obligation. For the self-realizationist the concept of value is basic in ethics. Judgments of obligation and right conduct are derivative in the sense that they presuppose prior critical determination of ends or goals deemed worthy of attainment.[12] In the second place, Royce's account thus far suggests two criteria, permanency and comprehensiveness, on the basis of which we are able to distinguish desires and interests deemed

---

[10] Unpublished papers, H.U.A.
[11] Urbana lectures, folio 76, lecture 2, p. 1.
[12] I shall consider certain objections to this teleological conception of obligation in the sequel.

worthy of pursuit from those which are not. (1) Those desires and interests whose satisfaction is found to be conducive to the more lasting well-being of the self as a whole are to be pursued in preference to those gratifying mere impulses of the moment. (2) Those desires and interests are to be pursued whose satisfaction is found to contribute to rather than hinder the satisfaction of other desires and interests deemed essential to the well-being of the self as a whole.[13] In the third place, the somewhat subjectivistic tenor of Royce's account so far should not overly disconcert the reader. Royce is maintaining only that the *first step* in the process of moral deliberation is the appraisal of single actions in the light of personal purposes and goals. Since in Royce's view the adoption of these purposes (and ultimately the individual's life plan) is as much a matter of voluntary decision as are the single acts performed in order to fulfill them, they are in turn subject to appropriate standards of moral appraisal and criticism.

But before we consider this more advanced stage of moral criticism, it is necessary to examine Royce's account of how the moral agent comes by his purposes in the first place.

To Royce it is a psychological fact that the mature individual desires above all a cohesive life plan, an all-encompassing purpose for his existence. For, without such a plan, there is, on Royce's view, no definable self. And the quest for selfhood, that is, the desire for self-possession or self-realization, is a fundamental concern of every rational human being. But an analysis of how we acquire our life plans, Royce finds, reveals something of a paradox.

While no purpose can be morally authoritative over against my own acts unless this purpose appears to me to be my own . . . that which I choose, we are nevertheless unable to define this purpose by merely looking within at our own instinctive preju-

---

[13] Other criteria are forthcoming as Royce gradually develops the third or "communal" dimension of his later ethical theory. Cf. Chapter Eight.

dices and desires. I am acting rightly if I live according to my purpose. But what is my purpose? My own natural desire, my own inherited nature, my own untrained self-will, these are all silent with regard to this question. Or rather, one may say, these all speak too volubably [sic] with an incoherent babble of voices . . . I have no innate unity of life plan . . . If I ask whither I am bound I find in my own natural disposition no means of deciding. Hence I must indeed look without me for guidance as to what I mean. My true self lies beyond the boundary of my present natural self, and I am always on a voyage of discovery to find what the true self is.[14]

Herewith Royce recognizes as one of the deepest paradoxes of the moral life that individual moral autonomy cannot be achieved without extensive submission to social influences. Again Royce draws on his psychology to account for the acquisition of purposes and ideals.

The compulsion to learn from without what the very ideal is that I shall afterwards from within voluntarily select as my own [is] no merely physical compulsion. I myself, in so far as I have yet to learn my ideals, am dissatisfied with my inner situation . . . It is I, then, who as a social being, continually require myself to look for guidance to my social world. My comrades, my teachers, my rivals, yes, even my enemies, teach me what it is that I want. Through imitation I at length learn self-mastery. Through my social docility I come to attain my independence. My very freedom, in so far as I ever attain such freedom, will be due to the fact that I am able to learn through social contact with others, what it is that I myself want to be.[15]

Royce concludes that the tension thus described between individual freedom and social conformity is crucial to an understanding of the moral life.

One need not wonder, then, at the union of independence and social plasticity which marks the life of every moral agent. The two truths, (1) that nothing is right for me unless I will the end which makes this act right, while, on the other hand, (2) I never discover my own purposes without constantly consulting my so-

[14] Urbana lectures, folio 76, lecture 2, pp. 8-9.   [15] Ibid., pp. 9-10.

cial order,—these truths are not inconsistent. Their union, their interplay, determines the whole nature of ethical truth.[16]

The individual must choose his ideals for himself. But "the act of choosing is a fine art. We learn it very slowly." On the one hand, the ability to make effective moral decisions requires elaborate social training. On the other hand, however, individual purposes cannot simply be copied from others. The complex differences between individual psychological makeups prevents out-and-out imitation of one another. "For every individual has a task that is in some respects unique, has instincts that nobody else possesses in just the same way, has a social training that nobody else repeats, and consequently comes to himself only by making decisions that nobody else can ever make."

From this last consideration Royce draws the inference that a fully codified, uniform, and universal moral law is, practically speaking, impossible and the quest for it misguided.

The notion of a moral law which is in all respects absolutely and abstractly the same for all of us is a notion that is simply unjust to the very nature of our individuality. Your duty to be yourself differs in some respect from the duty of anyone else, and therefore involves some truths that are simply inaccessible to any individual besides yourself.[17]

In fact, Royce contends, the precepts even of existing moral codes are much too abstract, are too much in the nature of generalizations, to provide me with the sort of individual guidance I need in order to formulate my life plan. More often than not I shall avail myself of the model of some personality I respect, some charismatic figure I admire, for personal guidance.[18]

---

[16] *Ibid.*, p. 10.   [17] *Ibid.*, p. 12.
[18] Royce, in the nineteenth-century language so characteristic of him, describes this process as follows: "The life of a fascinating hero becomes known to me. Perhaps I cannot be like him, but in him the problems of being an individual self, of determining acts by purposes, of succeeding in the

The process of personal moral deliberation, then, involves at least three stages or "moments." The first is marked by a growing self-awareness of desires and needs. The second is characterized by the critical appraisal and integration of these desires and interests by reference to an overarching purpose or life plan. The third, as Royce has suggested, involves the criticism of these purposes themselves. Royce's conception of how such criticism of individual life plans takes place remains to be examined. Inasmuch as this level of criticism is conducted for the most part in the social arena, the problem of the validity and effectiveness of interpersonal moral judgment is at once raised.

b. Interpersonal Moral Judgment

The individual's docility to social authority and social suggestion is a persistent theme, as we have seen, in Royce's analysis of the human person. The meaning and use of general ideas are taught him by society. His self-evaluation is largely dependent upon the evaluation made of him by others. Even the formulation of his life plan is accomplished with an eye to personally fascinating social models whom he is strongly drawn to emulate. But in spite of the individual's social dependency, he becomes a moral agent only when he chooses a life plan (however much this plan might be socially influenced) for himself. "The one inalienable possession of the self . . . is the choice of the self's own purpose, the determination of its own ideal. Concerning such matters the self may be endlessly instructed, but it cannot be compelled . . ."[19] It is Royce's belief that were it not for this choice, by each individual, of his own distinctive life plan,

---

acts of personality, seem to have been accomplished . . . Thus, watching my hero, I formulate my own will." In this manner, "the precepts of the customary code, when emphasized by the example of heroes, lose their abstractness. And this is the relation between hero worship and morality." (Urbana lectures, folio 76, lecture 2, pp. 23–24).

[19] *Ibid.*, pp. 5–6.

the very notion of moral autonomy would have no meaning. Royce's determination to defend individual moral autonomy leads him to adopt an unusual and, in the eyes of some moral philosophers, questionable view of the nature of moral obligation. Once the individual has chosen his own life plan, it is this plan that serves as the basis for deciding what his moral obligations are. In other words, the ultimate criterion for determining the rightness or wrongness of individual acts is the life plan or purpose to which the individual has voluntarily committed himself. Royce carries the principle of moral self-determination or self-legislation this far in no uncertain terms:

No external authority . . . can give one any reason why an act is truly right or wrong. Only a calm and reasonable view of what it is that I myself really will,—only this can decide such a question. My duty is simply my own will brought to my clear self-consciousness. That which I can rightly view as good for me is simply the object of my own deepest desire set plainly before my insight.[20]

It would seem, then, that interpersonal moral judgments, if they are to have any authority over the individual at all, must be made with reference to his own purposes or life plan. Royce does come to this conclusion—but with one important qualification. The individual, in spite of the moral autonomy ascribed to him, may not at a given moment be aware of his real interests.[21] This gap between the individual's "deeper" interests and his conscious awareness of what these really are becomes, in Royce's analysis, the major area

[20] *The Philosophy of Loyalty* (New York, 1908), p. 25. Cf. "Yale Lectures on Ethics," given during the academic year 1907–08 (folio 77, lecture 2, pp. 29–31). Royce mentions these and the Urbana lectures as forming the background of *The Philosophy of Loyalty* (see the preface to the latter, pp. v–vii).
[21] Cf. *The Problem of Christianity*, 2 vols. (New York, 1913), I, 87. By this time Royce has come to declare categorically that "the natural man does not know his own true needs."

in which interpersonal moral judgment is both valid and, on occasion, effective.

Therefore, when we dogmatically say that what somebody else just now regards as right, is in truth wrong for him, our only rational warrant for this assertion must be the assurance that if he knew better what his own purposes are, he would himself see that the act which we criticize is in fact condemned by these purposes of his.[22]

Royce here gives two examples which indicate what is presupposed when one man takes it upon himself to judge the conduct of another. Suppose a student, accused by his teacher of laziness, claims that he means to be lazy. The teacher's only warrant for judging the boy's conduct to be wrong lies in his belief "that the student himself, as a rational human being, will inevitably discover, in the long run, that he is cheating himself by his own indolence, so that if he only knew it, since he really means to succeed, he really purposes what involves . . . labor." Royce's writing style is generally marked by sentences cluttered with qualifications and parenthetical clauses. In this instance at least the qualifications are worthy of close attention. For Royce is in effect declaring that valid interpersonal moral judgments must presuppose that the person judged is (1) rational; (2) equipped with a self-consciousness that enables him ideally to "span" a lifetime of activities and appraise its meaning; and (3) in possession at least latently of an overarching purpose which defines the meaning of his life.

The second example, while reminiscent of a nineteenth-century dime novel plot, makes these presuppositions even clearer. A pirate, "or captain of a slave ship, might insist that his view of life justified his own acts, because they conformed to his purpose." And, indeed, he will no doubt manifest some "valuable ethical attainments" such as courage, resolution, endurance, and fidelity to his crew.

[22] Urbana lectures, folio 76, lecture 2, p. 3.

Yet if . . . I persist in asserting that in fact he is a rascal, my comment is morally justified only by my respect for his actual humanity . . . In general . . . I shall find that he does perform a good many humane and faithful acts, and that he does consider such acts right. I shall consequently judge that he has latent in him purposes which are distinctly humane purposes, and which, if they came to his knowledge, would lead him to condemn his own acts as pirate . . . In brief I conceive him as De Foe conceived his Captain Singleton, as partly a victim of circumstances, partly a rational being imperfectly come to himself. I shall anticipate his awakening. And such anticipations alone can justify my presumption in attempting to decide what his duty is.[23]

Here again Royce is presupposing, as warrant for interpersonal judgment, the sort of latently rational and moral personality in terms of which he has defined the human "self" in its most significant sense. And once again Royce is required, it seems, to posit certain latent moral dispositions as constitutive of human nature in general.[24] Thus,

to call a man a rascal has this rational warrant and only this, namely, that I believe that the man himself possesses such a nature that if he realized his true purpose, he would agree with my judgment. If I do not think this to be the case, I ought to regard him merely as insane, or as hopelessly imbecile with regard to moral considerations.[25]

In this context, to call a man a rascal is not so much to insult him as to pay him a left-handed compliment. It is in effect to recognize that his potential worth as a human being far exceeds the evidence of it that he has thus far given.

Now it seems to me that Royce is properly calling attention to a significant aspect of interpersonal judgment. Occasionally we encounter a particularly recalcitrant individual who is adamant in his unwillingness to recognize an obligation claim we feel is binding upon him. In such instances we

---

[23] *Ibid.*, p. 4.
[24] Recall that Royce referred to the notion of the self in its most significant sense as an ethical category.
[25] Urbana lectures, folio 76, lecture 2, p. 5.

are nevertheless reluctant to retract our claim. We find ourselves forced back to rendering what might be called a quasipredictive moral judgment: *were* the individual in question to come to fuller self-consciousness, he *would* assent to the obligation claim made on him. Our judgment in such cases has a necessary reference to a latent moral disposition we ascribe to the person judged.

But does everyone in fact have such a latent moral disposition? Royce seems to think that everyone does. Can the universal existence of such a disposition in all men be established by empirical psychological investigation? To this question Royce's answer is not clear. He seems to think that at least some psychological evidence is available. We know of instances when men have sooner or later acknowledged obligation claims which they had refused to acknowledge before, thereby indicating, perhaps, that a latent moral disposition has become manifest. Nevertheless, it is unlikely that Royce would regard any amount of psychological evidence to the contrary as capable of disproving conclusively the existence of such a latent moral disposition in this or that individual. Royce, I believe, would remain unconvinced by a man who exhibited very little of such a disposition, or none at all, and who stubbornly disclaimed it under persistent questioning and criticism. If so, then Royce's positing of a deeper latent moral disposition in all men is of the nature of an hypothesis that can never be finally established or refuted on empirical grounds.

Thus, Royce seems committed to the view that beyond a certain point the justification of interpersonal moral judgments must rest on a hope that the person judged will eventually respond to the judgment rendered, and thereby acknowledge its validity in and by his own experience. I might add that Royce is not the only moral philosopher who has recognized, however reluctantly, that the process of justifying interpersonal moral judgments does sooner or later involve such an element of hope.

As far as the moral judge is concerned, the implication of Royce's view is that he must approximate as best he can the role of an ideal observer. His judgments must be second-personal in the sense that they have reference to the conceived moral well-being of the person judged, and not his own. He must make a disinterested appraisal of the latent moral capacities as well as of the actual life plan of the individual judged. Above all, therefore, he must respect the latter's moral autonomy and individuality as a person. When he ascribes moral responsibilities to the latter, these ascriptions must be in accord with the latter's own capacity for moral response and the uniqueness of his ideals.

c. The Nature and Ground of Obligation

It is unfortunate that Royce, apart from the views about moral deliberation and interpersonal moral judgment just discussed, does not offer a more explicit theory of the nature and ground of moral obligation in general. An attempt must be made, therefore, to piece together, from the doctrines previously examined, a general theory of obligation coherent with Royce's over-all position. Further investigation is required especially in regard to these three questions: (1) how the concept of rightness is to be understood and how it is related to the concept of goodness; (2) what is to serve as a criterion of rightness; and (3) how, if at all, obligation claims may be justified. The discussion of each of these questions in turn requires a consideration of objections that have been raised against the type of theory to which Royce seems committed.

(1) As we know, Royce regards the concept of value or goodness as the fundamental concept in ethics, and the concept of rightness or obligation as explicable in terms of the

realization of the good. Now I have interpreted Royce as holding that the meaning of goodness can be further elucidated in terms of other concepts to which it is necessarily related. Thus, goodness in its generic sense may be defined as that which satisfies desire, while goodness in its specifically moral sense has to do with what would satisfy the desires of the self as a whole. There is no question here of identifying goodness with desire. It is merely being asserted that goodness and desire are necessarily related, that whatever is good must give satisfaction to some persons in some degree.

Royce's views on moral deliberation and interpersonal moral judgment strongly suggest that the concepts of rightness and obligation are to be defined by reference to goodness conceived as the realization of the true self. Once again, this must not be taken as an assertion of identity. If an act's being right *meant* that it was an act realizing the true self, then the judgment that it is right to realize the true self would be a tautology asserting that to realize the true self is to realize the true self. Instead, rightness is to be regarded as bearing a synthetic but necessary relation to the realization of the good, just as goodness bears a synthetic but necessary relation to the ends of human desire.[26]

The view to which Royce seems to subscribe, then, may be stated as follows. Duties or obligations are moral claims that men regard as binding upon themselves. These claims are implicit in their conception of what is desirable, and what is desirable can be understood only in relation to the well-being of the true self or self as a whole. Underlying the conception of what ought to be done there must be the ideal of an ultimate good to be obtained. It is for this reason that judgments of obligation are not reducible to generalizations about what does in fact satisfy certain persons in certain situations. For the individual recognizes claims of obligation

[26] Cf. J. H. Muirhead, *Rule and End in Morals* (London, 1932), p. 45.

as binding upon him just at the point when he experiences within himself the conflict between his "lower self," conceived in terms of his momentary desires and particular satisfactions, and his "higher self" or self as a whole, conceived in terms of his permanent and comprehensive interests as a human being. The individual's conception of his duty, then, may be expressed in terms of the subjection of his lower self to the dictates of his higher self or self as a whole.[27]

If the terminology of higher and lower self is repugnant to the reader, one could restate the view just summarized more simply as follows. The individual, once he has committed himself to a life plan, binds himself to a general system of rules which he regards as necessary for the attainment of the good life. Right actions are henceforth conceived as actions performed in conformity with these self-imposed rules.

But there is good reason for preserving the self-realizationist's peculiar terminology. For it brings into sharper focus a feature of our experience of moral obligation that other ethical theorists have tended to ignore or misrepresent. The self-realizationist conceives of obligation under a double aspect.[28] While on the one hand the moral agent regards his obligations as requirements binding upon him independently of and even in opposition to his private wishes and inclinations, yet on the other hand he is conscious of having voluntarily laid these obligations upon himself. Thus it is

[27] Compare the following passage in F. H. Bradley's *Ethical Studies*, 2 ed. (Oxford, 1927), p. 146: "If our self were nothing above and beyond these coexistent and successive phenomena, then the word 'ought' could have no meaning. And again, if our self were a pure, unalloyed will, realizing itself apart from a sensuous element, the word 'ought' would still be meaningless. It is the antagonism of the two elements in one subject which is the essence of the ought . . . The ought is the command of the formal will, and duty is the obedience, or, more properly, the compulsion of the lower self by that will, or the realization of the form in and over against the recalcitrant matter of the desires."

[28] The influence of Kant on modern self-realization theory is unmistakable at this point. Cf. *Foundations of the Metaphysics of Morals* (Chicago, 1950), sec. 2.

possible for the moral agent both to feel his duties as externally imposed and to be conscious of them as self-imposed at the same time. The self-realizationist claims that he is able to account for this double aspect of obligation by the fact that what he calls the momentary self or will and the higher self or will may be and are distinguished in human experience even though they are aspects of one and the same self.

With this theory of the double aspect of obligation and the corresponding distinction within the self between a higher and lower will, the self-realizationist is attempting to reconcile two fundamental demands of the moral consciousness: the demand for moral autonomy and the demand for moral objectivity. We commonly believe that the ultimate justification for moral distinctions must lie in the autonomous will of the moral agent himself. At the same time, we believe that moral distinctions must have objective import at least to the extent that they validly impose obligations on men over and beyond their private inclinations and whims. We recall that the reconciliation of these two demands of the moral consciousness was precisely the task which Royce regarded as primary for ethical theory in *The Religious Aspect of Philosophy*. Royce's subsequent adoption of a self-realizationist doctrine brought him closer, it seems to me, to accomplishing this task than he had been in that earlier work.

We are now in a better position to understand Royce's somewhat unusual doctrine of interpersonal moral judgment. By insisting that B's judgment of A carries moral binding power only if it is in conformity with A's own ultimate purpose or life plan, Royce is seeking to defend the moral autonomy of the individual so judged. On the other hand, in recognizing that the person judged may not at the moment be aware of his own deeper interests, that is, that he may not always be conscious of the moral demands imposed upon him by his own higher self, Royce is allowing that moral judgments may be objectively valid over and against the momentary inclinations and impulses of the person judged. On Royce's view the moral agent would be fully cognizant of his own deeper interests only if he were fully enlightened, in possession of a universal point of view, and completely unbiased by his passions. Inasmuch as these are ideal conditions to which the moral agent can at best approximate, he always remains subject, in spite of the moral autonomy that is his in principle, to the moral criticism of his fellow men.

This view of moral obligation is, of course, not nearly objectivistic enough for those philosophers traditionally described as formalists or deontologists. The deontological intuitionists such as Prichard, Ross, and Broad have argued that moral obligations are determined by a unique and indefinable character inherent in certain situations in which men find themselves. They speak of the right act as being the one "appropriate" or "fitting" to the situation, and argue that the requirement imposed upon the individual by the situation is independent of any attitude or state of mind he may happen to have.[29] On their view, therefore, the moral requirement comes from outside the agent and is dependent upon some objective character of the situation. That would seem to entail a denial that moral rules are self-legislated.

This is hardly the place to attempt a resolution of a controversy that in one form or another has raged throughout the history of ethical theory.[30] Nevertheless one deontological criticism of the self-realizationist's position cannot go unanswered. It is that if moral rules are ultimately self-legislative in character, they cannot be universally binding on all men. They must therefore be arbitrary and the claim they

[29] Cf. H. A. Prichard, "Duty and Ignorance of Fact," in *Moral Obligation*, p. 21 and *passim;* W. D. Ross, *Foundations of Ethics* (Oxford, 1939), p. 51; C. D. Broad, *Five Types of Ethical Theory* (New York, 1934), pp. 164–165.

[30] For a searching discussion of it, see W. D. Falk, " 'Ought' and Motivation," in *Readings in Ethical Theory*, ed. W. Sellars and J. Hospers (New York, 1952), pp. 492–510.

impose on conduct can at best be relative and subjective. In replying to this criticism, the self-realizationist has several alternatives open to him. In the first place, he may argue, as does Royce, that objectivity and universality in the sense demanded by the deontologists are simply false to our moral experience. It is impossible to formulate a moral code or rule of right conduct that holds for all men at all times without exception. To suppose otherwise is tantamount to denying the uniqueness and individuality of persons. The ascription of duties and obligations requires a consideration not only of the situation (and no two situations are ever exactly alike) in which moral agents find themselves, but also of the unique life plan which each agent, according to his own lights, has formulated for himself.

In the second place, the self-realizationist may argue that his theory of obligation does in fact meet the requirements of objectivity and universality in the sense in which these are applicable to the moral life. The self-realizationist insists that where a duty exists for someone, it is a duty for him regardless of his opinion or attitude in regard to it. Thus, duties are objective at least in the sense that they override the claims of momentary feelings and momentary personal advantage. Moreover, the self-realizationist is fully prepared to honor the claim of moral common sense that if I have a duty to perform a certain action, then anyone in my circumstances would also have such a duty. The self-realizationist merely points out that no one else is ever precisely in my circumstances. There are, to be sure, certain moral obligations taken as *prima facie* binding on all men in certain circumstances. Among these are the familiar duties of promise keeping, truth telling, and the prevention of unnecessary suffering. But the possibility of conflict among these well-established obligations suggests to the self-realizationist that no one of them is absolute.

Finally, the self-realizationist himself holds at least one moral principle or rule to be absolutely binding on all men.

That is the principle to realize the good. Whereas particular obligations may be relative both to the varying circumstances in which moral agents find themselves and to the unique life plans of each, the obligation to realize the good is exhibited to the moral consciousness as a "categorical imperative." In addition, it is possible to interpret Royce's four formal constituents of the moral attitude—reasonableness, impartiality, respect for persons, and the harmonization of conflict, as ethical principles binding on all men at all times and in all circumstances. These principles could then be regarded as further elucidations of what is inherently involved in the absolute requirement to realize the good.

(2) We turn now to the problem of the criterion of rightness. Royce, along with other self-realizationists, is a teleologist in his conception of the relation between goodness and rightness. Thus he speaks of the common ground of obligation in general as being the realization of the good. More specifically, Royce seems to hold that the common characteristic of all right actions in virtue of which they are right is their capacity to fulfill the deeper purposes of a rational and voluntary being. In other words, Royce says that those actions are obligatory which are necessary to the realization of the self as a whole.

But Royce does not specify precisely how this criterion of right actions is to be understood. It is possible to interpret Royce as a nonhedonistic or "ideal" utilitarian. On this interpretation, those acts and only those acts having a tendency to produce the general good or good on the whole are to be considered obligatory. In spite of certain passages in Royce that support this interpretation,[31] it does not seem acceptable. Royce explicitly rejected the view that the rightness of actions may be assessed in terms of their consequences alone.[32]

---

[31] See, in particular, *The Philosophy of Loyalty*, p. 142.
[32] See Part I. Royce attacked Plato and the Hedonists for making virtue a means to something beyond itself.

It might seem, then, that Royce is maintaining two apparently conflicting conceptions of obligation at once. The first, commonly associated with the deontologists, is that at least some acts are right *per se*, independently of their consequences. The second, commonly associated with the utilitarians, is that acts are right only in so far as they are productive of the good.

The difficulty in question has been well stated by a more recent self-realizationist, H. W. B. Joseph. He writes:

> It is the difficulty, how to reconcile the conviction that the obligation to do an action does not arise merely from the goodness of some results or consequences of the action, with the conviction that the action that I recognize I ought to do cannot be without value in itself; how to maintain that obligation is neither derived from the goodness merely of the consequences of the action to which I am obliged, nor yet independent of relation to any goodness . . .[33]

Thus there is good reason to avoid both a deontological view holding that certain actions are right *per se*, independently of any relation to goodness, intrinsic or extrinsic, and a utilitarian view holding that the rightness of actions may be determined solely by the goodness of the consequences to which they lead.

It is my belief that Royce is attempting to reconcile these two conflicting positions by steering a path between them. On his view, as I interpret it, an act is morally right only in so far as it is also good. But the goodness which makes the act right may be inherent in the act itself and not merely a consequence of it.

This interpretation seems the most plausible in the light of Royce's self-realization theory in general. For this theory maintains a distinction between acts which, in one way or another, promote the realization of the self as a whole, and those acts which are more properly regarded as being by

[33] *Some Problems in Ethics* (London, 1933), pp. 26–27.

their very nature the acts of a higher self, or acts conceived to be of the sort that fit into the life plan of the self as a whole. The distinction in question is then between acts that are means to the desirable end and acts that are necessary ingredients or parts of the desirable end itself. On the basis of this distinction, Royce would be able to account for another distinction commonly made by moral philosophers, between formally or subjectively right actions and materially or objectively right actions. Actions motivated by the desire to realize the self as a whole would be deemed worthy of moral approval even while they are subject to further criticism from the point of view of whether or not they actually bring about the desirable end.

On Royce's view, however, no appraisal of the rightness of actions is complete unless both points of view are taken into account. In fact, Royce believes that an adequate appraisal of conduct involves at least three considerations: the motive of the action, the end for which the action is undertaken, and the actual or expected consequences of the action.[34] To judge an action by reference to its effects alone is, on Royce's view, to judge it in abstraction. All our moral judgments carry at least an implicit reference to the character and motives of the agent.

Perhaps the most serious objection to Royce's view thus interpreted has been made by the intuitionist H. A. Prichard. [35] It is Prichard's contention that any theory of obligation which puts forward as the criterion of right acts their extrinsic or intrinsic goodness reduces the moral ought to a nonmoral ought and is, therefore, no theory of moral obligation at all. Prichard distinguishes two forms of such theories. Theories of the first form hold that actions productive of what is good ought to be performed. Theories of the second

[34] See "Tests of Right and Wrong," in *Fugitive Essays*, ed. J. Loewenberg (Cambridge, Mass., 1920), pp. 206ff.
[35] "Does Moral Philosophy Rest on a Mistake?," *Mind*, n.s., 21:21–37 (1912). Quoted with permission of the editor.

form hold that certain actions are good in themselves and that their intrinsic goodness is the reason why they ought to be performed. Prichard claims that there are insuperable objections to theories in both forms. If he is correct, then Royce's theory of obligation, which I have interpreted as a combination of both forms, would be untenable.

Against theories of the first form, that is, theories that base the obligatoriness of actions on the goodness of the ends for which they are originated, Prichard argues that they

presuppose an intermediate link, *viz.,* the further thesis that what is good ought to be. The necessity of this link is obvious. An "ought," if it is to be derived at all, can only be derived from another "ought." Moreover, this link tacitly presupposes another, *viz.,* that the apprehension that something good which is not an action ought to be involves just the feeling of imperativeness or obligation which is to be aroused by the thought of the action which will originate it. Otherwise the argument will not lead us to feel the obligation to produce it by the action. And, surely, both this link and its implication are false. The word "ought" refers to actions and to actions alone.[36]

Prichard's argument, as I understand it, is that there are two unbridgeable gaps in theories of the form under discussion. The first gap is between the proposition "*x* is good" and the proposition "*x* ought to be." The second gap is between the proposition "*x* ought to be" and the proposition "*x* ought to be done." In support of this argument, Prichard asserts that the moral consciousness is immediately aware of both of these gaps. Now it seems clear that Prichard maintains the existence of these two gaps because he refuses to accept the relation between goodness and obligation which his opponents accept. Royce, in common with other self-realizationists, conceives goodness and obligation to be so closely related that further links between the two concepts are unnecessary. To him, it appears self-evident that what is ulti-

[36] *Ibid.*, p. 24.

mately and unconditionally good ought to be produced and furthered. The very idea of the good, Royce believes, presents itself to the moral consciousness in the form of an imperative, a demand to seek its fulfillment.

Stated in these terms, the issue at hand appears to resolve itself finally into a dispute over what it is, if anything, that the moral consciousness actually intuits. Prichard is claiming that what is good and what ought to be done are altogether separate notions. The self-realizationist is claiming that these two notions are not ultimately separable. It seems obvious that neither party to such a dispute is able to demonstrate the correctness of its respective position. Thus if Prichard's claim that the self-realizationist's theory of obligation is fallacious rests on an intuition, he may well be begging precisely the question at issue.

Against theories of the second form, that is, theories that base the obligatoriness of actions on the intrinsic goodness of the actions themselves, Prichard argues that a dilemma is involved. When we approve of actions as being intrinsically good, Prichard contends, we do so only with respect to their motives. Moreover, the motive in question is either the sense of obligation itself or an intrinsically good desire such as gratitude, affection, or public spirit. Prichard continues:

The dilemma is this: If the motive in respect of which we think an action good is the sense of obligation, then so far from the sense that we ought to do it being derived from our apprehension of its goodness, our apprehension of its goodness will presuppose the sense that we ought to do it. In other words, in this case the recognition that the act is good will plainly *presuppose* the recognition that the act is right, whereas the view under consideration is that the recognition of the goodness of the act *gives rise* to the recognition of its rightness. On the other hand, if the motive in respect of which we think an action good is some intrinsically good desire, such as the desire to help a friend, the recognition of the goodness of the act will equally fail to give rise to the sense of obligation to do it. For we cannot feel that we ought to do that the doing of which is *ex hypothesi* promoted solely by the desire to do it.[37]

Prichard then concludes:

The fallacy underlying the view is that while to base the rightness of an act upon its intrinsic goodness implies that the goodness in question is that of the motive, in reality the rightness or wrongness of an act has nothing to do with any question of motives at all. For, as any instance will show, the rightness of an action concerns an action not in the fuller sense of the term in which we include the motive in the action, but in the narrower and commoner sense in which we distinguish an action from its motive and mean by an action merely the conscious origination of something, an origination which on different occasions or in different people may be prompted by different motives.[38]

Now Royce's reply to this argument would, I believe, be somewhat as follows. There are certain actions which we approve as being intrinsically good, namely, those actions which by their very nature are the actions of a self seeking to fulfill his deeper purposes or life plan. But to suppose that the intrinsic goodness of such actions is determined exclusively by their motives involves an abstraction repugnant to the moral consciousness. For an action to be judged intrinsically good it is necessary that the end for which it is undertaken be good, that it be not merely a means to this end but an essential component part of it, and that it be motivated by the desire to realize it. Only when these conditions are satisfied may an act be regarded as intrinsically good and its intrinsic goodness serve as a criterion of its rightness.

To begin with, then, Royce would not accept the presupposition of Prichard's dilemma, namely, that the intrinsic goodness of an action is determined by its motive alone. On Royce's view, morality inevitably implies an end in itself to be realized. If a moral agent were ever to be motivated in his actions by a sense of obligation alone, it is likely that his

[37] *Ibid.*, p. 26.   [38] *Ibid.*, pp. 26–27.

often-repeated recognition of the action as being either conducive to or a part of the end for which it was undertaken would have led him to lose sight of the end itself. But were he to be asked for a *reason* or *justification* of the rightness of the act, he would refer to the goodness of the end and not to the sense of obligation motivating him. From Royce's point of view, therefore, the first horn of Prichard's dilemma involves a confusion between a question of moral psychology and what might be called a question of moral logic. It is psychologically possible for a man to perform an action for its own sake, motivated solely by a sense of duty. But in offering a reason why the action is right (or wrong), a reference to the end involved, beyond the mere sense of duty itself, is necessary.

As for the second horn of Prichard's dilemma, Royce would say, I believe, that an action motivated by an intrinsically good desire is good *in that respect*. But in order for the action to be regarded as right or obligatory, it must in addition be conceived as necessary to or inherent in the attainment of a morally worthy end.

Thus we may state Royce's position in contrast to Prichard's as follows. On the one hand, when the rightness of an act is based upon its intrinsic goodness, considerations other than and in addition to the goodness of its motive must be taken into account. On the other hand, an adequate appraisal of the rightness or wrongness of any act must take into account the character, and hence the motive, of the agent as well as the goodness of the end for which the action is initiated. To suppose otherwise is falsely to abstract the rightness of actions from the total context by reference to which our moral consciousness renders its judgments.

Prichard presents an additional objection that might be supposed to bear against the self-realizationist's psychology. In discussing an example designed to illustrate and support his contentions, Prichard writes:

Moreover, if we eventually pay our bills from fear of the county court, we shall still have done *what* we ought, even though we shall not have done it *as* we ought. The attempt to bring in the motive involves a mistake similar to that involved in supposing that we can will to will. To feel that I ought to pay my bills is to be *moved towards* paying them. But what I can be moved towards must always be an action in which I am moved in a particular way, therefore, an action from a particular motive; otherwise I should be moved towards being moved, which is impossible. Yet the view under consideration involves this impossibility, for it really resolves the sense that I ought to do so and so, into the sense that I ought to be moved in a particular way.[39]

While it may seem at first glance paradoxical to suppose that we can will to will, the view Prichard maintains here is, I submit, even more paradoxical. For if it is true that we are the passive victims of our desires and motives, having no voluntary control over them whatsoever, then it is difficult to see what justification we have for morally appraising one another's characters. No one, not even Prichard himself, would deny that the appraisal of motives plays a dominant role in the judgment of moral character. Yet if we are in any sense to be held morally responsible for our characters, we must at least to some extent be able to control and redirect our desires and motives.

Actually, from the self-realizationist's point of view, the contention that we can will to will, if properly understood, is not paradoxical at all. An analysis of the structure of the human personality reveals an ever-present contrast between the desires of the momentary, fragmented self and the desires or interests associated with an idealized life plan or self as a whole. When the momentary desires and the more comprehensive interests conflict, the individual has the power to control and redirect the former in behalf of the latter. When even the latter interests are subject to social criticism, the individual is further able to broaden, deepen, and recon-

[39] *Ibid.*, p. 27.

struct them as well. At the very least, he is able voluntarily to focus his attention on certain of these interests to the exclusion of others.[40] Were he unable to do so, it is difficult to see how moral responsibility and personal autonomy could be ascribed to him at all.

Perhaps a familiar example would help to clarify the self-realizationist's position. Suppose I contribute regularly to charity, motivated solely by the desire to further my reputation as benefactor in my community. Suppose further that I come to know a fellow contributor who, I gradually discover, is motivated by a disinterested desire for the welfare of the recipients of his gifts. Reluctantly I may come to feel that he is the better man and that his act is worthier of moral approval than mine. Little by little, through focussing attention upon the beneficiaries of my donations rather than upon my own good name, through deliberate efforts to see for myself the results of my contributions, I may come to make his motive my own. A process similar to this, I suggest, is a not uncommon occurrence in our everyday moral experience.

(3) We turn finally to the question of the extent to which obligation claims may be justified. Royce's general theory of obligation, as we have seen, rests on two cardinal principles. The first is that the rightness of actions is necessarily related to the ends conceived as worthy of attainment. The second is that in the final analysis duties must be self-imposed if the autonomy of individuals as moral agents is to be preserved. On this view, what accounts for the binding force that the moral consciousness regards as accompanying our conception of our duties? We recall Prichard's contention that a teleological theory of the sort Royce advances is in principle unable to account for the sense of imperativeness attaching to moral obligations. Is this contention justified?

The self-realizationist, for his part, does not think so. He

[40] See Chapter Four.

believes that the good of the self as a whole, once it is recognized as the supreme ethical principle, carries with it a unique moral claim. This moral claim arises out of the contrast between the desire for momentary and immediate satisfactions and the desire for the permanent, abiding realization of the self as a whole. Once the individual acknowledges the latter as his highest end, the obligation to do whatever is required to attain that end appears to him as self-evident.

Royce and the self-realizationists in general never pretend to be able to prove that the recognition of the ultimate good as they conceive it carries with it this unique moral claim. The most they can do is leave it up to the individual himself to decide whether he recognizes, upon reflection, that his duties are expressions of the self-realizationist principle. If this principle is indeed the supreme ethical principle, it cannot be derived from or justified in terms of any further ethical principle. It must carry its own binding force for the person who accepts its validity.

At least a measure of agreement is possible, therefore, between the self-realizationists and their deontologistic opponents. Beyond a certain point in the process of moral reflection, the question "Why ought I to do x?" is no longer legitimate—if it is a request for a *moral* answer. But when is this point reached? According to the self-realizationist, if the question is meant to challenge the supreme ethical principle ("Why ought I to do what the supreme principle says I ought to do?"), and if this principle is indeed supreme, then the question is either illegitimate, or else it is really a request for an extra-moral motivating reason or inducement to do what is right. In the former case, once it is granted that the ultimate moral end is that form of life conceived as constituting the well-being of the self as a whole, and if that form of life is a life lived under certain self-imposed obligations, then to ask for a further reason why one ought to be bound by these obligations is indeed senseless. In the latter case, the question is tantamount to asking "Why be moral?" Clearly an answer to such a question can be found, if at all, only beyond the pale of morality altogether.

Nevertheless, the self-realizationist must recognize that the question, "Why ought I to do x?" is legitimate whenever it is a request for justification of a *particular* obligation. This is a consequence of the necessary relation he believes to exist between rightness and goodness. Unlike the intuitionist, he does not regard the rightness of an act as a unique characteristic of the act itself independent of the good realized by the act. On his view, therefore, no particular obligation claim is self-evident. To ask "Why ought I to do so-and-so?" therefore, is a legitimate question demanding, as a reason for performing the act, evidence that it is truly conducive to or inherent in the realization of a morally worthy end.

Thus the self-realizationist's account of the justification of moral obligations differs from that of the deontologist in at least three ways. The self-realizationist accepts a supreme ethical principle which the deontologist rejects. He maintains a necessary mutual relation between rightness and goodness, between obligation and value, which the deontologist denies. And, finally, he makes a sharper distinction than does the deontologist between the question "Why ought I to do so-and-so?" conceived as a request for the justification of a particular obligation or claim, and the question "Why ought I to do what is right?" The self-realizationist considers the former question legitimate and answerable in terms of the goodness of the end involved. He considers the latter question unanswerable within the moral context.

Before we conclude this discussion of moral obligation, one further point should be stressed. When a moral philosopher has presented and defended a view as to the criterion of moral obligation, he has provided, in terms of his ethical theory as a whole, what he believes to be the rationale underlying moral judgments. But he has not thereby answered the question how, in concrete moral situations, the moral agent is to determine his duties. The question "What is the criterion of obligation?" and the question "How do I know what is right?" although they are related, are not identical. The former is a theoretical question to be answered by the moral philosopher, whereas the latter is a practical question to be answered by the moral agent in a particular case. The moral philosopher may, once he has presented a theory of the moral criterion, go on to propose substantive moral principles designed to assist men in deciding, in concrete instances, what is valuable and what ought to be done to attain it. But he is then undertaking a different kind of ethical inquiry.

Now Royce's later ethical theory includes an elaborate and searching investigation of the latter sort, which we shall examine in the next chapter. His "philosophy of loyalty," for which he is best known as a moral philosopher, is an attempt to answer the practical demand of the moral agent for substantive principles capable of assisting him in his everyday moral decisions. Royce's development of these principles constitutes what I have called his third phase of ethical inquiry. This phase, however, is of crucial importance for the structure of Royce's ethical theory as a whole. For it is only now that Royce seriously undertakes to show that the realization of the self as a whole necessarily involves the fulfillment of certain social obligations.

Chapter Eight

LOYALTY AND THE COMMUNITY

IN the previous two chapters we have examined two phases of Royce's mature ethical theory. The first involved an attempt to define the moral attitude from a formal point of view. This attitude, whose elucidation is logically prior to a critical determination of substantive principles of moral value and moral conduct, was seen to consist in the adoption of certain regulative principles which govern the domain of moral activity and moral appraisal as a whole. The second phase of ethical inquiry was concerned with the effort to establish the principle of self-realization as the individual's criterion of moral value and obligation.

With this much accomplished, Royce's later ethical theory is still, however, incomplete. At least two important problems remain to be faced. One is that the principle of self-realization has not as yet been connected with the social requirements of morality as demanded by our moral consciousness. It is imperative upon Royce to show that the ideal of self-realization cannot be attained independently of the social context of which the individual is necessarily a part. The principle of self-realization must therefore be exhibited as imposing upon the individual moral agent certain duties toward his fellow men and toward society at large.

The other problem, more substantive in nature, has to do with practical principles designed to enable the moral agent to know what is good and to do what is right in concrete moral situations. Royce is well aware of the impossibility of formulating a complete set of practical principles adequate to every existing, not to speak of every conceivable, moral situation. Nevertheless, his analysis of the human self makes it especially incumbent upon him to develop what substantive principles he can. For even though the individual must in the end be conceived as morally autonomous, he is required, on Royce's view, to look in the first instance beyond himself for his life plan, for his ideal ends, and for an understanding of his duties. We might even say that the character of Royce's third or "communal" dimension of ethical inquiry is determined by his conception of the paradox of moral autonomy and social dependency in the human individual.

The present chapter is divided into three sections. The first examines Royce's principle of loyalty to a social cause as the practical determinant of moral value and of right conduct for the individual. The second is concerned with the principle of loyalty to loyalty as a test of the worthiness of social causes and as a method of adjudicating among conflicting loyalties. The third section treats of Royce's conception of the ideal "Community of Interpretation" as constituting the ultimate fulfillment of man's desire for self-realization and the highest object of his loyal devotion.

1. Loyalty

a. The Need for Loyalty

In Royce's account of moral deliberation, discussed in the previous chapter, the paradoxical nature of the quest for personal moral autonomy was brought to light. The individual, on Royce's view, must achieve a sense of self before he can become a moral agent. This sense of self is conditional on his ability to formulate for himself a life plan by reference to which he can then order the pursuit of his interests and evaluate his conduct. But the very life plan that is to endow the individual with moral autonomy, Royce insisted, is attainable only through constant reference to social norms and socially prevalent ideals of personality. Social conformity was seen to be the necessary albeit insufficient condition of individual moral autonomy.

In the opening chapter of *The Philosophy of Loyalty* (1908), Royce's analysis of the paradox of moral autonomy is considerably deepened. The individual, when confronted with the problem of deciding what he ought to do, what is right for him, must consult his own will. Royce stands committed to the principle that no external authority, be it society or, for the religious man, the will of God, can compel the individual's moral assent unless he is able to identify it with his own "deepest desire." But left to his own devices, the individual is unable to discover what this deepest desire is.

I can never find out what my will is by merely brooding over my natural desires, or by following my momentary caprices. For by nature I am a sort of meeting place of countless streams of ancestral tendency. From moment to moment, if you consider me apart from my training, I am a collection of impulses. There is no one desire that is always present to me. Left to myself alone, I can never find out what my will is.[1]

I have still to learn my own will, therefore, since "I have no inborn ideal naturally present within myself." And learning, as Royce taught in his psychology, is largely a matter of social conformity through imitation. It is

the social activities . . . that first tend to organize all of our instincts, to give unity to our passions and impulses, to transform our natural chaos of desires into some sort of order . . . It is our social existence, then, as imitative beings . . . that suggests to us the sort of plans of life which we get when we learn a calling, when we find a business in life, when we discover our place in the social world . . . We in so far learn what our own will is by first imitating the wills of others.[2]

However, the paradox of individual moral autonomy and social dependency is not so easily resolved. Social authority

[1] *The Philosophy of Loyalty* (New York, 1908), pp. 27f.
[2] *Ibid.*, pp. 31-33.

and social imitation in their turn fail, for two reasons, to satisfy adequately the individual's moral needs. The first reason is that social training presents us with a large variety of life plans, plans that frequently conflict, and from among which a choice must still be made. This limitation on the power of society to bring the individual to mature self-fulfillment was made explicit in Royce's theory earlier, as we saw in Part II. But there is a second and deeper reason which now becomes a part of Royce's doctrine for the first time: society breeds its own enemies, and thereby as it were sows the seeds of social antagonisms within its own bosom.

We never merely imitate. Conformity attracts, but also wearies us. Meanwhile, even by imitation, we often learn how to possess, and then carry out, our own self-will . . . Teach men customs, and you equip them with weapons for expressing their own personalities. As you train the social being, you make use of his natural submissiveness. But as a result of your training he forms plans; he interprets these plans with reference to his own personal interests; and he may end by becoming, if not original, then at least obstreperous.[3]

It is Royce's mature insight that the power with which society equips the individual to carry out its purposes may be and generally is turned against it in the long run.

Social conformity gives us social power. Such power brings us to a consciousness of who and what we are. Now, for the first time, we begin to have a real will of our own. And hereupon we may discover this will to be in sharp conflict with the will of society.[4]

[3] *The Philosophy of Loyalty,* p. 34.
[4] *Ibid.,* p. 35. I find this to be a somewhat more realistic view of the relation between the individual and society than, say, Plato's. At times in the *Republic* Plato seems to assume that all that is required to bring individuals into social harmony is the proper social training of their capacities. (Cf. George Sabine, *A History of Political Theory* [New York, 1937], p. 51.) Royce, of course, has the advantage afforded by 2500 years of the frustration of faith in social reform fully to resolve interpersonal conflict.

In Royce's estimation, the individual's tendency to rebel against the dictates of the social order is not only natural but to a certain extent justified. The individual who in every instance accepts the requirements of the social order as his way of life betrays his moral autonomy. If you act solely on the principle of conformity, Royce writes,

you find yourself without any determinate way of expressing your own individuality. For if the social order is indeed not as chaotic in its activities as by nature you yourself are, it is quite unable of itself to do more than make of you, in one way or another, a link in its mechanism, or a member of one of its numerous herds, in any case a mere vehicle for carrying out its various influences. Against this fate, as an ethical individual, you justly revolt.[5]

Neither in isolated self-assertiveness nor in submissive social conformity is the moral agent able to achieve genuine self-fulfillment.

The circle of frustration thus engendered by the individual's search, alternately within himself and in society, for a life plan that at one and the same time promises satisfaction of his deepest needs and harmonizes with those of his fellows can only be broken, Royce believes, by a happy conjunction of circumstances. Suppose I have the good fortune to become so attracted by a social activity, say the furthering of my country's interests, that I become willing to enlist my services in this activity as though it were my cause. When this happens, I find myself on the one hand obedient and submissive to whatever the cause requires for its success. Perhaps I am prepared even to give my life for it. On the other hand, the cause, since I have chosen it, gives me at once the opportunity to satisfy my own will and the ability to identify with an enterprise loftier and more far-reaching than any that I could initiate on my own. In a situation like this, "conformity is no longer opposed to having one's own

[5] *The Philosophy of Loyalty*, p. 82.

will." [6] The antagonism between individual self-assertiveness and social docility has been reconciled. The individual has found a life plan for himself that involves by its very nature some measure of social cooperation.

This is what Royce understands by loyalty. Loyalty, in Royce's well-known but rather loosely formulated definition, is "the willing and practical and thoroughgoing devotion of a person to a cause." [7] By a cause Royce means simply the object of this devotion, be it an institution like Parliament, an ideal event like the "lost cause" of Zionism or the hoped-for second coming of Christ, or an ideal goal like universal brotherhood or the scientific community of truth and knowledge. [8] The recognition of such a wide range of possible causes makes it incumbent upon Royce to determine the common characteristics that render causes fitting objects of loyalty.

b. The Essential Characteristics of a Cause

In *The Philosophy of Loyalty* Royce initially offers three criteria that a cause, to be a fitting object of an individual's loyal devotion, must meet. In the first place, a cause must be capable of *engaging* my natural interest. "The cause that is to appeal to me at all must . . . have some elemental fascination for me. It must stir me, arouse me, please me, and in the end possess me." [9] Loyalties, according to Royce, take their rise within the ambit of the individual's everyday circumstances and needs.

I shall serve causes such as my natural temperament and my social opportunities suggest to me. I shall choose friends whom I like. My family, my community, my country will be served partly because I find it interesting to be loyal to them. [10]

[6] *The Philosophy of Loyalty*, p. 41.   [7] *Ibid.*, p. 51.
[8] *Ibid.*, pp. 103–107; cf. *The Problem of Christianity* (New York, 1913), I, 232, and *William James and Other Essays* (New York, 1912), pp. 83–87.
[9] *The Philosophy of Loyalty*, pp. 119f.
[10] *Ibid.*, pp. 131f. Cf. Urbana lectures (1907), folio 76, lecture 3, p. 42:

The first condition that a cause properly so called must satisfy, therefore, is that it have moving appeal for the individual who adopts it as his own.

In the second place, a cause must be capable of *holding* my interest. Since it is in terms of a cause that I am to define my life plan, such a cause must be rich enough to harness the various energies I have at my disposal, and to fulfill over a long period of time my growing and changing desires and needs. To meet this requirement a cause must have the magnitude of a project that I in my loyalty to it can never quite complete, of a goal that I can never fully achieve. "Even because of this vastness of my ideal, even because that to which I am loyal is so much greater than I ever become . . . can my ideal unify my life . . ."[11] It is necessary, moreover, that I maintain my belief in the worthiness of the cause even if my own personal efforts to bring about its realization should fail.

Thirdly, the cause must be *social* in nature. It is of course possible to be loyal to an individual: thus a mother to her child, or lovers to each other. But loyalty, in the special sense in which Royce uses the term, is always loyalty to a social cause. Since a cause is to furnish the individual with an enduring life plan, and since, from a psychological point of view, the individual is inclined to choose a cause suggested to him by existing social ideals in accordance with his natural affections, such a cause will of necessity be a social enterprise. It will "unite him with other persons by some social tie, such as personal friendship, or his family, or the state may, in a given case, represent."[12] Personal affection is perhaps a necessary but never a sufficient condition for the

---

"Natural ties and natural affections will suggest such objects [of loyalty] . . . nobody can say to another man: 'This is the object to which you ought to be loyal.' Each must choose for himself . . . The inalienable privilege and duty to choose our objects of loyalty leaves open an endless range for a wise individualism."

[11] *The Philosophy of Loyalty,* p. 173.   [12] *Ibid.,* p. 52.

expression of loyalty. In the case of lovers, for example, "one is loyal . . . not merely to the individual, but to the tie, to the relation, as well as to *some larger whole* in which the beloved and the lover have their places." [13]

Unfortunately, Royce never makes clear, in *The Philosophy of Loyalty*, precisely what he means by this "larger whole." The book is cluttered with romantic and metaphorical language, metaphysical in its overtones,[14] designed for the most part, I believe, to inspire in the reader a belief in such a larger whole rather than to analyze its structure. In one of his more suggestive passages on this point Royce claims that a cause is to be regarded as

superpersonal, because it links several human selves, perhaps a large number of selves, into some higher social unity. You cannot be loyal to a merely impersonal abstraction; and you also cannot be loyal simply to a collection of various separate persons, viewed merely as a collection. Where there is an object of loyalty, there is, then, a union of various selves into one life.[15]

But the clarification of what Royce understands by this "higher social unity" had to await the formulation of his theory of the community during the last years of his life. In fairness to Royce, I think it is best to defer discussion of the problem here raised until this theory has been explicated. Our immediate concern is with the ethical status of loyalty and its objects.

---

[13] Urbana lectures, folio 76, lecture 3, pp. 16–17. Italics added. Cf. *William James and Other Essays,* p. 75, where Royce goes so far as to claim that in the bond of friendship there is created "a new spiritual person on a higher level."

[14] To give just one example: "Loyalty . . . is an effort to conceive human life in an essentially superhuman way, to view our social organizations as actual personal unities of consciousness, unities wherein exists an actual experience of that good which, in our loyalty, we only partially apprehend" (p. 310).

[15] *Ibid.,* p. 52; cf. *William James and Other Essays,* p. 58.

c. Loyalty as an Intrinsic Good

We recall that according to Royce the source of value for the individual lies in his ability to achieve a sense of selfhood, which in turn is dependent upon his ability to discover a life plan. In the light of the interplay of individual autonomy and social dependency involved in the discovery of a life plan, Royce now contends that such a plan becomes accessible to the individual only when he is able to be loyal to a cause. "Whatever cause thus appeals to a man meets therefore one of his deepest personal needs; namely, the need of a life task that is at once voluntary, and to his mind worthy." [16] Since loyalty provides the individual with an overarching purpose for his existence, and since such a purpose is a necessary condition of self-realization, Royce is prepared to argue that loyalty is the concrete embodiment of the supreme good for the individual. Thus,

loyalty is for the loyal man not only a good, but for him the chief amongst all the moral goods of his life, because it furnishes to him a personal solution of the hardest of human practical problems, the problem: "For what do I live?" [17]

For Royce, therefore, loyalty is an intrinsic good. The possession of the loyal attitude as such has inherent moral

[16] *The Philosophy of Loyalty*, p. 59.

[17] *Ibid.*, p. 57; cf. p. 152. Professor J. Loewenberg has suggested that loyalty may be regarded as Royce's principle of individuation on the ethical plane. Since selfhood for Royce is an ideal to be achieved and not a given, and since it is attained only through a chosen loyalty to a cause, this uniquely expressed loyalty defines one's moral individuality. See *Royce's Synoptic Vision* (Baltimore, 1955), p. 26. The following passage in *The Philosophy of Loyalty* tends to bear out Loewenberg's interpretation: "A self is a life in so far as it is unified by a single purpose. Our loyalties furnish such purposes, and hence make of us conscious and unified moral persons. Where loyalty has not yet come to any sort of definiteness, there is so far present only a kind of inarticulate striving to be an individual self. This very search for one's true self is already a sort of life-purpose, which, as far as it goes, individuates the life of the person in question, and gives him a task. But loyalty brings the individual to full moral self-consciousness" (pp. 171–172).

value. "Whoever is loyal, whatever be his cause, is devoted, is active, surrenders his private self-will, controls himself, is in love with his cause, and believes in it. The loyal man is thus in a state of mind which has its own value for himself." [18] Moreover, loyalty is a necessary aspect, if not the whole, of the ideal end of self-realization itself. Loyalty "tends to unify life, to give it centre, fixity, stability." It frees its possessor of "inner dissatisfaction" and disharmony. It is "the universal form in which the human Self fulfils its individual and social function." [19]

Nevertheless, while every loyalty has some measure of intrinsic goodness, it is plain that some loyalties are better than others—better both from the point of view of which ones best afford self-realization to the individual, and from the point of view of which ones best harmonize with the loyalties of others.[20] Hence initially chosen loyalties remain open to further perspectives of moral appraisal and criticism. These perspectives will be examined in section 2.

d. My Cause as Practical Determinant of My Duty

If loyalty is the concrete moral good for the individual, the object of his loyalty, his cause, determines in practice what is morally right for him. For the cause is the objective expression or embodiment of the individual's personal ideal, in terms of which he judges his particular purposes, his single acts, and his momentary impulses. Royce writes that once you have found your cause, "it must become your conscience, must tell you the truth about your duty, and must unify, as from without and from above, your motives, your special ideals, and your plans." [21]

It would be well at this point to retrace the steps by which

---

[18] *The Philosophy of Loyalty*, p. 22.
[19] Urbana lectures, folio 76, lecture 3, pp. 24f.
[20] These points of view are, of course, inseparable, inasmuch as the interpersonal conflict of loyalties leads to the frustration of the individual's ends.
[21] *The Philosophy of Loyalty*, p. 47; cf. pp. 44, 173–177.

Royce arrives at this position. Royce's analysis of the individual moral agent revealed that his acts and impulses are judged right or wrong in the first instance by reference to his avowed purpose. However, this purpose, as we saw in Chapter Seven, may itself be immoral (thus in the example of the pirate). Royce found it necessary, therefore, to posit a "deeper" desire or more ultimate purpose, frequently only latent, in every individual to which it is possible to appeal as a basis for criticizing his avowed purpose. This deeper purpose was broadly characterized as the desire for rational self-possession. Now the fulfillment of this desire for self-possession is made possible, on Royce's analysis, only through loyalty to a cause, since the individual is unable to discover within himself what it is that he really wants.

But in thus freely allowing a cause beyond himself to become the expression of his own will, the individual voluntarily transfers the highest court of moral judgment from himself to something outside himself and to that extent "objective," namely his cause. An adequate cause, Royce claims, will by its very nature require the individual to perform actions in conformity with the social demands of the moral consciousness. It will demand of him that he keep his promises, tell the truth, act justly and faithfully, respect the rights of others, and the like. It is Royce's thesis that "when rightly interpreted, loyalty is the whole duty of man." [22]

If Royce can substantiate this claim, he will have taken a major step in connecting the principle of self-realization with the social obligations held to be mandatory by our reflective moral consciousness. We shall evaluate this claim when it recurs in the context of Royce's principle of loyalty to loyalty, the subject of the next section. At present, let us examine another claim closely connected with the one just mentioned, namely, that the individual's moral conscience may be exhibited in terms of the cause to which he is loyal.

[22] *Ibid.*, pp. 139–140.

Royce contends that when the individual voluntarily adopts a cause as his personal ideal, he also and by that very fact delegates to his cause the role of serving as his personal moral conscience. "When I look to my cause, it furnishes me with a conscience; for it sets before me a plan or ideal of life, and then constantly bids me contrast this plan, this ideal, with my transient and momentary impulses."²³ Since my cause can become my conscience, Royce is more strongly inclined than ever to insist that the moral conscience is not innate. "On the contrary, it is the flower rather than the root of the moral life." Nor, on this view, is conscience to be regarded as infallible.

My conscience is precisely as fallible or as infallible as my choice of a cause is subject to error, or is of such nature as to lead me aright. Since loyalty, in so far as it is loyalty, is always a good, the conscience of any loyal self is never wholly a false guide. Since loyalty may be in many respects blind, one's conscience also may be in many respects misleading.²⁴

This passage strongly suggests that Royce's account of the individual's moral conscience runs closely parallel to his account of the formation of the life plan that is to constitute the individual's deeper self. Neither is innate in the individual. Both must be acquired through complex processes of learning, through imitation, already existing social norms and ideals. But by the time an individual has achieved a mature awareness of selfhood, both his life plan and his conscience may be said to be uniquely his own. The development of conscience, then, just like the acquisition of a life plan, has its matrix in what Royce has described as the tension between individual moral autonomy and social dependency.

²³ *The Philosophy of Loyalty*, p. 174.   ²⁴ *Ibid.*, pp. 177–178.

e. Summary

As we remarked at the beginning of this chapter, Royce's construction of a theory of moral value and moral obligation in terms of the principle of self-realization left two major problems unresolved. The first is that the principle of self-realization as such is in need of supplementation by substantive principles enabling the individual to determine within the fabric of his experience what is his good and what his conduct ought to be. The second is that the principle of self-realization must be exhibited as being in conformity with the social norms of value and right conduct expressive of our reflective moral consciousness. Royce's doctrine of loyalty attempts to resolve both these problems.

The moral agent, in order to realize the good, must develop for himself a life plan capable of fulfilling the abiding needs of his self as a whole. His own immediate desires and interests fail to suggest such a plan to him, for they are too conflicting and too chaotic. His ordinary social environment fails equally to provide him with such a plan, for in training his moral consciousness it also trains his self-will, his tendency to resist and oppose the collective will. What he requires is a voluntary identification of his deeper will with an enterprise of sufficient magnitude to engage and hold his interests and to satisfy his growing needs. In short, his capacities as a human being can best be fulfilled in loyalty to a cause. Through his loyalty he is able concretely to express his value as a person. Through his cause he is able to determine practically what his duties are.

Moreover, since a cause is by its very nature a social enterprise, since the individual freely chooses a cause to function as surrogate for the expression of his own deepest will, and since this cause then assumes the role of his moral conscience or judge, Royce appears to have found a way of submitting individual behavior to standards of moral criticism derived from beyond the individual while still preserving his moral autonomy. One's cause, involving as it invariably does the cooperation of many men for its achievement, commits one to the preservation and improvement of the social relations binding its members together. A cause by its very nature requires of its devotees that they deal with one another justly, honor obligations contracted in the name of the cause, and mutually respect individual rights the possession of which is essential to the furthering of the cause.

Thus it is Royce's contention that loyalty, as he understands it, is capable of arresting the spiral of increasing self-assertiveness and interpersonal divisiveness which he finds to be characteristic of ordinary social relations in advanced civilizations. When men are loyal to a cause, their self-will is transformed into the will of the cause. Their pride, their ambition, their struggle for power, for recognition, and for success are all transfigured, so to speak, in the cause. It is only to be expected that the social relations obtaining among members of a cause will have a moral quality not to be found in ordinary social relations.

So much, at any rate, is what Royce claims for his doctrine of loyalty. But the question whether or not these claims are justified cannot be adequately answered as yet. For by his own admission [25] the doctrine of loyalty thus far formulated is inadequate and incomplete. On Royce's view, although any loyalty to any cause affords a measure of intrinsic goodness for the individual, not every cause is genuinely worthy of his lasting devotion. By allowing a cause of his own choosing to serve as surrogate for his moral conscience and his deeper will, the individual is in effect recognizing that he himself lacks the overarching vision or vantage point required to know what in the long run would fulfill the needs of his self as a whole. But by the same token he has only a hope, at best a reasona-

[25] *The Philosophy of Loyalty,* pp. 56f, and *passim.*

ble expectation, that his cause will lead him to the fulfillment of his deeper ends. He is easily lured by unsatisfactory objects of loyalty, and he may soon discover that a cause he has chosen is unworthy of his abiding devotion. If, in addition, as Royce insists, personal moral fulfillment necessarily entails interpersonal cooperation and harmony, the need for a further criterion of the worthiness of causes is that much intensified. Royce writes:

> Loyalty is a good for the loyal man; but it may be mischievous for those whom the cause assails. Conflicting loyalties may mean general social disturbances; and the fact that loyalty is good for the loyal does not of itself decide whose cause is right when various causes stand opposed to one another. And if . . . we declare that the best form of loyalty, for the loyal individual, is the one that he freely chooses for himself, so much the greater seems to be the complication of the moral world, and so much the more numerous become the chances that the loyalties of various people will conflict with one another.[26]

The principle of loyalty to loyalty, which we shall examine in the next section, constitutes Royce's effort to furnish the additional criterion needed to determine the worthiness of the several causes.

We might conclude this section by pointing out that the principle of loyalty suggests a possible solution to a dilemma encountered by the self-realizationist. According to the self-realizationist, the criterion for determining which desires and interests are genuinely worthy of pursuit is the conceived well-being of the self as a whole. In some sense and to some degree, therefore, the theory claims self-realization to be the end of human striving. Yet most self-realizationists have recognized that, paradoxically, a man cannot attain the ideal of self-realization by consciously and deliberately making it the end he pursues in and for itself. When he does so he tends to find his efforts self-defeating. An overweening

[26] *Ibid.*, p. 111.

spiritual pride and restless discontent are the common fruits of his endeavors. When, on the other hand, he focuses his attention on and directs his energies toward the well-being of others, he tends to find that self-fulfillment and happiness accrue to him of their own accord.[27] In short, most self-realizationists are at one with the Christian tradition in recognizing that the best way to win the self is to lose it.

Royce's doctrine of loyalty, it seems to me, may be regarded as a particularly striking effort to resolve this familiar paradox of human experience. In loyalty to a cause the individual identifies his highest end with that of an ideal social enterprise vastly richer, more meaningful, and more valuable than his own private self. It is not his own advantage that he seeks, but the furtherance of something outside and beyond himself. Yet his loyalty to his cause alone brings him what measure of happiness and self-fulfillment he may attain. Ideally, the life of loyalty is a life of self-fulfillment through self-surrender.

2. Loyalty to Loyalty

a. The Need for a Criterion of Worthy Causes

It is Royce's contention that the individual can find self-fulfillment only in loyalty to a cause. But not every cause will secure for the individual the satisfaction of his deepest needs. Two compelling motives prompt Royce to seek an additional moral criterion by which the value of causes themselves may be judged. The first has to do with the welfare of the individual as such. The insight necessary in order to see the meaning of his life as a whole is, on Royce's view, denied the individual. It is precisely for this reason that the individual entrusts his cause with moral control over his own destiny. By the same token, just because a cause must be

---

[27] See A. C. Garnett, *Can Ideals and Norms Be Justified?* (Stockton, Calif., 1955), pp. 66, 91, for a searching discussion of this paradox.

rich and complex enough to meet an individual's lifetime of growing needs, both the value of such a cause and the manner in which it may or may not bring the individual to self-realization are beyond his power to perceive and to anticipate at any given moment.[28] He is, therefore, deeply in need of a standard by which he can distinguish the causes more likely to bring him lasting satisfaction.

The second motive prompting the establishment of a criterion of worthy causes has to do with the welfare of society as a whole. When many men choose causes freely in accordance with their own lights, their loyalties can be expected to issue in interpersonal conflict. Such conflict, of course, threatens to destroy precisely what is the supreme good for each antagonist involved: the opportunity to express his loyalty. Royce perceives the irony of the situation in which the intensification of parochial loyalties results in the wholesale crushing of loyalty itself. "Where such a conflict occurs, the best, namely loyalty, is used as an instrument in order to encompass the worst, namely, the destruction of loyalty."[29] A principle of determining those causes most likely to harmonize rather than conflict with the causes of others is therefore needed.

In order to meet both of these needs, Royce proposes the principle of loyalty to loyalty itself as the ultimate criterion of the worth of particular causes. The individual can fulfill himself in loyalty only when his loyalty can be saved from destructive conflict with the loyalties of other men. In choosing his cause, therefore, he ought to decide for the cause most likely to further, rather than frustrate, the loyalties of his fellow men. Royce, in fact, specifies the cause of univer-

---

[28] Cf. *The Philosophy of Loyalty*, p. 254: "Your true good can never be won and verified by you in terms to which the present form and scope of human experience is adequate. The best that you can get lies in self-surrender, and in your personal assurance that the cause to which you surrender yourself is indeed good."

[29] *Ibid.*, p. 117.

sal loyalty as the highest and most general cause the moral agent can and ought to serve. The individual who serves this cause is furthering not only his own supreme good, but that of mankind as a whole. Thus the principle of loyalty to loyalty becomes, in Royce's later moral philosophy, the supreme ethical principle which is to guide the individual in his quest for self-fulfillment.

b. The Criterion Applied

No doubt the question uppermost in the mind of the reader at this point is precisely how the cause of universal loyalty is to be served. If the principle of loyalty to loyalty is to be of any practical use, it must help me resolve my moral doubts as to which of several conflicting causes I should adopt. Royce is well aware of the familiar reproach "that moral philosophers have fine-sounding principles to report, but can never tell us how these principles practically apply, except when the cases are such as common sense has already decided . . ." [30] The problem which Royce faces is not only how interpersonal conflicts of loyalties are to be resolved, for loyalties conflict within the purview of the single individual as well. Royce writes:

By virtue of my nature and of my social training, I belong to a family, to a community, to a calling, to a state, to humanity. In order to be loyal to loyalty, and in order to be a person at all, I must indeed unify my loyalty. In the meantime, however, I must also choose special causes to serve; and if these causes are to interest me, if they are to engross and possess me, they must be such as together appeal to many diverse sides of my nature; they must involve me in numerous and often conflicting social tasks; they can form one cause only in so far as they constitute an entire system of causes. My loyalty will be subject, therefore, to the ancient difficulty regarding the one and the many. Unless it is one in its ultimate aim, it will be no loyalty to universal loyalty; unless

[30] *The Philosophy of Loyalty*, p. 165.

it is just to the varied instincts and to the manifold social interests of a being such as I am, it cannot engross me.[31]

Royce has no easy solution to offer to this problem. In attempting to defend his principle of loyalty to loyalty against the charge of empty formalism, he specifies two standards of loyal conduct which, he believes, are implied by his principle. They are decisiveness and fidelity. My moral doubt is likely to take the following form:

> I hesitate at the critical moment between conflicting loyalties. For the sake of loyalty to loyalty, which one of the two conflicting causes shall I henceforth undertake to serve? . . . If I knew what is to be the outcome, I could at once easily choose. I am ignorant of the outcome. In so far I indeed cannot tell which to choose.[32]

Nevertheless, Royce argues, the principle of loyalty to loyalty, since it commits me to the cause of furthering loyalty itself, requires of me that I choose service to one or the other conflicting special cause in spite of my ignorance. "It forbids me to play Hamlet's part." Acknowledging indebtedness to William James' notion of "the will to believe," Royce continues:

> The point where I am to make this choice is determined by the obvious fact that, after a certain waiting to find out whatever I can find out, I always reach the moment when further indecision would of itself constitute a sort of decision,—a decision, namely, to do nothing, and so not to serve at all. Such a decision to do nothing, my loyalty to loyalty forbids.

According to Royce, therefore, loyalty to loyalty demands decisiveness. A choice must be made, even if it must be made blindly. Royce adds, however, that decisiveness is pointless unless it involves a further characteristic, namely, fidelity to the chosen cause. Since to abandon a cause is at once "to destroy the unity of your own purpose, and to set

[31] *Ibid.*, pp. 180–181.   [32] *Ibid.*, pp. 188–189.

the social model of disloyalty before your fellows," the only justification for rejecting a cause once chosen is the subsequent realization "that further service to that special cause would henceforth involve unquestionable disloyalty to universal loyalty." [33] Thus, the principle of loyalty to loyalty carries with it the practical injunctions to be decisive in the choice of a cause and to be faithful in its service once the choice has been made.

By Royce's own admission, the principle of loyalty to loyalty gives us only limited practical guidance in choosing among conflicting causes. The principle requires of the individual that, in his quest for a life plan, he order his particular loyalties into a coherent pattern. Presumably, therefore, he is enjoined to cultivate only those among his special loyalties which tend, during the course of his experience, to cohere into a system of causes. The principle further demands that the individual choose social causes that, so far as he is able to determine, contribute to rather than defeat the overarching cause of universal loyalty among men. When his ignorance prevents him from knowing which of several conflicting causes will fulfill the preceding requirements, the principle dictates that even if he must choose arbitrarily he should do so decisively, and should remain faithful to his chosen cause until such a time as its undesirability becomes manifest to him. But in view of the complexity of the human situation and the relative ignorance in which the moral agent confronts it, the principle of loyalty to loyalty cannot give him further guidance.

c. Loyalty and Interpersonal Moral Judgment

Royce now reconsiders the scope and limitations of interpersonal moral judgment in the light of his doctrine of loyalty. On the one hand, I have the right to subject my fellow man to moral criticism if he (1) fails altogether to be loyal to a

[33] *Ibid.*, p. 190.

cause; (2) fails to organize his special loyalties into a unified system of causes, and thus into a coherent life plan, to the best of his abilities; (3) fails to be decisive in his choice of causes and faithful to his cause once he has chosen it; or (4) fails to choose the cause that, to the best of his knowledge, advances rather than frustrates the cause of universal loyalty among mankind at large.[34] On the other hand, however, I must respect my fellow man's right to choose his own causes in accordance with his own lights and his own unique capacities and needs. I have no right, therefore, to criticize him because (1) his cause is different from my own; (2) I have no sympathy with the objects of his loyalty; (3) if I did what he does, I would be disloyal to causes I accept; (4) my failure to understand the object of his loyalty leads me to believe that he has no cause at all; (5) his cause could, if he were differently constituted, be broader than it now is; or even because (6) he neglects natural opportunities for loyalties that would compel my interests but do not seem to attract him.[35]

Royce places these limitations upon interpersonal moral judgment not only because he wishes to safeguard the moral autonomy of the individual, although that is one of his primary concerns. He also insists, as we have seen, that an adequate moral judgment requires a complex process of determining the capacities and character of the moral agent, the nature of the ends for which he acts, and the consequences, immediate and remote, of his actions for himself and for his fellow men. The man able to judge his fellow's loyalties accurately in all three of these respects must indeed be an "ideal observer."

d. Loyalty as a Moral Code

Royce would have us believe that on the basis of the two principles of loyalty and of loyalty to loyalty, a code of

[34] *Ibid.*, p. 201. [35] *Ibid.*, pp. 205–206.

moral conduct may be formulated that is as complete and as adequate as the human condition allows. Royce explicitly makes this claim more than once.

My thesis is that all those duties which we have learned to recognize as the fundamental duties of the civilized man . . . are to be rightly interpreted as special instances of loyalty to loyalty. In other words, all the recognized virtues can be defined in terms of our concept of loyalty. And this is why I assert that, when rightly interpreted, loyalty is the whole duty of man.[36]

In *The Sources of Religious Insight* [37] he maintains that the principle of loyalty to loyalty is "fit to be made the basis of a universal moral code. There is no duty, there is no virtue whose warrant and whose value you cannot deduce from this one principle." On several occasions Royce even attempts to carry through such a "deduction." The most striking of these is summarized in the following passage from *The Philosophy of Loyalty:*

Thus all unnecessary personal aggression upon what we commonly call the rights of other individuals is excluded by my formula, simply because in case I deprive my fellow of his property, his life, or his physical integrity, I take away from him the only means whereby he can express in a practical way whatever loyalty he has. Hence such aggression . . . involves disloyalty to the general loyalty of mankind . . . Such is the range of judgment that we have a right to use in our moral estimates of other people. The range just indicated is . . . large enough to enable us to define all rationally defensible principles regarding right and wrong acts. Murder, lying, evil speaking, unkindness, are all from this point of view simply forms of disloyalty.[38]

[36] *Ibid.*, pp. 139–140; cf. pp. 129–130. Cf. the Urbana lectures, folio 76, lecture 3, p. 40: "Charity, justice, truthfulness, self-sacrifice, self-realization,—all these virtues and ideals are . . . fully expressible in terms of loyalty, and of loyalty to loyalty." See also the Pittsburgh lectures on the doctrine of loyalty (1908), folio 82, lecture 3, pp. 1–3.

[37] (New York, 1912), p. 203. There follows a long list of duties and virtues allegedly inferrable from this principle.

[38] *The Philosophy of Loyalty*, pp. 204–205. Cf. Pittsburgh lectures, folio 82, lecture 2, pp. 24–40, where Royce attempts a "casuistry of truth-telling" on the basis of the principle of loyalty.

In this manner Royce seeks to connect the principle of self-realization with the social obligations commonly recognized by the moral consciousness as binding upon all men. Royce's argument, freely interpreted, is this: (1) self-realization, the highest good for the individual, requires a commitment on his part to a coherent life plan; (2) such a life plan is accessible to the individual only in a freely chosen loyalty to a cause; (3) the free expression of this loyalty requires that the individual's cause be integrated and harmonized with those of his fellow men; (4) hence the individual's highest moral commitment is to the cause of universal loyalty itself; (5) but that cause, in turn, requires for its furtherance the performance of the very moral duties and the recognition of the very moral rights demanded by our enlightened moral consciousness. Those special social duties and rights have thus been given an independent justification on the basis of the principle of self-realization, made concrete in terms of the principles of loyalty.

We shall consider certain objections to this "deduction" of rights and duties in the general evaluation which follows.

e. Evaluation

I think it can fairly be said that the "philosophy of loyalty" constitutes one of Royce's distinctive contributions to moral philosophy. As a substantive theory of the individual's highest good, it elucidates one of the outstanding ways recognized in the Western tradition of bringing man to fulfillment as a moral agent. As a doctrine of right conduct, it imposes stringent obligations on the individual while at the same time acknowledging that ultimately these obligations are self-imposed. The loyal man, as Royce describes him, on the one hand submits to the authority of an institutionalized social cause; but on the other hand, he does so by a free choice in conformity with his own natural impulses, capacities, and needs.

Moreover, the doctrine of loyalty as Royce formulates it suggests a plausible way of harmonizing and reconciling the good of the individual with the welfare of mankind as a whole. The more comprehensive the cause to which the moral agent commits himself, the more likely it is that his loyalty will answer his varied needs and at the same time engage the loyal cooperation of other men, thereby helping to fulfill their deeper needs as well. And, finally, the doctrine of loyalty reduces to a few relatively simple, easily understood, and universally applicable moral principles the welter of conflicting value and obligation claims characteristic of the moral life as we know it.

Nevertheless, it seems to me that Royce's presentation of the doctrine of loyalty is unsatisfactory in regard to at least two important issues. The first has to do with Royce's claim that all of the rights and obligations recognized by the moral consciousness as binding upon the moral agent can be "deduced" from his principles of loyalty. The second concerns Royce's claim that the principle of loyalty to loyalty can serve as a practical criterion for determining the relative worthiness of the causes to which moral agents commit themselves.

Surely Royce's claim that all recognized rights and duties can be "deduced" from his principles of loyalty is exaggerated. In the first place, he does not really mean that they can be so deduced in any strictly logical sense. What he does mean is that the principles of loyalty provide their justification or ground. Thus the moral agent loyal to the cause of promoting universal loyalty may, and no doubt will, recognize that the realization of his cause requires that he keep his promises, tell the truth, respect the integrity of his fellow men, and so forth. But in that case the connection between these particular obligations and the principle of loyalty is better described as an existential rather than as a logical relation.

Even then, there is an ambiguity in Royce's conception of the loyal individual's rights and obligations. Several of the passages I have quoted suggest that the rights and duties traditionally recognized by moral common sense are the ones Royce takes to be justified by his principles of loyalty. But other passages suggest the view that particular rights and duties are determined for the individual exclusively and for the first time by the cause to which he commits himself. Royce's strongest statement of the latter position is the following: "Your rights are your duties to the cause; and your duties are, in the end, your only rights." [39]

If the first interpretation is taken to be closest to Royce's real intention, the suspicion arises that Royce has simply attempted to incorporate the traditional body of Western morals into his principles of loyalty at the outset, instead of having "deduced" such a code from them as he claims.[40] This suspicion is strengthened when we find Royce characterizing the loyalist as a man who is decisive and faithful, just and kind, humble yet self-assertive, reasonable in his dedication to a well-established, institutionalized cause, and yet original in his ability to adapt his loyalty to novel situations.[41] What emerges here is a loosely conceived ideal of Western man, compounded from a *potpourri* of traditionally acclaimed virtues.

If, on the other hand, we accept the second interpretation as decisive for Royce, an even more serious objection presents itself. It is generally supposed that men have rights (to life, to property, and so forth) belonging to them and duties (to ameliorate suffering, to keep promises, and so forth) re-

[39] Pittsburgh lectures, folio 82, lecture 1, p. 27. Cf. *The Philosophy of Loyalty*, p. 143: "My rights are morally the outcome of my loyalty."
[40] Cf. Professor Frank Thilly's review of *The Philosophy of Loyalty*, in *Philosophical Review* 7:541–548 (September 1908). In Thilly's opinion, "Loyalty is not a principle; it is a general label for all the virtues."
[41] *The Philosophy of Loyalty*, pp. 105, 159, 196; Pittsburgh lectures, folio 82, lecture 2, p. 32; lecture 3, p. 43; *The Sources of Religious Insight*, p. 200.

quired of them, simply as men, and not only as servants of causes. A man who has no cause to which he is loyal may, on Royce's theory, be morally required to find one. But in the meantime we would still feel that he has certain moral rights and responsibilities quite apart from the "will" of the cause which is not yet his own. In reply, Royce would probably argue that he has discovered the supreme good for man, namely loyalty, and that to attempt to define rights and duties without reference to the *summum bonum* is to put the cart before the horse. But an answer of this sort would ignore common moral practices in society as we know it. The complicated business of defining, establishing, and enforcing rights and duties has been carried on for centuries, sometimes in the face of acknowledged ignorance of what the highest good for man might be. Royce's probable rejoinder, that this procedure is theoretically unjustifiable and therefore philosophically unsound, would be weakened by the ambiguity in his own position. For he has not made it clear whether he means to justify traditionally accepted rights and duties by reference to his highest moral principle, or whether he means to define, normatively, a new set of rights and responsibilities peculiar to his own ideal moral agent, the loyal man.

Actually, the former alternative is the more plausible of the two. Royce is not a moral prophet. His primary intention is not to propose reform of accepted moral standards, but to render them more coherent, more unified, and simpler to follow in practice by organizing them around the principles of loyalty. But then one might grant that Royce's reformulation of our accepted moral code in terms of loyalty is reasonable and useful, and still deny that the principles of loyalty in any strict sense justify that moral code. In its most plausible form, I believe, Royce's claim reduces to the contention that in living a life of loyalty the moral agent again and again confirms, in his own experience, the validity and binding force of the obligations traditionally recognized by the reflective moral consciousness.

Turning now to the second issue, we recall that Royce proposed the principle of loyalty to loyalty both as the test of the rightness of a moral agent's choice of causes, and as a criterion for determining the relative worthiness of causes as such. While there is some ground for supposing the principle capable of performing the former task, I do not see how it can satisfactorily perform the latter task. It should be emphasized that these two tasks are quite distinct, although Royce was not always careful to preserve the distinction. In its first application, the principle of loyalty to loyalty is supposed to serve as a criterion of *subjective* rightness—that is, as a rule for determining whether a moral agent has done all that is in his power to discover the good and to act in order to attain it. In its second application, the principle is designed to function as a criterion of *objective* rightness—that is, as a standard for appraising the inherent capacities of a given cause to promote the supreme good.

When evaluating his own chosen loyalty to a specific cause, Royce maintains, the moral agent must ask himself whether his loyalty is in harmony with or at least not needlessly destructive of the loyalties of other men—whether, in short, it advances the cause of universal loyalty. This question, Royce admitted, is frequently difficult or even impossible to answer. Confronted with the need for deciding between two equally attractive but conflicting causes, the individual may find that he is unable to anticipate the results of either choice, and that therefore he simply does not know which cause will best further universal loyalty. Royce imagines that this is the situation in which Robert E. Lee probably found himself prior to the outbreak of the Civil War.[42] Lee was unquestionably loyal to his country. In his eyes the Northern and Southern causes had equal claim to be serving

[42] *The Philosophy of Loyalty*, pp. 183, 193.

the cause of the nation as a whole. How was he to decide which of the conflicting special causes to serve?

Royce has argued that two considerations implied by the principle of loyalty to loyalty can assist in the making of such a decision: the need to be decisive and the need to be faithful. The former prohibits neutrality because ultimately that involves the decision not to serve at all, and thereby a betrayal of the cause of loyalty as such. The latter counsels that in the absence of further knowledge, the cause to which one is already committed by natural ties and affections, and which one is best equipped to serve, has a prior binding claim on the individual. Presumably, then, when the moral agent finds, upon a thorough examination of conscience,[43] that he is serving his cause decisively and faithfully and that this cause, to the best of his knowledge, is consistent with the furthering of universal loyalty, he has done all that he can to ensure that his course of action is morally right. That is, his conduct is subjectively right and to that extent worthy of moral approval.[44]

As a criterion of the subjective rightness of conduct, it seems to me, Royce's principle has much to recommend it. But Royce also insists that loyalty to loyalty is a useful criterion for the evaluation of diverse causes as such. The highest good for each individual is attained in loyalty to a cause. Therefore a cause that furthers loyalty among all mankind is to be judged good; a cause that is unnecessarily destructive of universal loyalty is to be judged evil. Let us grant that Royce's principle is of use in evaluating some of the more obviously desirable and undesirable causes familiar to our

---

[43] It should be pointed out that Royce's account of the role of conscience in this connection may involve circular reasoning. The very same conscience that Royce alleges is developed only in and through loyalty to a cause is at the same time supposed to be our best guide in choosing causes in the first place. (Cf. *The Philosophy of Loyalty*, pp. 195–196.) It is difficult to see how Royce can have it both ways. However, see note 47 below.

[44] I suspect that this analysis explains rather well the universal admiration and esteem that Lee has been accorded.

culture. Thus the cause of world peace, since it works toward the mutual cooperation of loyal men everywhere, is approved by the principle of loyalty to loyalty. The same principle condemns the cause, if it can be called that, of an organized crime syndicate, since it seeks to satisfy the more venal interests of a few at the expense of the many. But surely such enterprises can be and are evaluated just as effectively on the basis of moral principles other than loyalty to loyalty.

On the other hand, consider a cause such as nineteenth-century England's expansion of empire or twentieth-century Algeria's revolutionary reform movement. In both instances certain benefits are to be attained, but at a considerable expense in lives, property—and loyalties—to the several parties concerned. It is difficult to see how Royce's principle can be of use in evaluating such causes. Royce's principle prohibits unwarranted infringement upon personal rights and unnecessary aggression against other loyalties. But how are we to define "unwarranted" and "unnecessary" when obvious benefits such as a higher standard of living and political and social reform are at stake?

Here Royce leaves us quite in the dark, and for good reason. Loyalty to the cause of universal loyalty has as its goal the attainment of a pattern of harmonious social relations among all the loyal. But by Royce's own admission men lack the conspectus, lack the ability to predict the manifold consequences of their actions that is necessary for them to know what such an eventual pattern would be and hence what action will help to bring it about. But if that is so, then the principle of loyalty to loyalty is not the dependable criterion of the objective worthiness of causes that he would have us believe it to be.

Finally, it should be pointed out that the cause of furthering universal loyalty as such is not only somewhat ill-defined but extremely abstract as well. A cause such as universal peace, the curing of a dreaded disease, or the realization of Zion on earth may well have so compelling an attraction for this or that individual that it becomes for him the embodiment of his "self writ large." But surely the cause of universal loyalty lacks the immediacy and the content needed to engage and to hold an individual's natural interests. The principle of loyalty to loyalty may serve as a limiting conception of man's moral obligations to his fellow men. But to call universal loyalty itself a "cause" is to extend the meaning of that term well beyond the range of intelligible application Royce claimed for it.

No doubt himself aware of this difficulty, Royce in his last years made a final effort to render what he thought to be the highest object of human loyalty more intelligible and more concrete. For the abstract conception of the cause of universal loyalty as such he substituted the notion of a "community of interpretation" as the social cause by devotion to which men have the greatest chance of realizing their highest good in common. An examination of Royce's doctrine of the community follows.

3. The Community of Interpretation

a. The Need for Community

Royce's mature ethical theory, as we have seen, is dominated by the concept of self-realization. Now Royce's successive efforts to render this concept more intelligible and more concrete may be said to be determined by his deepening awareness of the complex relations between individual and society. Already prior to the turn of the century, Royce had maintained that the human self in its most significant sense is not a given but an achievement, not an innate possession of the individual but a task to be accomplished over the extent of his entire life. The mature experience of selfhood presupposes commitment to a life plan, which in turn is the result of a certain reciprocal interaction between social conformity and personal initiative. Thus the individual in quest of a life plan first patterns his ideal ends and his standards of moral conduct upon the models afforded him by his society, then chooses among these models and adapts them to his own unique capacities and needs.

In *The Philosophy of Loyalty* (1908), Royce showed that society, in the very process of educating its individual members to social responsibility, equips them with the power of self-will capable of rising in rebellion against society. Thus, the mature individual is likely to find himself alienated from and opposed to the very environment that made his maturing possible. Royce went on to argue that the dialectical process of individual estrangement from society can be arrested only if and when the individual is able to discover a social cause to which he can voluntarily give his loyalty.

Five years later, in *The Problem of Christianity*, Royce presents his most extended analysis of the relation between individual and society—this time, however, to demonstrate the human need for communal organization of a distinctive kind.

Royce now characterizes the context in which the moral agent seeks self-fulfillment as consisting in the interplay of three factors: the self-conscious individual with his own unique capacities and needs, his fellow men who serve as his models and critics, and what Royce calls the "social will" in general. Ordinary conduct, Royce points out, can be molded by any sort of environment, animate or inanimate. But the self-consciousness characteristic of human conduct in its higher forms requires the nurture of a specific kind of social environment. It is the society of our fellow men

who first startle us out of our natural unconsciousness about our own conduct; and who then, by an endless series of processes of setting us attractive but difficult models, and of socially interfering with our own doings, train us to higher and higher grades and to more and more complex types of self-consciousness regarding what we do and why we do it. Play and conflict, rivalry and emulation, conscious imitation and conscious social contrasts between man and man—these are the source of each man's consciousness about his own conduct.[45]

Self-consciousness develops further when what happens to us in our "literal social life" is "repeated with endless variations in our memory and imagination." Memory and imagination enable us to conjure up "ideal fellow-beings" of all sorts—past and present, historical and fictional, human and divine—with whom we "compare and contrast ourselves and our own conduct." Socrates, a personal God, the hero of a novel, a contemporary public figure whom we have not met may be among these idealized personalities.

In addition, however, the form taken by our efforts to achieve self-fulfillment is deeply influenced by what Royce calls the "social will." The term is perhaps unfortunate, since it suggests the somewhat mysterious entity hypostatized in the writings of Rousseau, Hegel, and others. But Royce understands by the social will simply the collective wisdom of centuries of human experience as it is embodied in social institutions, customs, conventions, mores, and moral standards. We may find ourselves obeying or resisting the social will just as we may find ourselves in or out of harmony with our fellow men. Royce describes the relation between the maturing individual and the social will as one of reciprocal interaction. Thus, "the more we know of the social will, the more highly conscious of ourselves we become; while the better we know ourselves, the more clearly we estimate the dignity and the authority of the social will." [46]

The inevitable felt need of the individual moral agent at once to imitate, to oppose, and to integrate with his own the activities of his fellow men and of the social will leads him at last to formulate consciously a life plan or ideal of his own.

[45] *The Problem of Christianity*, I, 132.   [46] *Ibid.*, p. 134.

Thus, Royce reiterates the doctrine which he first propounded in his social psychology some twenty years earlier: "our moral self-consciousness is a product of our social life." He adds that

our developed conscience, psychologically speaking, is the product of endless efforts to clear up, to simplify, and to reduce to some sort of unity and harmony, the equally endless contrasts between the self, the fellow-man, and the social will in general . . .[47]

Royce, however, is even more skeptical in 1913 than he was in 1908 about the ability of individuals to achieve interpersonal harmony and fulfillment of their deepest moral ideals within the context of ordinary social relations. For these relations are marked by rivalry, contentiousness, and the pervasive instability resulting from unresolved tension between social submissiveness and personal self-assertiveness. Royce is firmly convinced that this spiraling conflict between conformity and self-will is beyond the power of the social structure, as we know it, to arrest. To some extent, indeed, the social will provides the moral agent with rules prescribing how he ought to act to promote social harmony. But these rules must be

taught to us as conscious rules of conduct. They can only be taught to us by first teaching us to be more considerate, more self-observant, more formally conscientious than we were before. But to accomplish this aim is to bring us to some higher level of our general self-consciousness concerning our own doings. And this can be done, as a rule, only by applying to us some new form of social discipline which, in general, introduces still new and more complex kinds of tension . . . between the general will and our own will . . .[48]

[47] *Ibid.*, pp. 134–135. This somewhat broader view of moral conscience would seem to avoid the circle mentioned in note 43 above. For on this view the individual's conscience cannot be fully identified with the cause to which he commits himself.

[48] *Ibid.*, pp. 140–141.

The conclusion is inescapable that

our social training thus teaches us to know ourselves through a
process which arouses our self-will; and this tendency grows with
what it feeds upon. The higher the training and the more cultivated and elaborate is our socially trained conscience,—the more
highly conscious our estimate of our own value becomes, and so,
in general, the stronger grows our self-will.

Moreover, Royce warns, external conformity of behavior
is no indication of true social harmony. As the social order
becomes more highly cultivated, more complex, the individual finds himself confronted by a social will that is "oppres-
sively vast" and "impersonal." "He may obey. That is conduct. But he will naturally revolt inwardly; and that is his
inevitable form of spiritual self-assertion, so long as he is
trained to self-consciousness in this way . . ." [49]

Where St. Paul as theologian preached the original sin of
a fallen human nature, Royce as social philosopher, although
unwilling to shackle the individual with a racial guilt inherited at birth, nevertheless insists upon "the original sin of
social contentiousness." [50] Royce understands the latter, unlike the "legend" of Adam's fall, to be an empirical analysis
of the relation between man and society as we know it. Inherent in the process of socialization undergone by each
individual, and inseparable from the development of civilization as a whole, there is a growing tendency toward divisiveness within and between persons. Royce finds that in his
own time new labels have been applied to this spiral of so-

[49] *The Problem of Christianity,* p. 143.
[50] *Ibid.,* p. 144. *The Problem of Christianity* has been read by several
commentators as a reinterpretation of Pauline theology in contemporary ethi-
cal and psychological terms. See Paul Ramsey, "The Idealistic View of
Moral Evil: Josiah Royce and Bernard Bosanquet," in *Philosophy and
Phenomenological Research* 6: 554–589 (1945–1946). Cf. also Professor
Ramsey's doctoral dissertation, "The Nature of Man in the Philosophy of
Josiah Royce and Bernard Bosanquet" (Yale University, 1943). Compare
S. G. Brown, ed., *The Social Philosophy of Josiah Royce* (Syracuse, 1950),
p. 16.

cial antagonism: "individualism and collectivism are tendencies, each of which, as our social order grows, intensifies the other." [51] With considerable psychological insight, Royce observes that the modern individualist, aware that to express himself he requires power and that power resides in large segments of the vast collective will, finds himself in the ironical position of "heaping up new burdens of social control,—control that he indeed intends to have others feel rather than himself." [52]

It is possible that Royce, throughout his life an unregenerate idealist in both the philosophical and the popular senses of the term, was constitutionally unable to let unsynthesized dualisms and unresolved dilemmas stand. Be that as it may, he refused in 1913, just as he did in 1908, to rest content with the essentially pessimistic view of society to which he had been led. There is, he continues to insist, a way beyond the dialectic of social divisiveness that promises individual self-possession and interpersonal reconciliation. This way is, once again, the way of loyalty. But *The Problem of Christianity* proposes a significant addition to the Roycean doctrine of loyalty: loyalty in its more encompassing form, previously defined as loyalty to the furthering of universal loyalty as such, is given a concrete object which it had previously lacked. That object is the "community" in Royce's special sense of the term.

Loyalty, Royce now contends, "involves an essentially new type of self-consciousness,—the consciousness of one who loves a community as a person. Not social training, but the miracle of this love, creates the new type of self-consciousness." [53] The term "community" now replaces the term "cause" in the very definition of loyalty: "by loyalty," Royce says, "I mean the practically devoted love of an individual for a community . . ." [54]

[51] *The Problem of Christianity*, I, 152. The quotation appears in italics.
[52] *Ibid.*, pp. 154f.   [53] *Ibid.*, p. 158.   [54] *Ibid.*, p. xviii.

The remainder of this chapter will attempt to explicate the role of the community in Royce's moral philosophy.

b. The Criteria of a Genuine Community

In the second volume of *The Problem of Christianity*,[55] Royce introduces the concept of the community through a discussion of two apparently conflicting sets of facts regarding social experience. On the one side are the facts which seem to separate individual persons from one another. These facts tend to fall into three groups generally recognized as such by common sense. The first group involves "the empirical sundering of the feelings,—that is, of the immediate experiences" of individuals. Their physical organisms remain private domains in respect to pain and the like. The most intuitive and imaginative sympathy cannot fully enter these domains. The second group refers to our more highly developed ideas. Each man's opinions, intentions, and plans "are secrets, except in so far as his physical organism indirectly reveals them." Our minds, as well as our physical organisms and the feelings that accompany them, seem to belong exclusively to ourselves. The third group of facts is particularly pertinent to our ethical common sense. My deeds, my voluntary decisions, my ideals, my worth as an individual, my rights and duties are thought to be my own inalienable possessions. Were this not the case, the notion of individual moral responsibility would be unintelligible.

Thus the phenomena of individualism—or, in Royce's terms, of "social pluralism"—seem to have a solid empirical basis. On this account, human individuals "appear to resemble Leibnizian monads," windowless but for the expressive movements of their physical organisms.

On the other side, however, every society exhibits certain phenomena that seem to depend on what, from the perspec-

---

[55] The material in this and the following three paragraphs is from volume II, pp. 19–29.

tive of social pluralism, must be an incomprehensibly high degree of interpersonal cooperation. Among the most common of these phenomena are languages, customs, and religions. "Yet a language, a custom, or a religion is not a collection of discrete psychological phenomena, each of which corresponds to some separate individual mind to which that one mental fact belongs, or is due." The English language, Royce insists, is a "mental product . . . possessing intelligent unity," which therefore presupposes that its creator is also, "in some sense, a single intelligence." Somehow the English people as a whole create the English language. It is not incorrect, therefore, to speak of the English people as "some sort of mental unity with a mind of its own."

Thus, whereas the facts of "social pluralism" lead to a conception of human individuals on the analogy of monads that have no windows, the equally impressive facts of what Royce might well have called "social monism" make these individual monads "appear as if they had no walls."

So far Royce is merely echoing the tendency of his pioneering contemporaries in social psychology, men such as Wundt, Durkheim, and Tarde, to insist that if a group of men behaves as a mental unit it must be a mental unit, "however its inner coherence may be constituted."[56] But it is precisely the constitution of these alleged social entities that Royce thinks has not received adequate attention from philosophers and social theorists. Nor does Royce deem it sufficient to allow analogy and metaphor to substitute for analysis when such an important question is at stake. In one of his more important unpublished papers, Royce remarks: "I have no disposition to press to any extreme those analogies between a social group and a living animal organism

---

[56] *The Problem of Christianity*, II, 30. Compare C. S. Peirce, who maintains that such instances of "corporate personality" as are manifested in esprit de corps, national sentiment, and the like, "are no mere metaphors" (*Collected Papers of Charles Sanders Peirce*, 8 vols. [Cambridge, Mass., 1931–1960], 6.371).

upon which some writers have laid doubtless too much stress." [57] Such analogies break down already, Royce notes, when it is observed that a social group has no sense organs but those of its individual members.

In beginning his analysis of the structure of "group minds," Royce distinguishes between what he calls a genuine community and a mere crowd. A crowd, whether in the form of a mob or a picnic gathering, is a more or less haphazard and accidental collection of individuals assembled in behalf of some activity of the moment. "It has a mind, but no institutions, no organization, no coherent unity, no history, no traditions." [58] The sort of unity that it has might best be described, in William James' terms, as a "mere blending of various consciousnesses,—a sort of mystical loss of personality on the part of its members." Royce describes the social mind of a mob as being "emotional, forgetful, thoughtless, hysterical . . . pathological." [59] Where there is a genuine community,

the result of the interaction of individuals is that the social group may show itself wiser than any of its individuals. In the mere crowd, on the other hand, the social group may be, and generally is, more stupid than any of its individual members. [60]

Royce asks us to compare a successful town meeting, "in which individuality is respected, even while social loyalty is demanded," with a street mob or the run-of-the-mill political convention.

A genuine community, as Royce understands it, consists of individuals engaged in certain coherent and consciously chosen activities which are rooted in a historical process. Its

---

[57] "Thoughts on Various Aspects of the Social Mind," folio 91, p. 18. The paper is undated, but appears to have been written some time after 1903.
[58] *The Problem of Christianity*, II, 37.
[59] "Thoughts on Various Aspects of the Social Mind," folio 91, p. 29.
[60] *Race Questions, Provincialism and Other American Problems* (New York, 1908), p. 88.

unity is the result of a history and destiny shared by its members. These members were brought together in the first place by the discovery that they participated in a common heritage of past events, real or ideal, and that they shared certain goals or hopes for the future which could be realized only through concerted action. One of Royce's favorite examples of a community is that inspired by the genius of St. Paul in the early days of Christianity. It acknowledged as its ancestry the lineage of the human race from Adam to Moses to Christ. It expected and worked for a future in which the salvation of its members was to be achieved. Royce assures us that the fact that "the memory of this community was in part legendary is beside the point. Its memory was essential to its life . . ."[61]

In an effort to tighten his analysis of the community, Royce specifies three conditions without which a community could not exist.[62] The first he calls "the power of an individual self to extend his life, in ideal fashion, so as to regard it as including past and future events which lie far away in time, and which he does not now personally remember." The second is the existence of "a number of distinct selves capable of social communication, and, in general, engaged in communication." The third requires "that the ideally extended past and future selves include at least some events which are, for all these selves, identical." Let us consider each of these conditions in turn.

The first condition, that of the individual's capacity for "ideal self-extension," represents the culmination of a life-long effort on Royce's part to define human personality in a manner consistent with psychological and moral experience. The development of Royce's concept of the self has been

---

[61] *The Problem of Christianity*, II, 38. By the same token, it would seem (although Royce never explicitly says so) that the possibility of its anticipated future being mythical or unattainable is also irrelevant, so long as its members continue to believe in and struggle in behalf of its attainment.
[62] *Ibid.*, pp. 61–68.

discussed at some length in previous chapters. This concept is reiterated in *The Problem of Christianity*. It is necessary here merely to indicate how Royce's notion of the community is dependent upon this concept.

"The rule," Royce says, "that time is needed for the formation of a conscious community is a rule which finds its extremely familiar analogy within the life of every individual self." [63] One term of the analogy, the individual person, is to be understood, as we have seen, not as a discrete collection of momentary states of consciousness, but rather as a coherent life creating out of its remembered past and anticipated future a plan or purpose for its existence. Thus, "my idea of myself is an interpretation of my past,—linked also with an interpretation of my hopes and intentions as to my future." [64] The results of these acts of interpretation are what Royce calls "ideal self-extensions," a generic term for the intentional activities of regretting, expecting, accepting responsibility, and so on, which when taken together help to determine one's conception of one's self. These self-extensions take place whenever an individual is able to say: "That former happening or achievement so predetermined the sense and the destiny that are now mine, that I am moved to regard it as belonging to my own past." Or again: "For that coming event I wait and hope as an event of my own future." [65] The other term of the analogy, the community, is simply the result of such ideal self-extensions when two or more individuals make them with regard to the same event(s), as we shall see presently.

The second condition for the existence of a genuine community, the requirement that its members be distinct individuals capable of and engaging in communication with one another, might seem at first glance an obvious truism requir-

[63] *Ibid.*, p. 40. Royce seems to press this analogy to the point of regarding the community as a veritable person in its own right (*ibid.*, pp. 166ff.). This in spite of his stricture against analogies.
[64] *Ibid.*, p. 42.   [65] *Ibid.*, p. 59.

ing no further analysis. But such a view would ignore the deeper implications of "social pluralism" which Royce was compelled to recognize. Royce was well aware that his psychological explanation of the learning process (outlined in Chapter Three) does not adequately account for the higher levels of interpersonal communication. Individuals first learn to cope with their physical environment through imitation of their fellow men. In this process they discover the existence of other minds as well. Thus a primitive basis for communication is established. But, as Royce insisted, mature individuals reflect, and reflection is largely a private matter, generating ideas about one's self and one's surroundings which are not easily communicated. Both the objects of what we come to call the "real world" and the life plans in terms of which we achieve a sense of personal identity require endless, complex, "mediating" processes of cognition. Royce's long search for an adequate way to account for these more elaborate cognitive processes culminated in the theory of interpretation which we discussed in Chapter Five. In light of this theory, Royce was led to argue that the very existence of a community presupposes the willingness of its members to reconcile their diverse interests, needs, and goals through a continuous process of mutual interpretation. According to Royce, therefore, a community in his sense of the term is by its very nature a "community of interpretation." We shall return to this notion in section c.

The third condition for the existence of a genuine community is that its members be able to recognize at least to some extent a history and destiny that they share in common. For Royce this is the decisive reason for calling a community a genuine unit.

Let the various ideal extensions, forwards and backwards, include at least one common event, so that each of these selves regards that event as a part of his own life. *Then, with reference to the ideal common past and future in question, I say that these*

selves constitute a community. This is henceforth to be our definition of a community.[66]

Thus the bond of the early Christian communities was assured when the death and resurrection of Christ became,
"for each believer, an acknowledged occurrence in his own
past." In that event the salvation of each member was supposed to have been made possible. The Last Supper afforded
Paul a commemorative act whereby the shared memory of
the community members would constantly be revitalized.
Moreover, the future of the community was assured by the
common hope for the coming end of the world, which was to
mark the realization of the ideal of the "united Church tri-
umphant." The community's common history and destiny
must not be allowed, however, to obliterate the individuality
of its members, that is, the variety of and contrast among
their unique capacities and needs as persons. For the
strength and richness of the community requires the diversity, as much as the unity, of its members. Royce praises the
genius of Paul for the careful preservation of individual plurality within the monistic character of his community. Each
member's personal salvation is at stake; but only in and
through the life of the community can it be achieved.

While Royce does not list it as such, there is a fourth
condition for the existence of a genuine community which
raises a considerable problem in his theory as a whole. This
added condition is the need for love. The existence of a community, Royce believes, is jeopardized both from within and
from without. The former danger has to do with the "all-too-
human" character of its members. In a passage worth quoting at length, Royce shows how realistic he can be with
regard to his proposals for human salvation.

A community, like an individual self, must learn to keep the
consciousness of its unity through the vicissitudes of an endlessly

[66] *Ibid.*, pp. 59–60. Italics in text.

shifting and often dreary fortune. The monotony of insignificant events, the chaos of lesser conflicts, the friction and the bickerings of the members, the individual failures and the mutual misunderstandings which make the members of a community forget the common past and future,—all these things work against the conscious unity of the life of a community. Memory and hope are alike clouded by multitudes of such passing events. The individual members cannot always recall the sense in which they identify their own lives with what has been, or with what is yet to come.[67]

Royce believes that only an abiding love for the community, a love capable of forgiving failures, reconciling antagonisms, and renewing energies, can see its members through these vicissitudes of communal life.

But the threat to the community from without is even more serious and, in Royce's estimation, an even stronger love is required to meet it. Both ordinary society as we know it, and that special, ideal society which Royce has defined as the community is based upon cooperation. It is undeniable that in society in general commerce, industry, art, custom, and language consist of vast cooperative complexes. But in most cases the type of cooperation needed for such enterprises is what Royce calls "external" or "mechanical." That is to say, the individuals who cooperate in these enterprises are not necessarily aware of why or how their various, relatively isolated activities bring these complicated enterprises to fruition. But the cooperation that characterizes a community, Royce contends, must be "organic" in nature. That is to say, the members of a community must consciously identify their own self-interest or self-fulfillment with the communal activities in which they take part. Cooperation in a community must involve that "ideal extension" of one's self which we have described above. The achievements of the community must appear to its member as his "own self writ large." For Royce this distinction between "mechanical" and "organic"

[67] *Ibid.*, p. 81.

cooperation forms the basis of his general distinction between society and community as he uses these terms.[68] It is largely because of this difference in the kind of cooperation attained that Royce regards every community as a social group, but not every social group as a community.

An even deeper threat to the existence of the community than the personal weaknesses of its members, therefore, is the tendency of "organic" cooperation to become "mechanical," due to the expansion and complexification of the social order itself. With the advance of technology the member of a community begins to lose the sense that his community's activities are ideal extensions of himself. Royce writes:

> He can no longer understand [his cooperative activities] in any detail. He takes part in them, willingly or unwillingly. He does so because he is social, and because he must. He works in his factory, or has his share . . . in the world's commercial activities. And his cooperations may be skilful . . . But his skill is largely due to external training, not to inner expansion of the ideals of the self. And the more complex the social order grows, the more all this cooperation must tend to appear to the individual as a mere process of nature, and not as his own work, as a mechanism and not as an ideal extension of himself,—unless indeed love supplies what individual wit can no longer accomplish.[69]

The threat of mechanical cooperation, with its attendant loss of voluntary commitment on the part of individuals, rendering them mere cogs in vast machines, can be met only by love. "If a social order, however complex it may be, actually wins and keeps the love of its members; so that—however little they are able to understand the details of their present cooperative activities,—they still . . . desire . . . that such cooperations go on"; if, in addition, the communal bonds of shared memories and hopes preserve their vitality, "—then

[68] Cf. Ferdinand Toennies, *Community and Society* (East Lansing, Michigan, 1957). Toennies' distinction, much more elaborately drawn, resembles Royce's in some respects.

[69] *The Problem of Christianity*, II, 90–91.

indeed love furnishes that basis for the consciousness of the community which intelligence . . . can no longer furnish."

Now Royce is quite aware that love is an emotion that tends toward a "mystical blending" of distinct individual personalities.[70] But such a loss of personal identity would in its own way destroy the community. For the community, according to Royce, requires for the realization of its goals the retention of individual initiative and self-consciousness precisely as individual. It is essential, therefore, to the preservation of the community that love should not attain the "mystical blending" which it sets out to achieve. Love must always be balanced by intelligent individual initiative. The community's loyal spirit depends upon the interplay between the longing for unity and the will to individual expression.

At this point Royce's analysis seems to be confused. When the growing complexity of modern society makes it difficult for the individual to maintain a conscious and intelligent sense of personal contribution to and identification with a cooperative enterprise, his only salvation can come through what Royce admits to be a more or less blind love. Having said that, however, Royce subsequently insists that love, without precisely the intelligent participation in an organically cooperative enterprise which love was supposed to be able to replace, is by itself inadequate to preserve the community.[71] Once again the refrain, "We don't know where we're going but we're on our way," seems to haunt Royce's uneasy scheme for social salvation.

An even more perplexing problem, one of which Royce is fully aware, concerns the notion of love in connection with the origin of the community. According to Royce, a person's

[70] *Ibid.*, p. 98.
[71] Professor John E. Smith points out that Royce came close to interpreting love as a form of insight in its own right (*Royce's Social Infinite* [New York, 1950], p. 77). Royce's considered opinion, however, would seem to exclude so rationalistic an interpretation.

love for a community far transcends his instinctive tendency to love one or another of his fellow men. The origin of the former cannot, therefore, be explained as a natural outgrowth of the latter.[72] How, then, does this higher love originate? It is tempting to suppose that the community by its very nature elicits a form of love previously unknown in the individual's experience. But the origin of such a community is in turn conditional upon the love of its members. Royce recognizes that "one moves thus in a circle":

The unity of love must pervade [the community], before the individual member can find it lovable. Yet unless the individuals first love it, how can the unity of love come to pervade it? [73]

Unable to accept literally St. Paul's theological solution in terms of divine intercession, Royce is compelled to conclude that the origin of the "transforming love" so essential to the life of the community is "psychologically inexplicable"—that it is, in fact, a mystery.

Love, when it comes, comes as from above. Especially is this true of the love of the ideal community of all mankind. I can be genuinely in love with the community only in case I have somehow fallen in love with the universe. The solution of the problem, if it comes at all, will be, in its meaning, superhuman, and divine, if there be anything divine.[74]

Even "a metaphysical study of the question whether the universe is a community," which Royce proposes to undertake later in the volume, "will be as powerless as the foregoing analysis of the real nature of human communities to explain the origin of love, or to make anyone fall in love with the universe."

It is of course possible that human beings do on occasion

---

[72] *The Problem of Christianity*, II, 101.   [73] *Ibid.*, I, 183–185.
[74] *Ibid.*, II, 102.

experience this "transforming love." It is also possible that no empirical, and not even a metaphysical explanation of the source of this experience can be given. But in making such an experience an integral part of his analysis of the community, Royce has made an important concession to what in *The World and the Individual* he classified and then rejected as "the Second Conception of Being"—namely mysticism.[75]

Summarizing Royce's conception of the community thus far, we may say that a community is a type of social organism composed of individual persons who manifest a degree of cooperative activity not found in ordinary social relations. A community comes into being when two or more persons, through their ability to extend their consciousness of self backwards and forwards into an ideal past and future, discover that they have, to some extent at least, a common history and destiny, and determine henceforth to work in concert toward the achievement of shared goals. While ordinary social activities may involve modes of cooperation that are involuntary, blind, and mechanical, the members of a community cooperate freely to achieve goals that each understands and desires for himself. While familiar social enterprises are permeated with interpersonal rivalry and individual self-assertiveness, a community is characterized by a bond of love: the love of each member for the community and its welfare as if it were his own self magnified.

We must now inquire into the role of the community in Royce's ethical theory. For it is Royce's contention that a certain kind of community, namely an unlimited "Community of Interpretation," is the ideal social cause to which the individual person's ultimate moral commitment is due.

[75] For further discussion of this point, see Wayne L. Sprague, "The Community and the Individual in the Later Philosophy of Josiah Royce," unpublished doctoral dissertation (Boston University, 1953), ch. iii. Cf. also W. E. Hocking, "On Royce's Empiricism," *Journal of Philosophy* 53:57–63 (February 1956).

c. The Unlimited Community of Interpretation as the Ideal Social Cause

At the end of the previous section I argued that Royce's highest substantive ethical principle—loyalty to the cause of furthering universal loyalty among all men—was unsatisfactory on several grounds. The "cause" of universal loyalty as such is highly abstract and indeterminate. It is difficult to see how such a "cause" could satisfy the criteria of a cause as Royce specified them, namely, that it must engage and hold the natural interests of this or that moral agent. In addition, Royce was hard-pressed to furnish practical guidelines as to how universal loyalty may be furthered.

Now in *The Problem of Christianity* Royce asserts categorically that "the 'Community' is the object to which loyalty is due." [76] Moreover, he claims that his doctrine of loyalty to the community marks an advance in concreteness and intelligibility over the formalistic notion of loyalty to loyalty presented earlier in *The Philosophy of Loyalty*. The reason for this claim is that the community as Royce conceives it, namely, as a "Community of Interpretation," unlike the abstract cause of loyalty to loyalty, has a definite structure and definite goals.

According to Royce, the particular form of cooperative activity that distinguishes communal relations from ordinary social relations is the voluntary commitment made by the community's members to engage in unlimited processes of mutual interpretation. As we saw in Chapter Five of this study, Royce described rational human endeavor in general as the effort to achieve an orderly and coherent experience —of ourselves as subsistent personalities organized around a life plan, of other persons as similarly subsistent personalities, and of a world of physical objects whose nature and laws are subject to social processes of verification—that is

[76] *The Problem of Christianity,* I, xxxviii.

beyond the limited powers of any one man to attain through his own cognitive acts of perception and conception. Royce thereupon argued that distinctive cognitive processes of interpretation, by their nature social and potentially unlimited, alone make accessible the kinds of experience in question.

On the basis of his analysis of social relations Royce at last reaches the conclusion that the goals of these interpretative processes can be achieved, if at all, only by an unlimited "Community of Interpretation" whose members are consciously and voluntarily committed to their realization. Since our social experience provides us constantly with novel situations and since the result of any limited process of interpretation may in turn become an object requiring further interpretation, Royce concludes that the Community of Interpretation is unlimited in respect to the number of its human members and to the extent of its activity.

In the light of this theory of ends and of the means whereby alone they might be realized, Royce now reformulates what he takes to be the ultimate substantive principle of moral obligation. In place of the injunction to be loyal to the cause of universal loyalty, we now find the injunction to interpret.[77]

Royce offers no single coherent argument in support of this obligation claim. The following is an attempt to piece such an argument together from various passages in *The Problem of Christianity*.

(1) All men desire rationality, coherence, and continuity in their own lives and in their environment as a whole, both physical and social.

(2) The limitations inherent in individual human experience tend to restrict it to the apprehension of relatively discrete and fragmentary phenomena and to the attainment of limited and unsatisfactory goals.

[77] *Ibid.*, vol. II, lecture 12, especially p. 218.

(3) To overcome these limitations, a vast communal enterprise involving an unlimited cooperative process of interpretation on the part of the human race as a whole is required.

(4) Consequently, participation in an unlimited Community of Interpretation, whose ideal goal is the final determination of what is real, what is true, and what is good, is the moral obligation in the broadest sense incumbent upon each reasonable man.

d. Evaluation

Assuming that this pattern of argument accurately represents Royce's thought, how convincing is it? The first step involves, on the face of it, an appeal to a psychological fact. All men, it is alleged, have a desire to bring harmony, coherence, rationality, and unity of insight into their lives and into their world. Now undoubtedly many people do have such a desire—Royce being one of them. To establish by empirical investigation that *all* men have it would seem to be a rather difficult undertaking. Royce, as we saw in the previous chapter, admitted that individuals might be found who exhibit little or nothing of such a desire, and who disclaim it under questioning. Nevertheless, he contended that all men possess this desire at least latently. The question was then raised whether Royce would ever accept psychological evidence to the contrary as conclusive. It was thought that he would not. But then his universality claim amounts to no more than a hope that any given individual would sooner or later acknowledge that he did in fact sincerely desire what Royce alleges he desires.

Granted for the moment that all men have such a desire, latently or manifestly, there is a further question as to whether this desire is to be given preeminence as worthy of fulfillment. Somewhere in this chain of reasoning Royce must effect a transition from fact to value, from what is desired to what is desirable. It is fairly obvious that the transition is implicitly attempted in the first step. Several alternatives suggest themselves. One might contend that all human desires are *ipso facto* worthy of fulfillment. This alternative Royce, as we have seen, emphatically rejects. The fulfillment of some desires is destructive of personal integrity and interpersonal harmony; such desires are to be suppressed. Another possibility might be to disregard altogether what men in fact desire, and to establish what they ought to desire on independent grounds. Thus Royce might argue, somewhat in the manner of Kant, that man has a moral destiny to achieve rationality, coherence, and so forth, for himself and in communion with his fellow men—regardless of and even in opposition to his natural desires and inclinations. But this way of grounding moral imperatives is also foreign to Royce's intention. He did not devote many years of his life to psychological inquiry for nothing. It is quite clear that he was looking for the moving appeal his substantive ethical principles might have for the individual person as he is, not as he ideally ought to be in the eyes of some moral philosopher. Passage after passage in Royce's writings bears this out. He never supposed for a moment that a moral obligation could be imposed on a man who was basically irrational or who did not have quasi-moral dispositions to begin with.

The alternative that Royce does seem to choose avoids both of these extreme positions. It might be stated in the form of a conjunction. Men in fact desire rationality, harmony, and so on—*and* these desires are worthiest of fulfillment because they express the deepest needs of the human person as a moral agent. The remainder of Royce's argument then involves an appraisal of the means whereby this end might best be attained. Royce is asking the individual to reflect upon his own limitations. If, as Royce asserts, these limitations can be overcome only in and by a community of men dedicated to the mutual interpretation of their experience in the conviction that thus alone may they ever attain what they want—insight into reality, knowledge of the truth, and enjoyment of the good—then it seems reasonable to obligate them morally to become active members of such a community.

Nevertheless, Royce observes (wisely, I think) that the binding force of such a moral obligation is limited, depending as it does upon the individual's implicit and ultimate assent. This assent may take two distinguishable but perhaps finally inseparable forms. Rational reflection may convince a man that the attainment of his most far-reaching goals necessitates his moral commitment to the Community of Interpretation. A less rational, more emotional form of assent is also possible. The individual may find himself to be in love with the community as a richer and worthier being than himself. Royce is well aware, as we have seen, that this love cannot be commanded, that it must be freely given, and moreover that its origin cannot even be explained. Nevertheless, he insists that the continued existence of the Community of Interpretation depends upon the love of its members.

In the light of this analysis, I should think that Royce's argument in support of the obligation to the Community must be conceded some plausibility. The premise, asserting a synthetic necessary connection between a certain allegedly universal desire and the desirability of fulfilling it, is in no way demonstrable. Nevertheless, many, perhaps most of us, would be inclined to accept it. Should the premise be accepted, the force of the conclusion is further dependent upon the correctness of the intermediate steps, which purport to show that the goal stated in the premise can be attained only in a certain way. These intermediate steps presuppose a theory of knowledge in which interpretation is given the stature of a fundamental and distinct form of cognition. The investigation of this doctrine in Part II suggests that while it is in need of greater precision and clarification at certain points, the existence of a cognitive process like that which Royce describes as interpretation is amply confirmed in our experience.

Royce's Community of Interpretation, it seems to me, affords a more convincing object for moral commitment than he had presented previously. There is an echo, in the community doctrine, of Royce's earliest effort to establish a moral commitment to a "world of consciousness." [78] But now Royce is able, as he was not then, to offer cogent reasons why we ought to acknowledge such a commitment and how we are to act once we have made it. Similarly, the two questions, why and how, seem to be answered more plausibly and more concretely when Royce demands loyalty to the Community of Interpretation than when he asked for loyalty to the "cause of loyalty itself." A certain tentativeness characteristic of the doctrine of universal loyalty recurs in the doctrine of the community. But whereas in the former this tentativeness was at least in part due to the vagueness of Royce's formulation, that involved in the community theory is much more justly attributable to the nature of reality as Royce sees it. Adequate knowledge of what is true and full realization of what is good are now seen as painfully remote goals whose possible achievement is contingent upon a thoroughgoing commitment to a vast and energetic communal enterprise.[79] The Community of Interpretation may have to begin its work by groping in the dark. It may require of its members commitments to special ideals, and to methods of attaining them, that are as yet tentative and badly in need of

[78] See Chapter Two, section 4.

[79] Compare the well-known remark by C. S. Peirce in regard to scientific investigation: "the idea of science is to pile the ground before the foot of the outworks of truth with the carcasses of this generation, and perhaps others to come after it, until some future generation, by treading on them, can storm the citadel" (*Collected Papers*, 6.3).

further specification. But now for the first time Royce offers the consolation, if consolation it be, that the commitment to this groping procedure is the only reasonable path open to men who seek to fulfill their deepest needs.

One of the most striking features of Royce's doctrine of the community is the close connection it seeks to establish between the moral life and the life of reason. The interpretative process is alleged to be the ideal way at once to the attainment of knowledge and to the realization of value. The individual is held to be morally obligated to an unlimited Community of Interpretation because that community represents his only *reasonable* hope of attaining what he most desires.[80] The goal of this community is thought to be that final interpretation in which each truth would be known in relation to every other truth, and each value or interest that has survived the critical scrutiny of the community as a whole would be harmonized with every other similarly established value or interest.

Such is Royce's conception of the ideal of rational moral conduct in its broadest sense. I see no better way to determine its plausibility further than to let the reader decide whether or not he finds that it expresses his own goals in life at those times when he conceives them with greatest clarity. This much, I think, may be said in Royce's favor: observation of human nature tends to indicate that, whereas on the one hand no proposed end of human striving can be expected to engage an individual's vital concern unless it holds out the promise of eventual realization, on the other hand the goals which *persist* in eliciting the commitment of reasonable men tend to be of the infinitely rich, vast, and re-

[80] On this point Royce and Peirce are in the closest agreement. See *Collected Papers*, 1.615, where Peirce contends that "the ideal of conduct will be to execute our little function in the operation of the creation by giving a hand toward rendering the world more reasonable . . ." Cf. 2.654f., where Peirce tries to show that selfishness is illogical and that the "identification of one's interests with those of an unlimited community" is the only reasonable mode of conduct open to an individual. (See also 5.354ff.)

mote kind. The following passage conveys, to my mind, a profound insight into human nature on Royce's part—an insight which he, of course, shared with Kant and other moral philosophers.

Just because the true issues of human life are brought to a finish not in time but in eternity it is necessary that in our temporal existence what is most worthy should appear to us as an ideal, as an Ought, rather than as something that is already in our hands. The old saying about the bird in the hand being worth two in the bush does not rightly apply to the ideal goods of a moral agent working under human limitations. For him the very value of life includes the fact that its goal as something infinite can never at any one instant be attained. In this fact the moral agent glories, for it means that he has something to do.[81]

Royce's preoccupation with the ultimate goals of human striving and with the unlimited Community of Interpretation should not, however, obscure the fact that he made continual efforts to keep his moral philosophy on a practical plane. Loyalty, Royce consistently maintained, begins at home. A lengthy and complicated "socialization" process is required to train the individual in the expression of his loyalty. Since his immediate environment is naturally the first to elicit his interests, his concerns, and his moral commitments, Royce felt that the best training grounds for larger loyalties are local communities with limited and definite objectives, such as religious and civic groups, commercial organizations like banking and insurance, and even clubs of various sorts. It is in these limited communities that the institutions, customs, and habits so essential for loftier concerted enterprises are first established. It is in these as well that the emotionally charged symbols, rituals, and ceremonies are developed which furnish the imagination with the vision needed for projecting larger enterprises and broader ideals of social action. And it is in these that the all-

[81] *Race Questions*, p. 101.

important art of interpretation, so essential to the "inner expansion of the ideals of the self," [82] is first and most fully learned. The metaphor that best characterizes Royce's conception of the ideal social order is, I think, a series of expanding circles or spheres of loyalty.

Actually, expanding spheres of loyalty is more than a mere metaphor for Royce. During the last two years of his life, he placed more and more emphasis on the role of limited communities in training moral capacities and in promoting social reform. In one of his last books, *War and Insurance,* Royce describes a situation in which only two individuals are involved as an "essentially dangerous community." [83] Buyer and seller, borrower and lender, plaintiff and defendant are "dangerous pairs" between whom friction almost inevitably occurs and moreover "tends to increase, unless some other relation intervenes." The intervening relation required is institutional in character and involves once again the mediating role of interpretation. Royce sees that in a dual relation between borrower and lender, "borrowing tends to become a concealed . . . substitute for theft,—a gaining of the lender's aid through false pretenses." Lending, in turn, "tends to become a device for despoiling the borrower through using his transient needs or his false hopes as a means to his undoing." [84] The introduction of the institution of banking, however, manages to "change this natural situation, and transform its vicious tendencies." Between borrower and lender there intervenes a third person, the banker. The fulfillment of his own interests depends upon the satisfaction of both members of the dangerous pair. The result of his intervention is that instead of one or both of the two initial parties finding their interests thwarted, three men find themselves the gainers.

[82] *The Problem of Christianity,* II, 90.
[83] (New York, 1914), pp. 30–35.
[84] "The Spirit of the Community," an unpublished essay apparently written at the same time as *War and Insurance* (folio 91, p. 31).

Royce is quick to generalize from this instance. Whenever there is introduced into a "dangerous community" of two a third party whose interests can be furthered by reconciling theirs, this third party may be regarded as the interpreter in what Royce calls a new "special community of interpretation." In a typical business transaction this interpreter will be the agent who represents his principal to a prospective client. In a judicial community this interpreter or mediator is the judge who arbitrates between plaintiff and defendant. In a community of insurance the insurer protects a beneficiary against any loss incurred through the risk of his benefactor. In each of these situations, as in the case of the banker, an institutional modification is successfully introduced into an unstable and potentially immoral relation between two individuals—a modification that tends almost of itself to civilize and "moralize" the parties involved. Thus, in the banking community, "the greed that deceives or despoils may indeed continue to exist; but it will have no necessary place. It will at least tend to disappear." [85] Commercial, judicial, and other institutions, merely by replacing dyadic relations with triadic ones, make possible a whole dimension of moral reform and interpersonal reconciliation otherwise inaccessible to private individuals.

Thus the reader for whom the unlimited Community of Interpretation is too remote or too impractical an ideal may find Royce's conception of the limited community much more appealing. Even more appealing, perhaps, is Royce's proposal that limited communities in another form, that of "provinces," be encouraged in order to safeguard personal integrity and individuality. By 1908, Royce had begun to feel a genuine concern for individual variety of expression in the face of the mammoth and unwieldy modern national

[85] "The Spirit of the Community," p. 31. Cf. *The Hope of the Great Community* (New York, 1916), where Royce proposes a scheme of international insurance as a safeguard against war.

states that threaten its suppression. In order that the individual may not lose "his right, his self-consciousness, and his dignity" in the presence of the "incomprehensible monster" the modern nation tends to become, Royce proposed a "wholesome" or "wise provincialism."

For me, then, a province shall mean any one part of a national domain, which is, geographically and socially, sufficiently unified to have a true consciousness of its own unity, to feel a pride in its own ideals and customs, and to possess a sense of its distinction from other parts of the country. And by the term "provincialism" I shall mean, first, the tendency of such a province to possess its own customs and ideals; secondly, the totality of these customs or ideals themselves; and thirdly, the love and pride which leads the inhabitants of a province to cherish as their own these traditions, beliefs, and aspirations.[86]

A "wise provincialism," Royce believes, would ensure that a certain amount of social power would continue to reside in groups small enough to permit deliberation, criticism, and integration of the diverse concrete interests of its members. It would counteract the "levelling tendency," the danger of "mob-spirit," and the growing centralization inherent in modern civilization. It would nurture most immediately and most effectively the bonds of love required by communal activity at all levels.

Now it seems to me that Royce's doctrine of loyalty to the unlimited Community of Interpretation would have gained in concreteness and intelligibility had he more explicitly connected it with his conception of the two kinds of limited communities just discussed. The Universal Community might then be understood as the ideal limit of a series of expanding circles of loyal activity. This series would begin whenever two individuals, finding themselves in a problematic situation or in a situation threatening conflict, realized the wisdom of seeking as intermediary a third

[86] *Race Questions,* p. 61.

party or interpreter able to resolve their problem or reconcile their conflict. Whenever they did so, a special little community of interpretation, one in which a triadic relation replaces the "dangerous pair," would be created. Sundry commercial, judicial, service, and other institutions could be regarded as limited communities operating on the same principle. These special communities would then be conceived as forming the basis of somewhat larger but still limited communities, namely, the "provinces" structured along regional rather than functional lines. In these provinces, loyalties would be broadened in proportion to the development of more complex processes of mutual interpretation in behalf of more inclusive, long-range goals. Finally, the self-transcending character of individual human consciousness as well as of the social institutions men create would gradually bring into view an unlimited Community of Interpretation as the object of their ultimate loyalty.

APPENDIX: A Guess at a Riddle

If a philosopher is entitled to at least one good riddle, his commentator, I should think, is entitled to one guess as to how it might be resolved. The riddle in Royce is whether or not his later substitution of the "Community of Interpretation" for the "Absolute Mind" or "Absolute Will" of earlier years signifies an abandoning of the absolutistic aspects of his philosophical idealism.[1] My guess is that Royce did in effect abandon his absolutism. Unfortunately, I have space for no more than a brief sketch of the evidence in support of my guess. The salient features of the contrast between Royce's earlier [2] and later position might be summarized schematically as follows.

I. METAPHYSICS
  A. Early Position
    1. The real is defined as the object of an all-embracing Absolute Mind, or Experience. In *The Religious Aspect of Philosophy* (1885),[3] this Absolute is described as "passionless eternal thought." In *The*

[1] Royce's own remarks merely add to the riddle. In the preface to *The Problem of Christianity* he writes: "In spirit I believe my present book to be in essential harmony with the bases of philosophical idealism set forth in various earlier volumes of my own . . ." Yet a page later he concedes that there is much in this book "which I did not expect to say when I began the task here accomplished." This task—"to consider the neglected philosophical problem of the sense in which the community and its Spirit are realities"—requires, Royce writes in his introduction, "a somewhat new form of Idealism, and, in particular, a new chapter in the theory of knowledge . . ." (p. xxxix). In volume II of the same work he claims to be presenting "simply a new mode of approach to the very problems which I have previously discussed" (p. 295). But in March 1916 he wrote to his student Mary Calkins that *The Problem of Christianity* "is the product of what for me is a new light, of a new experience, of ideas which are as new to me as the original form of my idealism was new to me when I first defined it." Cf. *Philosophical Review* 15:66–67 (May 1916); also W. H. Werkmeister, *A History of Philosophical Ideas in America* (New York, 1949), pp. 164–165.

[2] I include under the "earlier" position all of Royce's metaphysical views until roughly 1913, when he first developed his doctrine of the Community of Interpretation.

[3] (New York, 1885), p. 370; cf. pp. 443, 447, 482.

World and the Individual (1899),[4] it is characterized in more voluntaristic, activistic terms as the eternal fulfillment of finite purposes.

2. The existence of the Absolute is alleged to be logically demonstrable through the method of presupposition by denial.[5]

3. The reality of the temporal order can be asserted only from a finite or limited perspective. From the point of view of the Absolute, the world is what it is from all eternity. The good is eternally realized.[6] There is no room for contingency.[7]

B. Later Position

1. The real is defined as the ultimate object of the Community of Interpretation, conceived as a social organism made up of an unlimited number of finite human beings.[8]

2. The existence of the Community is not logically demonstrable. Moreover, it does not exist necessarily. Its inception is a contingent event, depending upon the initial loyalty of a devoted (and presumably human) individual, whose creative love is acknowledged to be mysterious in its origin.[9]

3. The temporal order is real. Indeed it is, apparently, the only real order. For the real is progressively determined by the interpretative activity of the Community. And that activity takes place radically in time. The Community requires for the achievement of its goals a lengthy social process, a history, and an open future.[10]

II. EPISTEMOLOGY

A. Early Position

1. The human knowing process consists in individual perceptions

---

[4] 2 vols. (New York, 1899), I, 359, 465, and *passim*.

[5] Cf. *The Religious Aspect of Philosophy*, pp. 384–435; *The World and the Individual*, I, 538–554; *The Conception of God* (New York, 1897), p. 43.

[6] *The Religious Aspect of Philosophy*, p. 465.

[7] In *The World and the Individual*, Royce sought to avoid the implications of metaphysical determinism and a "Block Universe" by insisting that the Absolute, as a *"totum simul"* or eternal "specious present," spans or includes the whole temporal order. (II, 138ff.) I doubt that this avoids the difficulty.

[8] Cf. *The Problem of Christianity*, 2 vols. (New York, 1913), II, *passim*. A commentator who shares my interpretation has observed that the term "Absolute" occurs only three times in this volume, and then in a changed meaning whose reference is to the Community itself as a "social universe." (W. L. Sprague, "The Community and the Individual in the Later Philosophy of Royce," unpublished doctoral dissertation [Boston University, 1953], ch. iv.)

[9] Cf. Chapter Eight, p. 244.

[10] *The Problem of Christianity*, II, 37ff.

and conceptions whose intended objects are the contents of an Absolute Consciousness.[11]

2. The criterion of truth is the agreement of our ideas with the Absolute Thought, an agreement of which only the latter can be aware.[12]

B. Later Position

1. The human knowing process consists for the most part in social processes of interpretation whose problematic objects are progressively determined by an unlimited Community of human investigators.[13]

2. The criterion of truth is the coherence of our limited interpretations of this or that problematic object with the whole of our experience, conceived in turn as a "universe of signs" demanding interpretation. Such coherence is established beyond question only in the ideal final interpretation by the unlimited Community.[14]

III. DOCTRINE OF MAN

A. Early Position

1. Finite individuals are related to something "beyond themselves" by being parts or fragments of an all-inclusive Absolute Self.[15]

2. Finite selfhood is defined as the unique expression of an Absolute Purpose.[16]

3. The individual is necessarily "included" in the Absolute in such a way that what evil he does is eternally overcome and "transfigured." [17]

B. Later Position

1. Finite individuals are related to something "beyond themselves" by becoming morally autonomous members of an unlimited Community of Interpretation, in which they seek to realize their far-reaching goals through concerted action.[18]

2. Finite selfhood is defined in terms of a unique life plan or purpose formed by the individual through a complex process of social imitation and contrast.[19]

3. The individual becomes a member of the Community only through a freely chosen commitment.[20] His obligations to the Com-

[11] Cf. *The World and the Individual*, I, lectures 7 and 8.
[12] Cf. *The Religious Aspect of Philosophy*, p. 371; *The World and the Individual*, I, lecture 8.
[13] Cf. *The Problem of Christianity*, II, 267ff.
[14] *Ibid.*, cf. pp. 290, 323f. Cf. *Royce's Logical Essays* (Dubuque, Iowa, 1951), pp. 118–124.
[15] *The World and the Individual*, I, 468; II, 135 and *passim*.
[16] *Ibid.*, pp. 466–470, 495, 588.   [17] *Ibid.*, II, lectures 8 and 9.
[18] *The Problem of Christianity, passim*.   [19] See Chapter Four above.
[20] *The Problem of Christianity*, II, 388.

munity are self-imposed, and he is able, through deliberate acts of disloyalty, seriously to impair the work of the Community and even destroy its bonds.

This outline may indicate why I believe that Royce did in effect abandon the Absolute in his last years. I am convinced, in any case, that his later position is much sounder than the one for which he is best known. The metaphysical implications of the doctrine of the Community as Royce conceives them—reality defined as the problematic object of an unlimited process of interpretation on the part of a Community of human investigators; the existence of such a Community viewed as a contingent event and supported by arguments of a nondemonstrative sort; the unhesitating ascription of full (and perhaps exclusive) reality to the temporal order—these metaphysical implications seem to me considerably more plausible and more sober than those of Royce's absolutistic period. Royce's later theory of knowledge, in which the attainment of knowledge is characterized as an unlimited process of interpreting communally the problematic objects of experience, and in which a coherence theory of truth is advanced, strikes me as a more reasonable view than the supposition that human knowing consists in the agreement, unknown to human knowers, of their isolated perceptions and conceptions with the contents of an Absolute Experience. Similarly, Royce's concept of man in Community as an autonomous moral agent who defines his own selfhood through the adoption of a life plan and who genuinely influences the course of events for good or ill, seems more in accord with our experience than does the view that we are emanations of an Absolute Will whose cosmic designs we cannot do otherwise than fulfill.

But I could not hope to deal adequately with the problem here raised in anything less than another full-length work. What I do wish to emphasize is that Royce's ethical theory, as I have presented it, appears to be fully compatible with his later position, whereas in all likelihood it is not compatible with his earlier position. Already during his own lifetime Royce's commentators urged that his conception of the Absolute precluded the genuine moral agency of finite individuals. Royce, obviously disturbed by this criticism, made several attempts to restate his absolute idealism in such a way that human moral responsibility could be accommodated.[21] But there are strong indications that he was himself dissatisfied with the results. In the last decade of his life, when ethical problems were unquestionably his deepest concern, Royce seemed more inclined to develop an over-all philosophical position accommodated to his ethical theory rather than the other way around. At any rate, it is surely easier to conceive of genuinely responsible moral agents as members of a human community progressively ap-

[21] Cf. Werkmeister, pp. 139–140, 157–159.

proximating far-reaching and shared human goals, than as fragments of an Absolute Will in which their purposes, being really Its purposes, are eternally realized.

If my guess is right, then perhaps Royce's later philosophy as a whole merits more careful examination. We might find that, instead of having to extract living fragments from the dead hulk of his metaphysical absolutism, there is a place in contemporary discussion for a "whole" Royce after all. Then his ghost—and my conscience—could both rest easier.

BIBLIOGRAPHY

I. Works by Royce

The Religious Aspect of Philosophy (Boston and New York: Houghton Mifflin, 1885).
The Spirit of Modern Philosophy (Boston and New York: Houghton Mifflin, 1892).
The Conception of God (New York: Macmillan, 1897).
Studies of Good and Evil (New York: Appleton, 1898).
The World and the Individual, 2 vols. (New York: Macmillan, 1899).
Outlines of Psychology (New York: Macmillan, 1906).
The Philosophy of Loyalty (New York: Macmillan, 1908).
Race Questions, Provincialism and Other American Problems (New York: Macmillan, 1908).
William James and Other Essays (New York: Macmillan, 1912).
The Sources of Religious Insight (New York: Charles Scribner's Sons, 1912).
The Problem of Christianity, 2 vols. (New York: Macmillan, 1913).
War and Insurance (New York: Macmillan, 1914).
The Hope of the Great Community (New York: Macmillan, 1916).
Fugitive Essays, ed. J. Loewenberg (Cambridge, Mass.: Harvard University Press, 1920).
The Social Philosophy of Josiah Royce, ed. S. G. Brown (Syracuse: Syracuse University Press, 1950).
Royce's Logical Essays, ed. Daniel S. Robinson (Dubuque, Iowa: William Brown, 1951).

II. Articles by Royce

"The Imitative Functions and Their Place in Human Nature," *Century Magazine* 48:137–145 (May 1894).
"The External World and the Social Consciousness," *Philosophical Review* 3:513–545 (September 1894).
"Preliminary Report on Imitation," *Psychological Review* 2:217–235 (May 1895).
"Mind," in *Encyclopedia of Religion and Ethics*, ed. James Hastings (New York: Charles Scribner's Sons, 1916), pp. 649–657.

III. Unpublished Papers by Royce
(Harvard University Archives)

"The Two-fold Nature of Knowledge: Imitative and Reflective" (1893), folio 62.
"Topics in Psychology of Interest to Teachers" (1893), folios 63–66.
"The Social Factors of the Human Intellect" (circa 1897), folio 68.
"Social Factors in the Development of the Individual Mind" (1898), folio 70.
"Some Aspects of Social Psychology" (1898), folio 70.
Urbana lectures on ethics (1907), folio 76.
Yale lectures on ethics (1907–1908), folio 77.
Pittsburgh lectures on the doctrine of loyalty (1908), folio 82.
"Thoughts on Various Aspects of the Social Mind" (circa 1903), folio 91.
"The Spirit of the Community" (circa 1914), folio 91.
Extension course on ethics (circa 1915), folio 94.

Note: For a more complete bibliography of Royce's writings, see that of Benjamin Rand in *Philosophical Review* 25:515–522 (May 1916). For fuller lists of Royce's unpublished material, see J. Loewenberg in *Philosophical Review* 26:578–582 (September 1917); J. Harry Cotton, *Royce on the Human Self* (Cambridge, Mass.: Harvard University Press, 1954).

IV. Works about Royce

Cotton, J. Harry, *Royce on the Human Self* (Cambridge, Mass.: Harvard University Press, 1954).
Hocking, W. E., "On Royce's Empiricism" *Journal of Philosophy* 53:57–63 (February 1956).
Loewenberg, J., *Royce's Synoptic Vision* (Baltimore: Johns Hopkins, Centennial Publishers, 1955).
Ramsey, Paul, "The Nature of Man in the Philosophy of Josiah Royce and Bernard Bosanquet," unpub. diss. (Yale University, 1943).
——— "The Idealistic View of Moral Evil: Josiah Royce and Bernard Bosanquet," *Philosophy and Phenomenological Research* 6:554–589 (1945–1946).
Smith, John E., *Royce's Social Infinite* (New York: Liberal Arts Press, 1950).
Sprague, W. L., "The Community and the Individual in the Later Philosophy of Josiah Royce," unpub. diss. (Boston University, 1953).

Thilly, Frank, Review of *The Philosophy of Loyalty*, in *Philosophical Review* 27:541–548 (September 1908).

Werkmeister, W. H., *A History of Philosophical Ideas in America* (New York: Ronald Press, 1949).

V. General Works

Aiken, Henry D., "Evaluation and Obligation" (1950), in *Readings in Ethical Theory*, ed. W. Sellars and J. Hospers (New York: Appleton-Century-Crofts, 1952).

———— "The Levels of Moral Discourse," *Ethics* 62: 235–248 (July 1952).

———— "Moral Reasoning," *Ethics* 64:24–37 (October 1953).

Balfour, Sir Arthur, *A Defence of Philosophic Doubt* (London: Macmillan, 1879). Cf. Appendix: "On the Idea of a Philosophy of Ethics," reprinted in *Readings in Ethical Theory*, ed. W. Sellars and J. Hospers (New York: Appleton-Century-Crofts, 1952).

Bradley, F. H., *Ethical Studies*, 2 ed. (Oxford: Clarendon Press, 1927).

Brandt, R. B., *Ethical Theory* (Englewood Cliffs, New Jersey: Prentice-Hall, 1959).

Broad, C. D., *Five Types of Ethical Theory* (New York: Harcourt, Brace, 1934).

Campbell, C. A., *Moral Intuition and the Principle of Self-Realization*, reprinted from *Proceedings of the British Academy*, vol. XXXIV (1948).

Dewey, John, "Theory of Valuation," in *International Encyclopedia of Unified Science*, II, no. 4 (Chicago: University of Chicago Press, 1952).

Falk, W. D., " 'Ought' and Motivation," in *Readings in Ethical Theory*, ed. W. Sellars and J. Hospers (New York: Appleton-Century-Crofts, 1952).

Freud, Sigmund, *Group Psychology and the Analysis of the Ego* (New York: Liveright, 1949).

Gallie, W. B., *Peirce and Pragmatism* (London: Penguin Books, 1952).

Garnett, A. C., *Can Ideals and Norms be Justified?* (Stockton, Calif.: College of the Pacific, 1955).

Hegel, G. W. F., *The Phenomenology of Mind*, rev. 2 ed., trans. J. B. Baillie (London: Allen and Unwin, 1949).

Hume, David, *A Treatise of Human Nature*, ed. L. A. Selby-Bigge (Oxford: Clarendon Press, 1902).

James, William, *Principles of Psychology* (New York: Henry Holt, 1890).

Joseph, H. W. B., *Some Problems in Ethics* (London: Oxford University Press, 1933).

Kant, Immanuel, *Foundations of the Metaphysics of Morals,* trans. Lewis White Beck (Chicago: University of Chicago Press, 1950).

McIver, Robert M., "The Deep Beauty of the Golden Rule," in *Moral Principles of Action,* ed. Ruth Anshen (New York: Harper, 1952).

Mill, John Stuart, *Utilitarianism* (London: Longmans, Green & Co., 1895).

Miller, Neal and Dollard, John, *Social Learning and Imitation* (New Haven: Yale University Press, 1941).

Moore, G. E., *Principia Ethica* (London: Cambridge University Press, 1960).

Muirhead, J. H., *The Elements of Ethics* (London: John Murray, 1892).

—————— *Rule and End in Morals* (London: Oxford University Press, 1932).

Peirce, C. S., *Collected Papers of Charles Sanders Peirce,* ed. Charles Hartshorne and Paul Weiss, 8 vols. (Cambridge, Mass.: Harvard University Press, 1931–1960).

Perry, R. B., *General Theory of Value* (Cambridge, Mass.: Harvard University Press, 1926).

Prichard, H. A., *Moral Obligation* (New York: Oxford University Press, 1950).

—————— "Does Moral Philosophy Rest on a Mistake?" *Mind,* n.s., 21:21–37 (1912).

Ross, W. D., *Foundations of Ethics* (Oxford: Clarendon Press, 1939).

Sabine, G. H., *A History of Political Theory* (New York: Henry Holt, 1937).

Toennies, Ferdinand, *Community and Society,* trans. Charles P. Loomis (East Lansing: Michigan State University Press, 1957).

Toulmin, Stephen, *An Examination of the Place of Reason in Ethics* (London: Cambridge University Press, 1953).

Wheelwright, Philip, *The Way of Philosophy,* rev. ed. (New York: Odyssey Press, 1954).

INDEX OF PROPER NAMES

INDEX OF TOPICS

DATE DUE